UGC NET Paper I Unlocked

Volume VII

People, Development and Environment

ANKIT SHARMA

A Complete Guide for UGC NET

TO THE POINT NOTES BASED ON PREVIOUS YEARS
QUESTION PAPERS

UGC NET Paper I Unlocked
Volume VII: People, Development and Environment

Author
Ankit Sharma

Publisher
NerdsTable

ISBN-13: 979-8897442355

Price: ₹999/-

First Edition: New Revised Edition
Printed in India

Table of Contents

Foreword

Preparing for UGC NET Paper I demands not only conceptual clarity but also smart planning, time efficiency, and strategic revision. Over the years, UGC NET Paper I Unlocked has earned the trust of thousands of aspirants by offering comprehensive coverage with detailed explanations of concepts and Previous Years' Questions (PYQs). While the earlier editions succeeded in depth and rigor, many students shared a genuine concern: the volume of content—spanning over 350 pages—often became difficult to complete within limited preparation time.

*UGC NET Paper I Unlocked Volume VII: People, Development and Environment is a thoughtful response to that concern. This new edition has been carefully redesigned with a learner-centric approach, focusing on **maximum exam relevance with minimum cognitive overload**. Without compromising academic integrity, the book adopts smarter strategies to make preparation more focused, faster, and more effective.*

*One of the most significant enhancements in this edition is the introduction of clearly marked **"Asked in Exam"** tags. These tags immediately signal high-priority concepts, enabling students to identify and concentrate on areas with proven examination relevance. In addition, PYQs from the **past ten years** have now been systematically placed at the end of each chapter, allowing learners to test their understanding once the concepts are complete—exactly how revision should work.*

*Another defining strength of this volume is the inclusion of the **Last-Minute Revision** section, a feature that has already proven its value in our other publications. Placed immediately after the PYQ section, this revision module presents all crucial points in a precise, exam-oriented order—only what has been asked, exactly how it has been asked. This not only reinforces learning but also builds confidence during the final days before the examination.*

*Remarkably, all of this has been achieved within **230 pages**, ensuring real comfort, better retention, and—most importantly—the confidence that the syllabus can be completed on time. This edition is not merely shorter; it is sharper, smarter, and more aligned with the realities of competitive exam preparation.*

This book is dedicated to aspirants who believe that success in UGC NET is not about reading more, but about reading right. May this volume serve as a reliable companion in your preparation journey and help you approach the examination with clarity, confidence, and control.

*Wishing you success on your journey to cracking the **UGC NET exam with confidence!***

Ankit Sharma

Author & Educator

Chapter 1

Development and Environment (MDGs, SDGs) & Human and Environment Interaction

The topic of Development and Environment holds significant importance in understanding the intersection between economic growth and environmental sustainability. While its direct relevance in question papers has fluctuated, ignoring it entirely would be unwise, as it continues to be a critical area of study in global discussions on sustainability and development policies.

In this section, we explore the **Millennium Development Goals (MDGs)** and the transition to the **Sustainable Development Goals (SDGs)**.

1. Millennium Development Goals (MDGs)

Overview:

The Millennium Development Goals (MDGs) were a set of eight international development goals for 2015. The United Nations Millennium Declaration was adopted following the Millennium Summit of the United Nations in 2000.

- ➢ Time Frame: The time frame for the implementation of Millennium Development Goals was 2000 – 2015. *(Asked in Exam)*
- ➢ Target Audience: Millennium Development Goals (MDGs) were mainly targeted at developing or poor countries. *(Asked in Exam)*
- ➢ Structure: Total 8 Goals in Millennium Development Goals. *(Asked in Exam)* and Total 21 targets in Millennium Development Goals. *(Asked in Exam)*
- ➢ Establishment: Millennium Development Goals (MDGs) were established during the Millennium Summit of the United Nations in the year 2000. *(Asked in Exam)*

> ➤ Deadline: The Millennium Development Goals (MDGs) were set to be achieved by 2015. *(Asked in Exam)*

The 8 Goals of MDGs:

The 191 member states of the United Nations and at least 22 international organizations committed to achieving the following:

1. **To eradicate extreme poverty and hunger.**
   - Goal 1 - Eradicate extreme poverty and hunger. *(Asked in Exam)*
   - Eradicate Extreme Poverty and Hunger – A key Millennium Development Goal (MDG). *(Asked in Exam)*
   - Reduce by half extreme poverty (1990-2015).
   - Reduce by half global hunger (1990-2015).

2. **To achieve universal primary education.**
   - Goal 2 - Achieve universal primary education. *(Asked in Exam)*
   - Under Goal 2 of Millennium Development Goals, UN member countries were to ensure that by 2015, children everywhere, boys and girls would be able to complete a full course of primary education. *(Asked in Exam)*

3. **To promote gender equality and empower women.**
   - Goal 3 - Promote gender equality and empower women. *(Asked in Exam)*
   - Eliminate gender disparity in education (2005/2015).

4. **To reduce child mortality.**
   - Goal 4 - Reduce child mortality. *(Asked in Exam)*
   - Reduce Child Mortality – Aims to lower under-five mortality rates. *(Asked in Exam)*

5. **To improve maternal health.**
   - Goal 5 - To improve maternal health. *(Asked in Exam)*
   - Reduce maternal mortality by three-quarters (1990-2015).

6. **To combat HIV/AIDS, malaria, and other diseases.**
   - Goal 6 - To combat HIV/AIDS, malaria, and other diseases. *(Asked in Exam)*
   - Halt and reverse HIV/AIDS spread (2015).

7. **To ensure environmental sustainability.**
   - Goal 7 - To ensure environmental sustainability. *(Asked in Exam)*

- o Ensure Environmental Sustainability – Focuses on sustainable resource management. *(Asked in Exam)*
- o Integrate sustainable development into policies.
- o Halve population without clean water & sanitation (2015).
- o Improve lives of 100 million slum-dwellers (2020).
- o *(Note: Energy targets are typically associated with SDG 7, though environmental sustainability is MDG 7).*

8. **To develop a global partnership for development.**
    - o Goal 8 - To develop a global partnership for development. *(Asked in Exam)*
    - o Developing a global partnership for development was one of the Millennium Development Goals. *(Asked in Exam)*

Summary of Scope:

- ➤ The Millennium Development Goals (MDGs) included the following relevant goals: Eradicating extreme poverty and hunger, improving maternal health, and promoting gender equity and empowerment of women. *(Asked in Exam)*
- ➤ Improving maternal health, improving the life of slum dwellers, and promoting gender equality and empowerment of women are related to Millennium Development Goals. *(Asked in Exam)*
- ➤ The Millennium Development Goals address child mortality, environmental sustainability, and primary education, but not human rights. *(Asked in Exam)*

Mnemonic to Remember MDGs:

Freedom from Poverty and Hunger, empowered by Education, fosters Gender Equality, reducing Child Mortality and improving Maternal Health. This strengthens the fight against HIV/AIDS, ensures Environmental Sustainability, and paves the way for Global Partnerships.

2. Sustainable Development Goals (SDGs)

Overview:

The Sustainable Development Goals (SDGs) or Global Goals consist of 17 interconnected global goals that serve as a "blueprint to achieve a better and more sustainable future for all". The SDGs replaced the MDGs in 2016.

- ➤ Adoption: Sustainable Development Goals (SDGs) were adopted in the year 2015. *(Asked in Exam)*

> Effect Date: The Sustainable Development Goals (SDGs) came into effect in January 2016. *(Asked in Exam)*

> Deadline: The Sustainable Development Goals (SDGs) were set to be achieved by 2030. *(Asked in Exam)*

> Agenda Name: Sustainable Development Goals (SDGs) are also known as Agenda 30. *(Asked in Exam)*

> Structure: Total 17 Goals in Sustainable Development Goals. *(Asked in Exam)*

> Targets & Indicators: Total 169 targets in Sustainable Development Goals. *(Asked in Exam)* and There are 232 indicators used to measure progress towards the targets. *(Asked in Exam)*

> Target Audience: Sustainable Development Goals (SDGs) are targeted at all countries whether developed, developing or poor. *(Asked in Exam)*

> Research Interest: The number of publications related to the SDGs can be numerous and continuously increasing, making it the highest number in this context. *(Asked in Exam)*

The 17 Goals of SDGs:

1. SDG 1: No Poverty. *(Asked in Exam)*
2. SDG 2: Zero Hunger. *(Asked in Exam)*
3. SDG 3: Good Health and Well-Being. *(Asked in Exam)*
   - "Ensure healthy lives and promote well-being for all at all ages" is a goal under the Sustainable Development Goals (SDGs), specifically Goal 3, which succeeded the MDGs. *(Asked in Exam)*

4. SDG 4: Quality Education. *(Asked in Exam)*
   - o Goal 4 of the 2030 Agenda for Sustainable Development... seeks to "ensure inclusive and equitable quality education and promote lifelong learning opportunities for all." *(Asked in Exam)*
5. SDG 5: Gender Equality. *(Asked in Exam)*
6. SDG 6: Clean Water and Sanitation. *(Asked in Exam)*
7. SDG 7: Affordable and Clean Energy. *(Asked in Exam)*
   - o Targets of Goal 7 of the Sustainable Development Goals (SDG) are: Universal access to modern energy, increase global percentage of renewable energy and double the improvement in energy efficiency. *(Asked in Exam)* *(Note: Original text attributed this to MDG, but these are specifically SDG 7 targets).*
   - o Ensuring energy security for all (This is more specifically addressed under the SDGs). *(Asked in Exam)*
8. SDG 8: Decent Work and Economic Growth. *(Asked in Exam)*
9. SDG 9: Industry, Innovation and Infrastructure. *(Asked in Exam)*
10. SDG 10: Reduced Inequality. *(Asked in Exam)*
11. SDG 11: Sustainable Cities and Communities. *(Asked in Exam)*
12. SDG 12: Responsible Consumption and Production. *(Asked in Exam)*
13. SDG 13: Climate Action. *(Asked in Exam)*
    - o Addressing climate change (This is more specifically addressed under the Sustainable Development Goals, SDGs, which succeeded the MDGs). *(Asked in Exam)*
14. SDG 14: Life Below Water. *(Asked in Exam)*
    - o Sustainable Development Goal - 'Life below water' aims at conserving and sustainably using Oceans, sea and marine resources. *(Asked in Exam)*
15. SDG 15: Life On Land. *(Asked in Exam)*
16. SDG 16: Peace, Justice, and Strong Institutions. *(Asked in Exam)*
17. SDG 17: Partnerships for the Goals. *(Asked in Exam)*

---

3. Comparison and Key Distinctions (MDGs vs. SDGs)

Commonalities:

Zero hunger, No Poverty, and Gender equality are common in both Millennium Development Goals (MDGs) and Sustainable Development Goals (SDGs). *(Asked in Exam)*

- **Zero hunger:** MDG 1 (Eradicate extreme poverty and hunger) → SDG 2 (Zero hunger). *(Asked in Exam)*
- **No poverty:** MDG 1 (Eradicate extreme poverty and hunger)→ SDG 1 (No poverty). *(Asked in Exam)*
- **Gender equality:** MDG 3 (Promote gender equality and empower women)→ SDG 5 (Gender equality). *(Asked in Exam)*

Shortcuts to Remember SDGs:

- **1-5:** Eradicating **Poverty** and **Hunger** through **Health** and **Education** fosters **Gender Equality**.
- **6-10: Clean Water** and **Energy** drive **Economic Growth**, strengthening **Industry and Infrastructure**, reducing **Inequality**.
- **11-15: Sustainable Cities** promote **Responsible Consumption**, tackling **Climate Change**, preserving **Life Below Water** and **Life on Land**.
- **16-17:** This foundation leads to **Peace, Justice**, and **Global Partnerships**.

UNDP Strategic Plan 2018-2021 (Key Highlights)

- ➢ Rooted in the **2030 Agenda for Sustainable Development**, emphasizing universality, equality, and social inclusion.
- ➢ Aims to **eradicate poverty** in all its forms and dimensions.
- ➢ Focuses on **accelerating structural transformations** for sustainable development.
- ➢ Enhances **resilience to crises and shocks** for sustainable progress.
- ➢ Serves as a **catalyst and facilitator** of UN System support.
- ➢ Strengthens partnerships with **governments, civil society, and the private sector**.
- ➢ Adapts to an **evolving development landscape** and changing needs of countries.
- ➢ Aligns with global efforts to **achieve Sustainable Development Goals (SDGs)**.
- ➢ Emphasizes **inclusive economic growth, governance, and resilience building**.
- ➢ Promotes **collaborative and innovative approaches** for sustainable impact.

UNDP Strategic Plan 2022-2025 (Key Highlights)

- ➢ Focuses on **three directions of change** to drive transformation.
- ➢ Introduces **six signature solutions** for global development challenges.
- ➢ Identifies **three enablers** to support implementation.
- ➢ Aims to increase **people's choices for a sustainable future**.
- ➢ Strengthens partnerships to **achieve SDGs effectively**.

> ➢ Adapts to **emerging challenges like climate change, inequality, and digital transformation**.
> ➢ Promotes **inclusive governance and sustainable economic growth**.
> ➢ Enhances **social protection systems and climate resilience**.
> ➢ Encourages **technological innovation and digital governance**.
> ➢ Provides a **clear framework for impactful global development efforts**.

Human and Environment Interaction:

The term 'human-environment interaction' describes how humans influence and are, in turn, influenced by their surrounding ecosystems. Humans can, for example, affect their environment by clearing trees from a forest to make farmland. We depend on the environment for food, air, and water. Studying humans and the environment will give me knowledge about the changes and problems of our natural environment and how individuals can positively play their environmental role.

There are **five general categories** of geography as defined by the 'Five themes of geography:

1. Location,
2. Place,
3. Human environment interaction,

4. Movement,
5. Region.

A human-environment interaction can be defined as the interaction between humans and their surroundings. Intricate adaptive systems exist within the human social system and the environment. There are many elements and correlations between environmental units and human social systems. An adaptive approach supports survival in continuously changing environments due to feedback systems. Interaction between humans and their environment is how people adapt to and modify their environment.

The 3 Types of Human Environmental Interaction

1. **Dependence on the Environment:** The way people depend on the environment for food, water, timber, and natural gas. To get essential resources, humans rely on the environment for survival (e.g. air, water, food, shelter).
2. **Modification of the Environment:** The way people modify the environment positively or negatively, like drilling holes and building dams.
3. **Adaptation to the Environment:** People adapt to the environment to fulfil their needs.

Environment:

The **natural environment** or **world** encompasses all living and non-living things occurring naturally, not artificial. The term is often applied to the Earth or some parts of Earth. In this context, the **environment refers to the interaction between all living species, the climate, the weather, and the natural resources that affect human survival and economic activity**.

➢ Complete ecological units function as natural systems without massive civilized human intervention, including all vegetation, microorganisms, soil, rocks, atmosphere, and natural phenomena within their boundaries and nature.
➢ The presence of universal physical phenomena and natural resources without clear boundaries. These, such as air, water,

climate, energy, radiation, electric charge, and magnetism, do not originate from civilized human actions.

The massive environmental changes of humanity in the Anthropocene have fundamentally affected all natural environments: Climate Change, Biodiversity loss and pollution from plastic and other chemicals in the air and water.

Component of Environment:

Several components make up the natural environment:

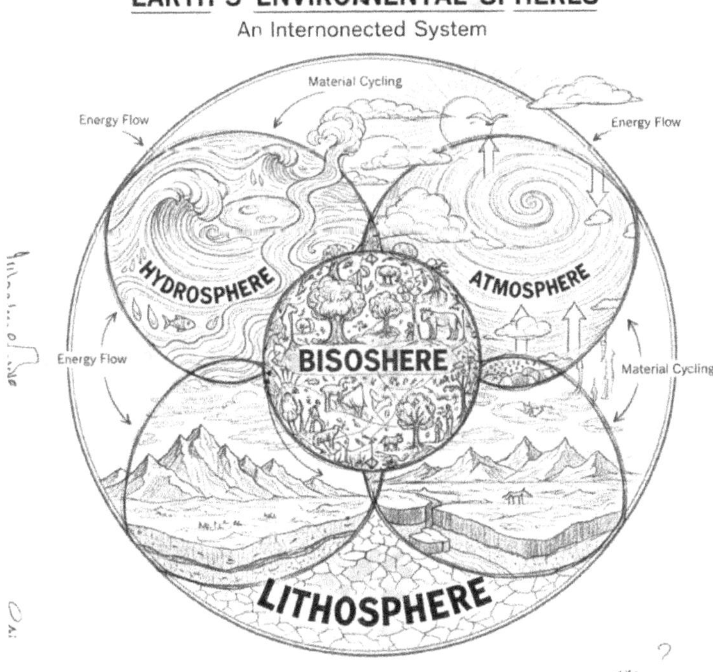

Lithosphere:

- ➢ Earth's outermost layer, called the crust.
- ➢ Composed of various minerals.
- ➢ Extends **up to 100 kilometers** deep.
- ➢ Exists as continental and oceanic crust.
- ➢ Continental crust is thicker, made of granite.
- ➢ Oceanic crust is thinner, made of basalt.
- ➢ The main component of the **lithosphere is Earth's tectonic plates**.

Hydrosphere:

- ➢ It consists of **all forms of water bodies on Earth.**
- ➢ **For instance, oceans, seas, rivers, lakes, ponds, streams etc.**
- ➢ The hydrosphere covers **70% of the Earth's surface**.
  - o The oceans contain 97.5% of the water on Earth.
  - o There is 2.5 percent freshwater on Earth.
    - ▪ 30.8% as groundwater,
    - ▪ 68.9% is in frozen forms, as in glaciers.
    - ▪ An amount of 0.3% is available in rivers, reservoirs and lakes and is easily accessible to man.

Atmosphere:

- ➢ It is a **gaseous layer of the Earth.**
- ➢ The atmosphere with **oxygen on Earth sustains life**.
- ➢ It mainly comprises:
  - o It contains **78.08%** nitrogen,
  - o It contains **20.95%** oxygen,
  - o It contains **0.93%** argon,
  - o It contains **0.038%** carbon dioxide and traces of hydrogen, helium, and noble gases.
- ➢ There is a variation in the amount of water vapour present.

Biosphere:

- ➢ **Biosphere**: Regions on Earth where life exists
- ➢ **Ecosystems**: Soil, air, water, and land support life
- ➢ **Term coined by** Edward Suess
- ➢ **Includes** all living matter (biomass/biota)
- ➢ **Life exists** from polar ice caps to the equator

Layers of the Atmosphere:

Troposphere:

- ➢ **Troposphere**: Lowest layer of Earth's atmosphere
- ➢ **Contains** 75% of atmospheric mass
- ➢ **Holds** 99% of water vapor & aerosols
- ➢ **Most weather phenomena** occur here
- ➢ **Height varies** by region:
  - o **18 km** in tropics
  - o **17 km** in middle latitudes
  - o **6 km** in polar regions (winter)

> ➤ **Average height**: 13 km (43,000 ft)

Stratosphere:

> ➤ **Stratosphere**: Second layer of Earth's atmosphere
> ➤ **Located** above troposphere, below mesosphere
> ➤ **Stratified layers**: Warm air high, cool air low
> ➤ **Close to** Earth's planetary surface
> ➤ **Temperature increases** with altitude
> ➤ **Ozone layer absorbs** UV radiation
> ➤ **Temperature inversion** contrasts troposphere

Mesosphere:

> ➤ **Mesosphere**: Third layer of Earth's atmosphere
> ➤ **Located above** stratosphere, below thermosphere
> ➤ **Temperature decreases** with altitude
> ➤ **Starts at** stratopause (top of stratosphere)
> ➤ **Ends at** mesopause (coldest atmospheric layer)
> ➤ **Temperature drops below** −143°C (−225°F)

Thermosphere:

> ➤ **Thermosphere**: Above mesosphere, below exosphere
> ➤ **Begins at** ~80 km altitude
> ➤ **UV radiation** causes photoionization
> ➤ **Major part** of the ionosphere
> ➤ **Gases stratified** by molecular weight (turbosphere)
> ➤ **Temperature increases** with altitude due to solar radiation

Exosphere:

> ➤ **Exosphere**: Outermost atmospheric layer
> ➤ **Thin, low-density gas volume** around a planet
> ➤ **Above the thermosphere**, merging with space
> ➤ **Molecules are gravitationally bound** but rarely collide
> ➤ **Main components**: Hydrogen & helium
> ➤ **Some heavier molecules** near the surface

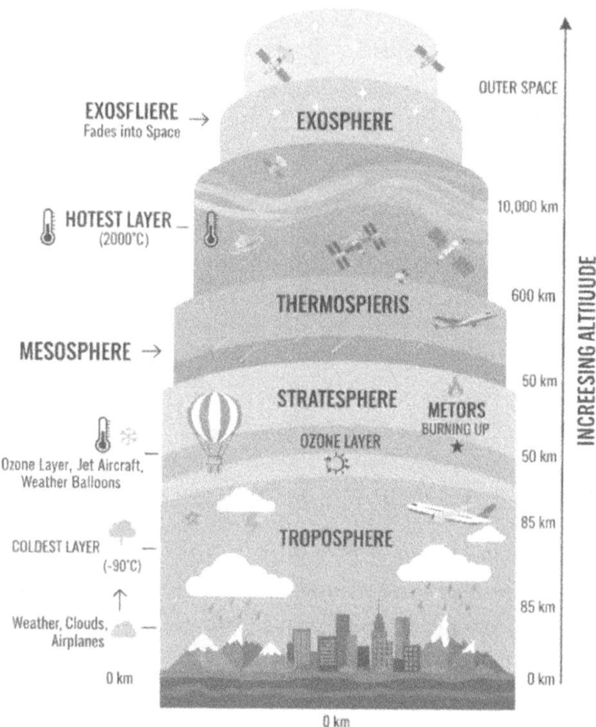

Biodiversity

- ➤ **Biodiversity**: Diversity of life on Earth
- ➤ **Measured at** genetic, species, and ecosystem levels
- ➤ **Defined as** total genes, species, and ecosystems
- ➤ **Unifies** traditional biological diversity types
    - ○ **Taxonomic Diversity**: Measured at the species level
    - ○ **Ecological Diversity**: Viewed as ecosystem diversity
    - ○ **Morphological Diversity**: Arises from genetic & molecular diversity
    - ○ **Functional Diversity**: Measures species' functional differences
- ➤ **Tropical forests**: Cover <10% of Earth, host >90% species
- ➤ **Marine biodiversity**: Highest along **Western Pacific coasts**
- ➤ **Species diversity**: Shows **latitudinal gradients**

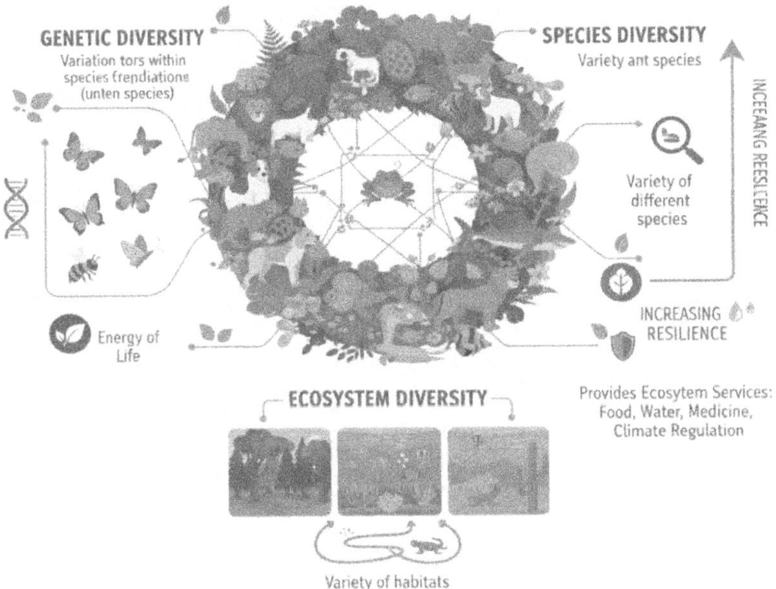

Biodiversity Hotspots:

- **Biodiversity hotspot**: Region with high biodiversity
- **Threatened by** destruction and deforestation
- **Essential for** ecosystem balance
- **Biodiversity clusters** in hotspots
- **Increasing but** may slow due to deforestation
- There are **four major biodiversity hotspots** in India:
    - **The Himalayas.**
    - **Indo-Burma Region.**
    - **The Western Ghats.**
    - **Sundaland**.
- It encompasses the evolutionary, ecological, and cultural processes that sustain life.

Holocene Extinction:

- **Biodiversity & genetic diversity** are declining
- **Holocene extinction**: Sixth mass extinction

- ➤ **Main cause**: Human impact & habitat destruction
- ➤ **Biodiversity loss** affects **human health**
- ➤ **Few adverse effects** are well studied

Ecosystems

- ➤ **Ecosystem**: Includes biotic & abiotic factors
- ➤ **Comprises** plants, animals, microorganisms
- ➤ **Defined by** relationships among organisms
- ➤ **Influenced by** environment & physical factors
- ➤ **Exists in** various geographical areas
- ➤ **Supports** biodiversity & ecological balance
- ➤ **Some Natural Ecosystems are:**
    - o Grassland Ecosystems.
    - o Tropical Rainforest Ecosystems.
    - o Temperate Forest Ecosystems.
    - o Taiga Ecosystems.
    - o Desert Ecosystems.
    - o Tundra Ecosystems.
    - o Freshwater Ecosystems.
    - o Marine Ecosystems.
    - o Hydrothermal Vents
    - o Coral Reefs

Food Chain

- ➤ **Food Chain**: Linear link of organisms in a food web
- ➤ **Producers**: Use **photosynthesis** (e.g., grass, trees)
- ➤ **Apex Predator**: Top consumer (e.g., grizzly bear, killer whale)
- ➤ **Detritivores**: Decomposers (e.g., earthworms, fungi, bacteria)
- ➤ **Illustrates** feeding relationships among organisms
- ➤ **Includes** different **trophic levels**
- ➤ **Food Chain vs. Food Web**: Chain is linear; web is interconnected
- ➤ The food chain only follows a direct, linear pathway of one animal at a time.
    - o **Food chain starts** with a **producer**
    - o **Primary consumer** eats the producer
    - o **Secondary consumer** eats the primary consumer
    - o **Tertiary consumer** may eat the secondary consumer
    - o **Quaternary consumers** are top predators
- ➤ **For Example:**

i.   **A** food chain might begin with a green plant as the producer.

ii.   A snail is the primary consumer of green plants.

iii.   The snail might then be the prey of a secondary consumer, a frog.

iv.   A tertiary consumer, such as a snake, may eat a frog.

v.   An eagle may consume a snake in turn.

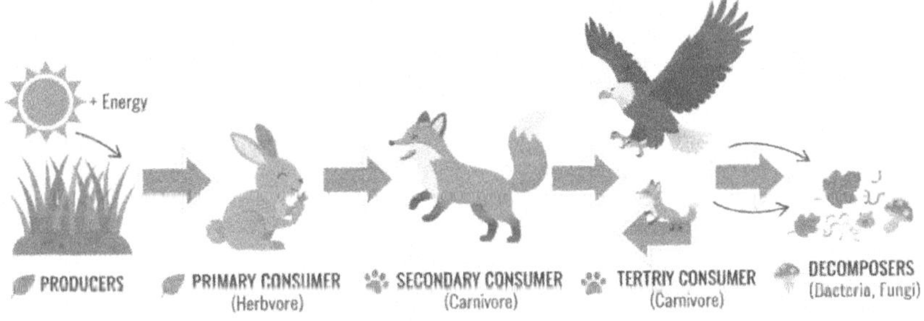

Anthropogenic Activities

Anthropogenic effects refer to environmental changes caused by human activities. With rapid economic development and an ever-growing population, significant stress is being placed on natural resources, infrastructure, and ecological balance. Industrial pollution, deforestation, soil erosion, urbanization, and land degradation have become critical concerns, exacerbating environmental degradation.

Various anthropogenic activities have led to notable environmental changes, including alterations in temperature regimes, radioactive contamination, toxic effluent discharge, nutrient inflows, and depletion of aquatic life. Additionally, excessive water consumption, habitat destruction, commercial exploitation of species, and large-scale construction projects, such as drilling rigs, have further intensified ecological damage.

For UGC NET aspirants, understanding anthropogenic effects is essential as it aligns with topics related to environmental sustainability, climate change, and ecological studies. Analyzing these human-induced changes provides insights into their long-term impact on regional and global ecosystems, a subject of increasing academic and policy relevance.

Human Impact on the environment

- **Anthropogenic impact**: Human effect on the environment
- **Alters** ecosystems, biodiversity, and natural resources
- **Global warming** and biodiversity loss threaten survival
- **Environmental modification** has severe consequences, including:
    - Global warming,
    - Environmental degradation (such as ocean acidification),
    - Mass extinction
    - Biodiversity loss:
    - The ecological crisis and ecological collapse.
- *The following are some examples of human activities that negatively affect the environment on a global scale, either directly or indirectly:*
    - Population growth,
    - Overconsumption,
    - Overexploitation,
    - Pollution,
    - Deforestation.

Climate Change or Global Warming

- **Climate change**: Includes global warming & weather shifts
- **Caused by** greenhouse gas emissions (CO_2, methane)
- **Main source**: Burning fossil fuels for energy
- **Other sources**: Agriculture, industry, deforestation
- **Greenhouse gases** trap heat near Earth's surface
- **Infrared radiation** absorbed, causing global warming

Environmental Degradation

Degradation of the environment is caused by the depletion of natural resources, such as air, water, and soil quality. It may include:

- **The destruction of ecosystems;**
- **The habitat destruction;**
- **The extinction of wildlife;**
- **The pollution.**

It is defined as any undesirable or harmful change to the environment. Environmental concerns can be defined as the harmful effects of any human activity on the environment. Some primary environmental challenges causing great concern are:

> **Air pollution**
> **Water pollution,**
> **Natural environment pollution,**
> **Rubbish pollution.**

Mass Extinction

> **Extinction event**: Also called mass extinction or biotic crisis
> **Biodiversity** is rapidly declining worldwide
> **Multicellular organisms** show reduced diversity & abundance
> **Happens when** extinction rate surpasses speciation rate
> **Past 540 million years** saw 5 to 20 mass extinctions
> **Differences arise** from defining "major" extinctions

Biodiversity Loss

> **Extinction**: Global loss of various species
> **Local extinction**: Species disappear from specific habitats
> **Sixth mass extinction**: Ongoing biodiversity crisis
> **Caused by** human activities exceeding planetary limits
> **Effects are** irreversible and threaten ecosystems

Deforestation

> **Deforestation**: Clearing forests for non-forest use
> **Converted into** farms, ranches, or urban areas
> **Tropical rainforests** are most affected
> **Forests cover** 31% of Earth's land today
> **One-third lower** than pre-agriculture levels
> **Half of forest loss** in the last century
> **15-18 million hectares** lost yearly (Bangladesh size)
> **2,400 trees** cut down every minute

Questions

Millennium Development Goals (MDGs)

Q 1. Which of the following goals is not a Millennium Development goal?

1. Eradicate extreme Poverty and Hunger
2. Reduce child Mortality
3. Climate Action
4. Ensure Environmental Sustainability

Answer: 3. Climate Action

Q 2. Which of the following are true about the Millennium Development Goals (MDGs)?

    A.   MDGs have 8 goals
    B.   MDGs have 40 targets
    C.   MDGs were to be achieved by the year 2015.
    D.   MDGs were the successor of Sustainable Development Goals (SDGs)

Choose the correct answer from the options given below:
1. A, B, and C only
2. A, and C only
3. B, and D only
4. B, C and D only

Answer: 2. A, and C only

Q 3. Targets of Goal 7 of the Millenium Development Goals (MDG) are
    A.   Control global warming
    B.   Universal access to modern energy
    C.   Increase global percentage of renewable energy
    D.   Mitigating air pollution
    E.   Double the improvement in energy efficiency

Choose the correct answer from the options given below:
1. A, B, C and D only
2. B, C and D only
3. B, C and E only
4. A, C, D and E only

Answer: 3. B, C and E only

Q 4. Match the column:

A. Goal 1	I. promote gender equality and empower women
B. Goal 2	II. reduce child mortality
C. Goal 3	III. eradicate extreme poverty and hunger
D. Goal 4	IV. achieve universal primary education

Choose the correct answer from the options given below:
1. A-Ill, B-IV, C-I, D-II
2. A-I, B-III, C-II, D-IV
3. A-II, B-IV, C-III, D-I
4. A-IV, B-II, C-I, D-III

Answer: 1. A-Ill, B-IV, C-I, D-II

Q 5. Which of the following was NOT an issue to be addressed under Millenium Development goal?
1. Child mortality
2. Environmental sustainability
3. Human rights
4. Primary education

Answer: 3. Human rights

Q 6. Under Goal 2 of Millenium Development Goals, UN member countries were to ensure that by 2015, children everywhere, boys and girls would be able to complete a full course of

1. Primary education
2. Secondary education
3. Tertiary education
4. Skill based education

Answer: 1. Primary education

Q 7. Which of the following are Millennium Development Goals?

A. Eradicating extreme poverty and hunger
B. Improving maternal health
C. Addressing climate change
D. Promoting gender equity and empowerment of women
E. Ensuring energy security for all

Choose the correct answer from the options given below:

1. A, B, C and D only
2. A, C, D and E only
3. A, B, C, D and E
4. A, B and D only

Answer: 4. A, B and D only

Q 8. Which of the following goals are related to millennium Development Goals?

A. Improving maternal health
B. Controlling depletion of ozone layer
C. Improving the life of slum dwellers
D. Creating smart city infrastructure
E. Promoting gender equality and empowerment of women

Choose the most appropriate answer from the options given below:

1. (A), (C) and (E) only
2. (A), (C), (D) and (E) only
3. (A), (B), (C) and (E) only
4. (A), (B), (D) and (E) only

Answer: 1. (A), (C) and (E) only

Q 9. Which of the following was not a Millennium Development Goal (MDG)?

1. Eradicate extreme poverty and hunger
2. Improve maternal health
3. Ensure healthy lives and promote wellbeing for all at all ages
4. Ensure environmental sustainability

Answer: 3. Ensure healthy lives and promote wellbeing for all at all ages

Q 10. Consider the following statements in the context of Millennium Development Goals (MDGs) adopted by the United Nations

a. Eradicate extreme poverty and hunger
b. Improve maternal health
c. Responsible consumption and production
d. Reduce child mortality

Choose the correct answer from the options given below
1. (b), (c) and (d)
2. (a), (c) and (d)
3. (a), (b) and (C)
4. (a), (b) and (d)

Answer: 4. (a), (b) and (d)

Q 11. Given below are two statements:
Statement I: The Millennium Development Goals were adopted in the United Nations in the year 2010
Statement II: Developing a global partnership for development was one of the Millennium Development Goals.
Which of the above statements is/are correct?
1. Only I
2. Only II
3. Both I and II
4. Neither I nor II

Answer: 2. Only II

Q 12. The time frame for the implementation of Millennium Development Goals was.
1. 2000 - 2005
2. 2005 - 2010
3. 2000 - 2015
4. 2000 - 2012

Answer: 3. 2000 - 2015

Q 13. Match the column:

List I (Goals/Targets of MDGs and SDGs)	List II (Number of Goals/Targets)
A. Goals in Millenium Development Goals	I. 8
B. Targets in Millenium Development Goals	II. 17
C. Goals in Sustainable Development Goals	III. 21
D. Targets Sustainable Development Goals	IV. 169

Choose the correct answer from the options given below
1. A-II B-I C-III D-IV
2. A-I B-III C-II D-IV
3. A-Ill B-I C-IV D-II
4. A-IV B-II C-I D-III

Answer: 2. A-I B-III C-II D-IV

Sustainable Development Goals (SDGs)

Q 14. Match the column:	
List I (Specific SDG)	**List II (Its Goal)**
A. SDG 12	(I) Life below water
B. SDG 13	(II) Life on land
C. SDG 14	(III) Responsible production and consumption
D. SDG 15	(IV) Climate Action

Choose the correct answer from the options given below

1. A-III, B-IV, C-I, D-II
2. A-III, B-IV, C-II, D-I
3. A-I, B-II, C-III, D-IV
4. A-I, B-II, C-IV, D-III

Answer: 1. A-III, B-IV, C-I, D-II

Q 15. Arrange the following themes of Sustainable Development Goals according to their goal number in increasing order.

A. Gender Equality
B. Zero Hunger
C. Peace and Justice
D. Climate Action
E. Quality Education

Choose the correct answer from the options given below

1. BEADC
2. ABDCE
3. CDAEB
4. BAEDC

Answer: 1. BEADC

Q 16. What is the correct sequence (from lower number to higher) of the following related to Sustainable Development Goals (SDGs)?

A. Number of Publications
B. Number of Goals
C. Number of Targets
D. Number of Indicators

Choose the correct answer from the options given below =

1. ABCD
2. BDCA
3. BCDA
4. CBAD

Answer: 3. BCDA

Q 17. 'Life below water' pertains to which of the SDGs?

1. SDG 13
2. SDG 14
3. SDG 15
4. SDG 12

Answer: 2. SDG 14

Q 18. Given below are two statements:
Statement (I): Millennium Development Goals (MDGs) were mainly targeted at developing or poor countries.
Statement (II): Sustainable Development Goals (SDGs) are targeted at all countries whether developed, developing or poor.
In the light of the above statements, choose the correct answer from the options given below:
1. Both Statement I and Statement II are correct.
2. Both Statement I and Statement II are incorrect.
3. Statement I is correct but Statement II is incorrect.
4. Statement I is incorrect but Statement II is correct.

Answer: 1. Both Statement I and Statement II are correct.

Q 19. Given below are two statements:
Statement I: Millennium Development Goals (MDGs) were set to be achieved by 2030.
Statement II: Sustainable Development Goals (SDGs) were set to be achieved by 2015.
In the light of the above statements, choose the correct answer from the options given below:
1. Both Statement I and Statement II are correct.
2. Both Statement I and Statement II are incorrect.
3. Statement I is correct but Statement II is incorrect.
4. Statement I is incorrect but Statement II is correct.

Answer: 2. Both Statement I and Statement II are incorrect.

Q 20. Given below are two statements:
Statement I: Millennium Development Goals (MDGs) were established during millennium summit of the United Nations in the year 2000.
Statement II: Sustainable Development Goals (SDGs) were adopted in the year 2015.
In the light of the above statements, choose the correct answer from the options given below:
1. Both Statement I and Statement II are correct.
2. Both Statement I and Statement II are incorrect.
3. Statement I is correct but Statement II is incorrect.
4. Statement I is incorrect but Statement II is correct.

Answer: 1. Both Statement I and Statement II are correct.

Q 21. Match the column:

A. sustainability development goal 2	I. sustainable cities and communities
B. sustainability development goal 3	II. zero hunger
C. sustainability development goal 6	III. good health and well being
D. sustainability development goal 11	IV. clean water and sanitation

Choose the correct answer from the options given below =
1. A-I B-III C-II D-IV
2. A-III B-II C-I D-IV

3.   A-II B-III C-IV D-I
4.   A-II B-III C-1 D-IV
Answer: 3. A-II B-III C-IV D-I

Q 22. Which one of the following is not a Sustainable Development Goal (SDG)?
1.   Decent work and economic growth
2.   Industry, Innovation and infrastructure
3.   Climate change
4.   Education to everyone
Answer: 4. Education to everyone

Q 23. The Sustainable Development Goals (SDGs) are intended to be achieved by the year
1. 2025
2. 2027
3. 2029
4. 2030
Answer: 4. 2030

Q 24. Sustainable Development Goals (SDGs) are also known as
1.   Agenda 30
2.   Agenda 35
3.   Agenda 17
4.   Agenda 10
Answer: 1. Agenda 30

Q 25. Which of the following are sustainable Development Goals (SDGs)?
A.   No poverty
B.   Zero hunger
C.   Employment to everyone
D.   Quality education
E.   Gender Equality
Choose the correct answer from the options given below =
1.   ABC
2.   ABCD
3.   ABDE
4.   CDE
Answer: 3. ABDE

Q 26. Which of the following are common in both Millennium Development Goals (MDGs) and Sustainable Development Goals (SDGs)?
A.   Zero hunger
B.   Life below water
C.   No Poverty
D.   Life on earth

E. Gender equality

Choose the correct answer from the options given below =
1. ABC
2. BCD
3. ADE
4. ACE

Answer: 4. ACE

Q 27. Which goal of the 2030 Agenda for Sustainable Development adopted by India in 2015 seeks to "ensure inclusive and equitable quality education and promote lifelong learning opportunities for all"?
1. Goa 12
2. Goal 4
3. Goal 6
4. Goal 15

Answer: 2. Goal 4

Q 28. The number of Sustainable Development Goals is
1. 13
2. 15
3. 17
4. 19

Answer: 3. 17

Q 29. Which one of the following Sustainable Development Goals (SDGs) is related to sustainable consumption and production patterns?
1. SDG 9
2. SDG 10
3. SDG 11
4. SDG 12

Answer: 4. SDG 12

Q 30. Which of the following goals are part of Sustainable Development Goals?
A. Industry. Innovation and Infrastructure
B. Universal higher education
C. Reduced Inequality
D. Partnerships to achieve goals
E. Clean air

Choose the correct answer from the options given below:
1. (A), (B), (C) and (D) only
2. (A), (B), (C) and (E) only
3. (A), (C) and (D) only
4. (B), (C), (D) and (E) only

Answer: 3. (A), (C) and (D) only

Q 31. Sustainable Development Goal - Life below water' aims at conserving and sustainably using
1. Groundwater resources
2. Rivers, streams, ponds and lake resources
3. Oceans, sea and marine resources
4. Wetland resources

Answer: 3. Oceans, sea and marine resources

Q 32. The Sustainable Development Goals (SDGs) set in 2015 by the United Nations are intended to be achieved by
1. 2025
2. 2030
3. 2035
4. 2040

Answer: 2. 2030

Q 33. Identify the objectives specific to sustainable Development Goals among the following?
A. Responsible consumption and production
B. Life on land
C. Improving maternal health
D. Ensuring environmental sustainability
E. Reduced inequality

Choose the correct answer from the options given below:
1. (A), (B) and (E)
2. (A), (C), (D) and (E)
3. (B), (C), (D) and (E)
4. (A), (B), (C), (D) and (E)

Answer: 1. (A), (B) and (E)

Q 34. Which of the following is not a Sustainable Development Goal?
1. Gender equity
2. Climate action
3. Protection of Ozone layer
4. Life below water

Answer: 3. Protection of Ozone layer

Q 35. The themes of some Sustainable Development Goals are
a) Climate action
b) Sustainable cities and communities
c) Peace, justice and strong institutions
d) Skill development and decent employment
e) Green agriculture
f) Responsible consumption and production

Choose the most appropriate from those given below
1. (a), (b), (c), (e) and (f)

    2.   (b), (c), (e) and (f)
    3.   (b), (c), (d), (e) and (f)
    4.   (a), (b), (c) and (f)
Answer: 4. (a), (b), (c) and (f)

Q 36. Consider the following statements
    a)   The Millennium Development Goals were to be achieved by 2015
    b)   The Sustainable Development Goals will guide United Nations Development Programme Policy until 2035
    c)   The Sustainable Development Goals came into effect in January 2016
Which of the above statements are correct?
    1.   (a) and (b) only
    2.   (b and (c) only
    3.   (a) and (c) only
    4.   (a), (b) and (c)
Answer: 3. (a) and (c) only

Q 37. Identify the Sustainable Development Goals from the list given below:
    i.   Zero Hunger
    ii.   Quality Education
    iii.   Universal Primary Education
    iv.   Clean Water and Sanitation
    v.   Green Agriculture
    vi.   Climate Action
Select correct answer from the options given below:
    1.   (i), (ii), (iii) and (iv)
    2.   (iii), (iv), (v) and (i)
    3.   (ii), (iii), (iv) and (v)
    4.   (i), (ii), (iv) and (vi)
Answer: 4. (i), (ii), (iv) and (vi)

Q 38. What is the correct sequence (from lower number to higher) of the following related to Sustain Development Goals (SDGs)?
    A. Number of Publications
    C. Number of Targets
    B. Number of Goals
    D. Number of Indicators
Choose the correct answer from the options given below
    1.   A, B, C, D
    2.   B, D, C, A
    3.   B, C, D, A
    4.   C, B, A, D
Answer: 3. B, C, D, A

Last Minute Revision

Millennium Development Goals (MDGs)

- ✓ Eradicate Extreme Poverty and Hunger – A key Millennium Development Goal (MDG). *(Asked in Exam)*
- ✓ Reduce Child Mortality – Aims to lower under-five mortality rates. *(Asked in Exam)*
- ✓ Ensure Environmental Sustainability – Focuses on sustainable resource management. *(Asked in Exam)*
- ✓ The Millennium Development Goals (MDGs) have 8 goals and were to be achieved by the year 2025. *(Asked in Exam)*
- ✓ Targets of Goal 7 of the Millenium Development Goals (MDG) are: Universal access to modern energy, increase global percentage of renewable energy and double the improvement in energy efficiency. *(Asked in Exam)*
- ✓ Goal 1 - Eradicate extreme poverty and hunger *(Asked in Exam)*
- ✓ Goal 2 - Achieve universal primary education *(Asked in Exam)*
- ✓ Goal 3 - Promote gender equality and empower women *(Asked in Exam)*
- ✓ Goal 4 - Reduce child mortality *(Asked in Exam)*
- ✓ Goal 5 - To improve maternal health *(Asked in Exam)*
- ✓ Goal 6 - To combat HIV/AIDS, malaria, and other diseases *(Asked in Exam)*
- ✓ Goal 7 - To ensure environmental sustainability *(Asked in Exam)*
- ✓ Goal 8 - To develop a global partnership for development *(Asked in Exam)*
- ✓ The Millennium Development Goals address child mortality, environmental sustainability, and primary education, but not human rights. *(Asked in Exam)*
- ✓ Under Goal 2 of Millenium Development Goals, UN member countries were to ensure that by 2015, children everywhere, boys and girls would be able to complete a full course of primary education. *(Asked in Exam)*
- ✓ The Millennium Development Goals (MDGs) included the following relevant goals: Eradicating extreme poverty and hunger, improving maternal health and Promoting gender equity and empowerment of women. *(Asked in Exam)*
- ✓ Improving maternal health, improving the life of slum dwellers and promoting gender equality and empowerment of women are related to millennium Development Goals. *(Asked in Exam)*
- ✓ The Millennium Development Goals (MDGs) set by the United Nations include eradicating extreme poverty and hunger, improving maternal health, and reducing child mortality. *(Asked in Exam)*
- ✓ Developing a global partnership for development was one of the Millennium Development Goals. *(Asked in Exam)*
- ✓ The time frame for the implementation of Millennium Development Goals was 2000 – 2015. *(Asked in Exam)*
- ✓ Total 8 Goals in Millennium Development Goals. *(Asked in Exam)*
- ✓ Total 21 targets in Millennium Development Goals. *(Asked in Exam)*
- ✓ Millennium Development Goals (MDGs) were mainly targeted at developing or poor countries. *(Asked in Exam)*

Sustainable Development Goals (SDGs)

- ✓ Addressing climate change (This is more specifically addressed under the Sustainable Development Goals, SDGs, which succeeded the MDGs) *(Asked in Exam)*

- ✓ Ensuring energy security for all (This is also more specifically addressed under the SDGs) *(Asked in Exam)*
- ✓ Ensure healthy lives and promote well-being for all at all ages" is a goal under the Sustainable Development Goals (SDGs), specifically Goal 3, which succeeded the MDGs. *(Asked in Exam)*
- ✓ Sustainable Development Goals (SDGs) are targeted at all countries whether developed, developing or poor. *(Asked in Exam)*
- ✓ Total 17 Goals in Sustainable Development Goals. *(Asked in Exam)*
- ✓ Total 169 targets in Sustainable Development Goals. *(Asked in Exam)*
- ✓ There are 232 indicators used to measure progress towards the targets. *(Asked in Exam)*
- ✓ Number of Publications: The number of publications related to SDGs can be numerous and continuously increasing, so it's considered the highest number in this context. *(Asked in Exam)*
- ✓ The number of publications related to the SDGs can be numerous and continuously increasing, making it the highest number in this context. *(Asked in Exam)*
- ✓ The Millennium Development Goals (MDGs) were set to be achieved by 2015 *(Asked in Exam)*
- ✓ The Sustainable Development Goals (SDGs) were set to be achieved by 2030. *(Asked in Exam)*
- ✓ Millennium Development Goals (MDGs) were established during millennium summit of the United Nations in the year 2000. *(Asked in Exam)*
- ✓ Sustainable Development Goals (SDGs) were adopted in the year 2015. *(Asked in Exam)*
- ✓ Sustainable Development Goals (SDGs) are also known as Agenda 30. *(Asked in Exam)*
- ✓ Zero hunger, No Poverty and Gender equalityare common in both Millennium Development Goals (MDGs) and Sustainable Development Goals (SDGs). *(Asked in Exam)*
- ✓ Zero hunger: MDG 1: Eradicate extreme poverty and hunger. SDG 2: Zero hunger. *(Asked in Exam)*
- ✓ No poverty: MDG 1: Eradicate extreme poverty and hunger. SDG 1: No poverty. *(Asked in Exam)*
- ✓ Gender equality: MDG 3: Promote gender equality and empower women. SDG 5: Gender equality. *(Asked in Exam)*
- ✓ Goal 4 of the 2030 Agenda for Sustainable Development, adopted by India and other United Nations member states in 2015, seeks to "ensure inclusive and equitable quality education and promote lifelong learning opportunities for all." *(Asked in Exam)*
- ✓ The Sustainable Development Goals (SDGs) came into effect in January 2016. *(Asked in Exam)*
- ✓ SDG 1: No poverty. *(Asked in Exam)*
- ✓ SDG 2: Zero Hunger *(Asked in Exam)*
- ✓ SDG 3: Good health and well-being. *(Asked in Exam)*
- ✓ SDG 4: Quality Education *(Asked in Exam)*
- ✓ SDG 5: Gender Equality. *(Asked in Exam)*
- ✓ SDG 6: Clean water and sanitation. *(Asked in Exam)*
- ✓ SDG 7: Affordable and Clean Energy. *(Asked in Exam)*

<table>
<tr><td>

✓   SDG 8: Decent Work and Economic Growth. *(Asked in Exam)*

✓   SDG 9: Industry, Innovation and Infrastructure. *(Asked in Exam)*

✓   SDG 10: Reduced inequality. *(Asked in Exam)*

✓   SDG 11: Sustainable cities and communities. *(Asked in Exam)*

✓   SDG 12: Responsible for Consumption and Production. *(Asked in Exam)*

✓   SDG 13: Climate Action. *(Asked in Exam)*

✓   SDG 14: Life Below Water. *(Asked in Exam)*

✓   SDG 15: Life On Land. *(Asked in Exam)*

✓   SDG 16: Peace and Justice. *(Asked in Exam)*

✓   SDG 17: Partnerships for the Goals. *(Asked in Exam)*

✓   Sustainable Development Goal - Life below water' aims at conserving and sustainably using Oceans, sea and marine resources. *(Asked in Exam)*

</td></tr>
</table>

Chapter 2

Environmental Issues: Water, Air, Soil and Noise Pollution

Environmental Issues: Overview

Definition & Scope:

Environmental issues refer to problems that disrupt the normal functioning of ecosystems, affecting biodiversity, climate stability, and resource availability. These issues may arise due to natural phenomena or, more commonly, due to human activities. When ecosystems lose their ability to recover, the impact becomes severe.

Levels of Impact:

Environmental issues exist at local, regional, and global levels:

- **Local:** Waste disposal, water scarcity, desertification. **In large parts of Eastern India, the groundwater is contaminated primarily by arsenic.** *(Asked in Exam)*
- **Regional & Global:** Climate change, ocean acidification, ozone depletion. These large-scale crises demand collective global action.

Pollution Sources:

- **Air pollution:** Industries, power plants, vehicles. *(Asked in Exam)*
- **Land pollution:** Excessive chemical fertilizers. *(Asked in Exam)*
- **Water pollution:** Industrial discharges and various sources. *(Asked in Exam)*
- **Noise pollution:** Roads, aircraft, industry, high-intensity sonar. *(Asked in Exam)*

Water

The Resource: Composition & Distribution

Water (H_2O) is clear, tasteless, and odorless. We get water from surface water (lakes, rivers) and groundwater (aquifers).

Global Water Distribution (Decreasing Order):

Correct Sequence in Decreasing Order of Percentage of Total World's Water: Ice caps and Glaciers – Groundwater - Lakes (Freshwater) – Atmosphere - Rivers and Streams. *(Asked in Exam)*

Freshwater Quantity (Increasing Order):

Water Bodies in Increasing Order of Quantity of Freshwater: Rivers and Streams - Freshwater Lakes and Reservoirs – Groundwater - Ice and Snow. *(Asked in Exam)*

Percentage Breakdown:

- ➢ Oceans: 97.25%
- ➢ Icecaps and Glaciers: 2.05%
- ➢ Groundwater: 0.68%
- ➢ Lakes: 0.01%
- ➢ Soil Moisture: 0.005%
- ➢ Atmosphere: 0.001%
- ➢ Streams and Rivers: 0.0001%
- ➢ Biosphere: 0.00004%

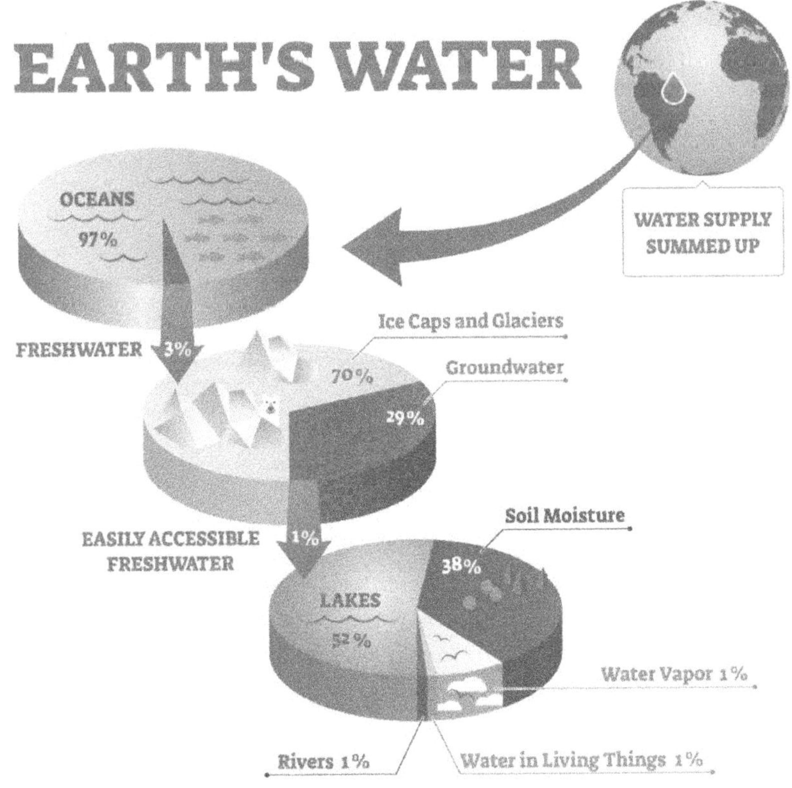

Water Pollution

Water pollution occurs when harmful substances contaminate water bodies.

Types of Pollution Sources:

1. **Point Source Pollution:**
   - Single identifiable source like pipes or ditches.
   - Major sources: industries, sewage plants, storm drains.
   - Easier to monitor and regulate.
2. **Nonpoint Source Pollution:**
   - No single source; spreads over large areas.
   - **Non-point sources of water pollution are diffuse, episodic, and difficult to monitor.** *(Asked in Exam)*
   - Includes farm runoff with pesticides & fertilizers, and urban runoff.

Specific Pollution Scenarios:

- **Thermal Power Plants: The hot water generated from thermal power plants is discharged into the nearby rivers.** *(Asked in Exam)* **Additionally, Bottom ash generated into the boilers of the thermal power plants is a major cause of nearby river pollution.** *(Asked in Exam)*
- **River Ganga Case Study: The Ganga is unlikely to become cleaner soon due to reduced flow, ineffective treatment plants, and rising sewage levels.** *(Asked in Exam)*
  - **Thinning of flow rate:** Reduces ability to dilute pollutants. *(Asked in Exam)*
  - **Failure of treatment plants:** Untreated wastewater discharge continues. *(Asked in Exam)*
  - **Increased sewage:** A major contributor. *(Asked in Exam)*

Key Contaminants

Organic Compounds:

- **Petroleum Hydrocarbons:** From oil spills and runoff.
- **Volatile Organic Compounds (VOCs):** From industrial solvents.
- **Per- and Polyfluoroalkyl Substances (PFAS):** Persistent "forever chemicals" from non-stick cookware and foams.
- **Polychlorinated Biphenyls (PCBs):**
  - **The full form of PCB is Poly Chlorinated Biphenyls.** *(Asked in Exam)*
  - Synthetic chemicals used in electrical transformers.
  - Bioaccumulate in fat tissues and cause cancer.
  - Restricted under the Stockholm Convention.

Inorganic Contaminants:

- **Ammonia:** From food processing waste.

> **Heavy Metals:** Lead, zinc, mercury, cadmium from emissions and industrial waste. **In large parts of Eastern India, the groundwater is contaminated by Arsenic.** *(Asked in Exam)*
> **Nitrates and Phosphates:** From fertilizers and sewage; cause eutrophication.
> **Silt (Sediment):** Increases turbidity. **Muddy water has the highest turbidity.** *(Asked in Exam)*
> **Salt:** From road de-icing and irrigation.

Pharmaceutical Pollutants (PPCPs):

> Includes medications and personal care products.
> Sewage plants often cannot remove them (requires fourth-stage treatment).
> Antibiotics from agriculture also contribute.

Solid Waste and Plastics:

> Enters via runoff and littering.
> Microplastics cause long-term contamination.

SOURCES OF WATER POLLUTION

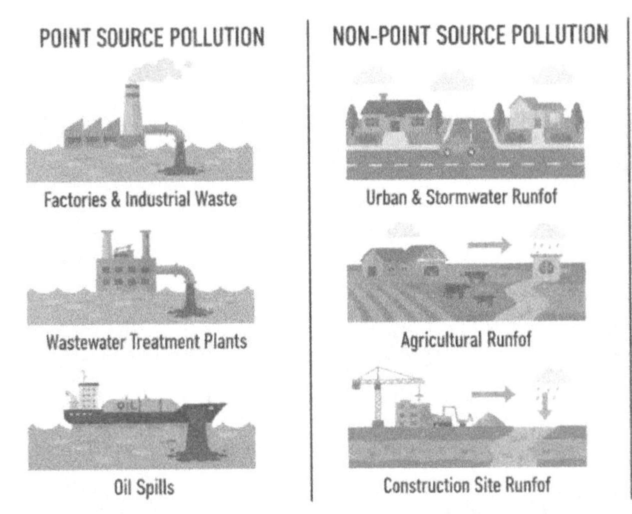

Mitigation Strategies

Mitigating water pollution requires a combination of technology, policy, and infrastructure:

> - **Sanitation & Treatment:** Improving wastewater treatment for industrial and agricultural sectors.
> - **Erosion Control:** Reducing sediment runoff.
> - **Sustainable Agriculture:** Reducing pesticide use and creating buffer zones.
> - **Regulation:** Enforcing laws on waste management and chemical discharge.

Marine Pollution

Overview:

Marine pollution is caused by industrial, agricultural, and residential waste. It includes harmful substances like plastics and chemicals. Excess carbon dioxide leads to ocean acidification, affecting marine life and ecosystem balance. This pollution damages the global economy through fisheries and tourism.

Specific Impacts:

> - Coral Reefs: Coral reefs are threatened because of release of sewage in ocean waters near them. *(Asked in Exam)*
> - Water Clarity: Release of sewage in oceans tends to reduce the clarity of ocean water. *(Asked in Exam)*

Sources of Marine Pollution:

> - **Land-Based Activities:** 80% of marine pollution originates from land. Household, industrial, and farm waste reach oceans. Fertilizers and pesticides wash into rivers and seas, while soil erosion adds sediments, harming marine habitats.
> - **Marine Transportation:** Ships release oil, waste, and noise pollution. Oil spills harm marine life, and ballast water introduces invasive species.
> - **Atmospheric Pollution:** Pollutants from the air (dust, sulfur, nitrogen) settle into the ocean. Carbonic acid contributes to ocean acidification.
> - **Continental Shelves:** Nearshore areas face the highest pollution levels due to industrial zones and urban wastewater.

Pathways of Pollution:

> - **Direct Discharge:** Waste dumped directly into the ocean.
> - **Land Runoff:** Pollutants carried by rainwater into rivers and then the ocean.
> - **Ship Pollution:** Waste and oil discharged from ships.
> - **Bilge Pollution:** Contaminants from the bilge water of ships.
> - **Atmospheric Pollution:** Pollutants from the air settling into the ocean.

> **Deep Sea Mining:** Potential future source of pollution.

Nutrient Pollution

Definition:

Nutrient pollution is caused by excess nitrogen and phosphorus in water, leading to eutrophication and harmful algal blooms. It reduces oxygen, harming aquatic ecosystems.

Sources:

> **Farm Runoff:** Fertilizers and animal waste wash into water. This is a major contributor to eutrophication.

> **Septic Tanks and Feedlots:** Leaks release nutrients, raising nitrogen and phosphorus levels.

> **Combustion Emissions:** Fossil fuel burning releases nitrogen compounds which settle into lakes and oceans.

> **Raw Sewage:** Untreated sewage contains high nutrient levels, encouraging algal blooms.

Environmental Impact:

> **Eutrophication:** Algae overgrowth depletes oxygen levels, causing fish kills. Algae blocks sunlight, harming aquatic plants.

> **Harmful Algal Blooms (HABs):** Certain algae produce toxins harmful to life, impacting fisheries and tourism.

> **Hypoxia (Dead Zones):** Low oxygen levels make water uninhabitable. A major dead zone exists in the Gulf of Mexico.

> **Acid Rain:** Excess nitrogen lowers pH levels in lakes and rivers.

> **Climate Change:** Nitrous oxide accelerates global warming.

Thermal Water Pollution

Definition:

Thermal pollution, also called "thermal enrichment," happens when human activities change the natural temperature of water. Unlike chemical pollution, it changes the physical properties of the water.

Causes:

> **Industrial Cooling:** Power plants and factories use water as a coolant and release it back at a higher temperature.

> **Urban Runoff:** Rainwater running off hot surfaces like rooftops and roads warms up natural water bodies.

> **Reservoirs:** Releasing very cold water from the bottom of reservoirs into warmer rivers.

Effects:
- ➤ **Oxygen Depletion:** Warm water holds less oxygen.
- ➤ **Thermal Shock:** A sudden change in temperature can kill fish and other wildlife accustomed to a specific range.

Endocrine-Disrupting Chemicals (EDCs)

Definition:

Endocrine-disrupting chemicals (EDCs) are chemicals that can interfere with the body's hormones. Most of the emerging contaminants of water are Endocrine Disrupting Chemicals (EDCs). *(Asked in Exam)*

Common Sources:
- ➤ Plastic bottles and containers.
- ➤ Liners of metal food cans.
- ➤ Detergents and cosmetics.
- ➤ **Flame retardant additives, found in the environment throughout the globe, are considered to be EDCs.** *(Asked in Exam)*

Emerging Concerns:

Many of the emerging contaminants have been observed to bioaccumulate in wildlife and humans. *(Asked in Exam)*

Bioaccumulation and Biomagnification

Concepts:

1. **Bioconcentration**: The tendency of a substance to accumulate in tissues directly from the surrounding environment (e.g., water). Bioconcentration is the tendency of hazardous substances to accumulate in human tissues. *(Asked in Exam)*
2. **Bioaccumulation**: When harmful substances, like pesticides, slowly build up in a single organism over time. Pesticides and Persistent Organic Pollutants (POPs) can be part of bioaccumulation/biomagnification. *(Asked in Exam)*
3. **Biomagnification**: Occurs when toxic substances move up the food chain, increasing in concentration.
   - ○ The effect of toxins is magnified in the environment through food webs. *(Asked in Exam)*
   - ○ Biomagnification occurs when toxins become more concentrated as they move up the food chain. The correct sequence starts with the smallest organisms and moves up to the largest: Bacteria - Zooplankton - Fish – Humans. *(Asked in Exam)*

- o Biomagnification occurs when the toxic burden of a large number of organisms at a lower trophic level is accumulated and concentrated in the organisms at a higher trophic level. *(Asked in Exam)* *(Note: Corrected for scientific accuracy; toxins move from lower to higher levels).*

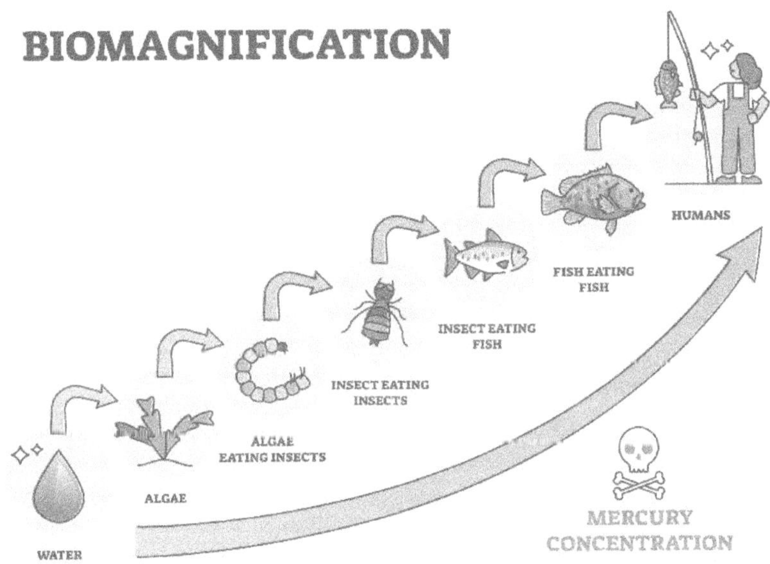

Distinction:

It is important to use the correct terminology. The correct term for the accumulation of hazardous substances in humans due to the consumption of contaminated fish is biomagnification, not bioconcentration. *(Asked in Exam)*

General Note on Pollutants

It is a misconception that only man-made things pollute. **Not all potential pollutants are synthetic chemicals. Natural substances, such as heavy metals (e.g., mercury, lead), and naturally occurring biological agents (e.g., bacteria, viruses) can also be significant pollutants.** *(Asked in Exam)*

Water Quality Parameters

There are three main categories of parameters used to measure water quality: physical, chemical, and biological.

1. Physical Parameters

Physical parameters describe the physical characteristics of water.

> ➢ Temperature, Turbidity, and TSS are physical parameters of water quality. *(Asked in Exam)*
> ➢ Temperature, Total Suspended Solids (TSS), and Conductivity are physical parameters to decide the water quality. *(Asked in Exam)*

Key Parameters:

- **Temperature:**

    - Measures the kinetic energy of water molecules. Warmer water has higher energy levels.
    - Influences aquatic ecosystems and chemical reactions.

- **Turbidity:**

    - Indicates the clarity of water.
    - High turbidity means more suspended particles, affecting light penetration and water quality.

- **Total Dissolved Solids (TDS) and Total Suspended Solids (TSS):**

    - The total solids (dissolved and suspended) in a wastewater sample are the materials left after water has evaporated from the sample. *(Asked in Exam)*
    - The dissolved solids fraction usually includes colloidal particles. *(Asked in Exam)*
    - TDS measures total dissolved substances (like in mineral water). High TDS may indicate contamination.

- **Electrical Conductivity (EC):**

    - Measures water's ability to conduct electricity.
    - Pure water has very low conductivity; seawater has high conductivity due to salts.

- **Salinity:**

    - Indicates salt content. Oceans have high salinity; rivers have low.

- **Colour, Taste, and Odor:**

    - Pure water should be transparent, tasteless, and odorless.
    - Discoloration (e.g., greenish for algae), metallic taste, or chlorine odor indicate contaminants.

2. Chemical Parameters

Chemical parameters reflect the chemical composition and the presence of dissolved substances. **pH, Hardness, DO, and BOD are chemical parameters of water quality.** *(Asked in Exam)*

pH Level

pH measures how acidic or basic water is by telling us how much hydrogen is in it.

- ➢ pH: An Important Water Quality Parameter. *(Asked in Exam)*
- ➢ pH represents the concentration of hydrogen ions. *(Asked in Exam)*
- ➢ pH refers to Acidic/Basic/Neutral nature of water. *(Asked in Exam)*

pH Scale & Ranges:

- ➢ pH can range from 0 to 14. *(Asked in Exam)*
- ➢ pH is a measure of acidity in water and a measure of basicity in water. *(Asked in Exam)*
- ➢ A pH of 0 indicates highly acidic and dangerous water. *(Asked in Exam)*
- ➢ Normal water typically has a pH level around 7, making it neutral. *(Asked in Exam)*
- ➢ Water with pH value between 5 to less than 7 is of acidic nature. *(Asked in Exam)*
- ➢ Rainwater tends to be slightly acidic due to dissolved atmospheric gases, with a pH range typically between 5 and 6. *(Asked in Exam)*
- ➢ Acid rainwater is more acidic than normal rainwater, with a pH level below 5, caused by pollutants such as sulfur dioxide and nitrogen oxides. *(Asked in Exam)*
- ➢ Ocean water has a pH level greater than 7, making it alkaline or basic. *(Asked in Exam)*

Impact on Life:

- ➢ **Water with a pH above 5 is not necessarily detrimental to aquatic life. In fact, many aquatic organisms thrive in water with a pH above 5. It is typically water with a pH below 5 that can be harmful to aquatic life.** *(Asked in Exam)*

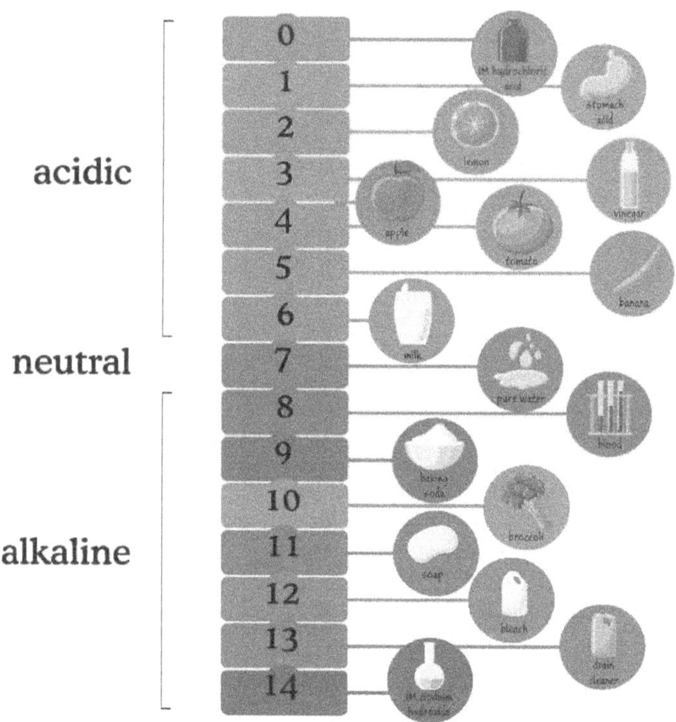

Dissolved Oxygen (DO), BOD, and COD

Dissolved Oxygen (DO):

- ➢ DO refers to the amount of oxygen in water. *(Asked in Exam)*
- ➢ Essential for fish and aquatic life survival. Higher in clear, flowing water bodies.

Biochemical Oxygen Demand (BOD):

- ➢ BOD refers to Oxygen consumed by microorganisms. *(Asked in Exam)*
- ➢ It measures the oxygen needed to decompose organic matter.
- ➢ The full form of CBOD is Carbonaceous Biochemical Oxygen Demand. *(Asked in Exam)*

Chemical Oxygen Demand (COD):

- ➢ COD refers to the strength of organic matter in water. *(Asked in Exam)*
- ➢ Measures oxygen required for chemical oxidation of all compounds (organic and inorganic).

Other Chemical Parameters

- ➢ **Water Hardness:** Caused by dissolved calcium and magnesium. Causes scale buildup in pipes.
- ➢ **Alkalinity:** Water's ability to neutralize acids.
- ➢ **Chlorides, Nitrates & Nitrites:** High levels indicate contamination; excess nitrates cause health issues.
- ➢ **Phosphates:** Can cause eutrophication and algal blooms.
- ➢ **Sulphates:** Affects taste.
- ➢ **Heavy Metals:** Lead, mercury, arsenic, cadmium.
- ➢ **Fluoride:** Excess leads to fluorosis.
- ➢ **Pesticides, Herbicides, VOCs:** Toxic pollutants from agriculture and industry.
- ➢ **Oil & Grease, Ammonia, Phenols, Cyanides:** Indicators of industrial/urban pollution.

3. Biological Parameters

Biological water quality parameters check for the presence of waterborne pathogens and other microorganisms like bacteria and viruses.

- ➢ **Real-life example:** Testing public swimming pools for *E. coli* to ensure safety.
- ➢ **Coliform Bacteria:** Often used as an indicator of fecal contamination.

Hardness of Water

Definition and Causes:

Water hardness is the amount of dissolved calcium and magnesium in the water. These minerals cause the hardness of water and are present as chlorides, sulfates, and bicarbonates.

- ➢ **Hardness of water is caused by the presence of cations in the water.** *(Asked in Exam)* The phenomenon is attributable to the presence of calcium ions (Ca^{2+}) and magnesium ions (Mg^{2+}).
- ➢ **Hardness in water is caused by carbonates of magnesium and calcium.**

Characteristics and Impact:

- ➢ Hardness in water can occur in both surface and underground waters. *(Asked in Exam)*
- ➢ Water hardness, due to calcium and magnesium ions, is classified as temporary or permanent. It leads to scale buildup in hot water pipes. *(Asked in Exam)*
- ➢ Hard water causes scaling in water distribution systems. *(Asked in Exam)*

> Hard water is considered safe for human consumption. *(Asked in Exam)*

Hard Water vs. Soft Water

Hard Water:

> High in dissolved minerals like calcium & magnesium.
> Reduces soap lathering and leaves a white residue.
> Contains common cations (Ca^{2+}) and (Mg^{2+}). from aquifers.

Soft Water:

> Low in minerals or dissolved ions.
> Rainwater & distilled water are typically soft.
> Prevents scaling and soap scum buildup.

Types of Hardness: Temporary vs. Permanent

1. Temporary Hardness:

> Caused by **bicarbonates** of calcium & magnesium.
> Removable by boiling.
> Forms white scale deposits (often seen in kettles when water is boiled).

2. Permanent Hardness:

> Caused by chlorides, sulfates, and nitrates.
> **Permanent hardness in water is caused by calcium and magnesium sulphates or chlorides.** *(Asked in Exam)*
> Cannot be removed by simple boiling.
> Requires water softeners or washing soda for removal.

Major Metal Water Pollutants

Heavy metals pose significant health risks when they contaminate water sources.

1. **Arsenic:**
   - Toxic element found in water & food; linked to cancer, heart disease, and diabetes.
   - **Groundwater contamination is a major issue** (especially in Eastern India).
2. **Methylmercury:**
   - Highly toxic form of mercury that accumulates in fish and shellfish.
   - **Methyl mercury in water can cause adverse human effects such as mental disturbance and impairment of speech, hearing, and vision.** *(Asked in Exam)*

       o   Pregnant women & infants are most vulnerable.

3. **Lead:**
   - Enters water via old pipes and industrial pollution.
   - **Lead exposure can affect various parts of the human body, but it has the most significant and harmful impact on the brain.** *(Asked in Exam)* Causes severe damage, especially in children.

4. **Fluoride:**
   - Added to water to prevent tooth decay, but **excess fluoride harms bones & joints** (skeletal fluorosis) and causes dental fluorosis (discolored teeth).

5. **Nitrates:**
   - Found in fertilizers; enters water through agricultural runoff.
   - **Nitrates are responsible for causing blue baby disease.** *(Asked in Exam)*
   - **In agricultural regions, groundwater can have significant concentrations of Nitrate.** *(Asked in Exam)*

Blue Baby Syndrome (Methemoglobinemia)

- **Definition:** Oxygen deficiency turns a baby's skin blue.
- **Cause: Caused by nitrate-contaminated drinking water.** Nitrites interfere with blood's oxygen transport.
- **Vulnerable Group:** Most common in infants under six months.
- **Prevention:** Requires nitrate-free drinking water.

Eutrophication and Nutrient Pollution

Nutrient Pollution:

Occurs when excess nutrients, mainly Nitrogen and Phosphorus, are added to water bodies. Nitrogen-phosphorus is a pair of elements that is most important for the eutrophication process. *(Asked in Exam)*

Eutrophication Process:

- Definition: When a water body gets enriched with nutrients, the process is called Eutrophication. *(Asked in Exam)*
- Impact: Eutrophication causes algae blooms, higher turbidity and odors, and makes it harder for aquatic life to thrive. *(Asked in Exam)*
- Human Impact: Cultural eutrophication is caused by increased nutrient input into the water body mainly due to human activities. *(Asked in Exam)* This accelerates the aging process of a water body.

Algae:

Simple plant-like organisms. A Eutrophic lake is rich in nutrients and has high algal blooms. *(Asked in Exam)*

> ➢ **Real-life example:** Green scum on a pond surface is likely an algal bloom.

Aquatic Weeds:

➢ **Aquatic weeds are fast growing weeds which can attain very high productivity when cultivated on nutrient rich wastewater such as domestic sewage.** *(Asked in Exam)*

➢ **Water hyacinth, salvinia, and duckweed are some examples of aquatic weeds.** *(Asked in Exam)*

Trophic States of Water Bodies

The water body exhibits varying nutrient status at different levels, classified as eutrophic, mesotrophic, or oligotrophic. *(Asked in Exam)*

1. **Oligotrophic Lakes:**
   - **When a water body is deficient in nutrients, it is known as Oligotrophic.** *(Asked in Exam)*
   - **If a water body is healthy and supports no significant biological activity, then its condition is called Oligotrophic.** *(Asked in Exam)*
   - Characteristics: Low nutrients, high oxygen, clear water.

2. **Mesotrophic Lakes:**
   - Moderate nutrients and balanced oxygen. A transition state.

3. **Eutrophic Lakes:**
   - **Eutrophic water bodies are those that have high nutrient levels and high biological productivity.** *(Asked in Exam)*
   - **Eutrophic lakes typically have high levels of nutrients, leading to high biomass production, especially algae and aquatic plants, which can make the water turbid and reduce clarity.** *(Asked in Exam)*

4. **Hypereutrophic Lakes:** Excessive nutrients, frequent algal blooms, poor water quality.

5. **Dystrophic Lakes:** Acidic, high organic matter, dark-colored water (tea-like), low productivity.

Dissolved Oxygen (DO) and Oxygen Demand

Dissolved Oxygen (DO):

➢ A decrease in dissolved oxygen (DO) in water threatens aquatic life, mainly due to oxygen-demanding wastes. *(Asked in Exam)*

➢ Turbulent and rapidly flowing waters are typically well-oxygenated. *(Asked in Exam)*

> Low dissolved oxygen in water, caused by oxygen-demanding wastes, can harm aquatic life and lead to unpleasant taste and odor. *(Asked in Exam)*

Oxygen Demanding Wastes:

> Oxygen demanding wastes decrease the oxygen level in water. *(Asked in Exam)*
> Oxygen-demanding wastes are substances that are oxidized in the receiving body of water. *(Asked in Exam)*
> Adding organic materials, such as sewage or paper pulp, to water stimulates activity and oxygen consumption by decomposers. *(Asked in Exam)*

Biochemical Oxygen Demand (BOD/CBOD/NBOD):

> **CBOD**: Carbonaceous Biological Oxygen Demand.
> **NBOD**: The full form of NBOD is Nitrogenous Biochemical Oxygen Demand. *(Asked in Exam)*
> **Decomposition**: As bacteria decompose oxygen-demanding wastes, they consume oxygen rather than release it. *(Asked in Exam)*

Waste Treatment: Aerobic vs. Anaerobic

Aerobic Digestion (Composting):

> Composting is aerobic degradation of organic materials under controlled conditions, yielding a marketable manure. *(Asked in Exam)*
> Both macro and micro-organisms play an important role in the composting process. *(Asked in Exam)*
> Aerobic digestion of sewage sludge requires lots of energy. *(Asked in Exam)*
> Aerobic digestion primarily produces carbon dioxide and water, not methane. *(Asked in Exam)*
> *Note on Nutrients:* While compost does contain important nutrients like nitrogen, phosphorus, and potassium, the concentrations of these nutrients in compost are generally lower than those found in commercial chemical fertilizers. *(Asked in Exam)*

Anaerobic Digestion:

> Anaerobic digestion of sewage sludge is an efficient method for treating organic solids. This process produces methane as a byproduct. *(Asked in Exam)*
> Produces biogas (methane & CO_2) for energy.

Biological Contaminants and Pathogens

Bacteria, nutrients, and metals are the primary pollutants responsible for lowering the water quality in rivers and streams. *(Asked in Exam)*

> **Pathogens:** Disease-causing organisms (viruses, bacteria, protozoa, helminths).
> **Viruses:** Cause Hepatitis A, gastroenteritis.
> **Bacteria:** *E. coli* causes diarrhea. Thrives in warm water.
> **Protozoa:** Cause giardiasis & dysentery.
> **Helminths:** Parasitic worms like schistosomes.

Diseases Caused by Polluted Water

Water-related diseases are classified based on how the water contributes to the transmission of the disease.

1. Water-borne Diseases (Ingested Polluted Water)

These diseases are caused by drinking water contaminated with human or animal excreta containing pathogens.

> **Cholera:**
>
> - Cholera is caused by the bacterium *Vibrio cholerae. (Asked in Exam)*
> - Transmission occurs via ingestion of contaminated water. *(Asked in Exam)*
> - Causes severe diarrhea & dehydration.

> **Typhoid Fever:**
>
> - Typhoid fever, a waterborne disease, is caused by Bacteria (*Salmonella typhi*) in contaminated water. *(Asked in Exam)*
> - Giardia, Amoebiasis, and Typhoid diseases are due to polluted water. *(Asked in Exam)*

> **Hepatitis (Viral):**
>
> - **Hepatitis, particularly hepatitis A, is caused by a virus and spread through contaminated water.** *(Asked in Exam)*
> - Transmitted via the fecal-oral route; causes liver inflammation and jaundice.

> **Polio:**
>
> - **Cholera, Acute Diarrhoea, Typhoid, and Polio are diseases caused by polluted water.** *(Asked in Exam)*

> **Diarrhea:**
>
> - **Diarrhea can be caused by a variety of pathogens, including viruses (rotavirus), bacteria (*E. coli, Salmonella*), and protozoa (*Giardia*).** *(Asked in Exam)*

> ➢ **Dysentery:**

>> ○ **Dysentery can be caused by protozoa such as *Entamoeba histolytica.*** *(Asked in Exam)*

2. Water-washed Diseases (Lack of Clean Water)

These infections occur due to a lack of water for personal hygiene (washing hands, face, etc.).

Trachoma:

> ➢ Water-washed disease Trachoma is related to lack of water for personal hygiene. *(Asked in Exam)*
> ➢ Trachoma: Associated with inadequate personal hygiene and insufficient water for cleaning. *(Asked in Exam)*
> ➢ Poor hygiene causes repeated eye infections which may lead to blindness.

3. Water-based Diseases (Contact with Polluted Water)

These are caused by parasites that spend part of their life cycle in water organisms (like snails) and enter the human body through skin contact.

Schistosomiasis (Bilharzia):

> ➢ Water-based disease Schistosomiasis results from contact with contaminated water. *(Asked in Exam)*
> ➢ Schistosomiasis is caused by parasitic worms (helminths). *(Asked in Exam)*
> ➢ Schistosomiasis, a common water contact disease, is spread by Cercaria (larval stage). *(Asked in Exam)*
> ➢ Schistosomiasis: Spread through skin contact with polluted water, not through ingestion. *(Asked in Exam)*

ASCARIS

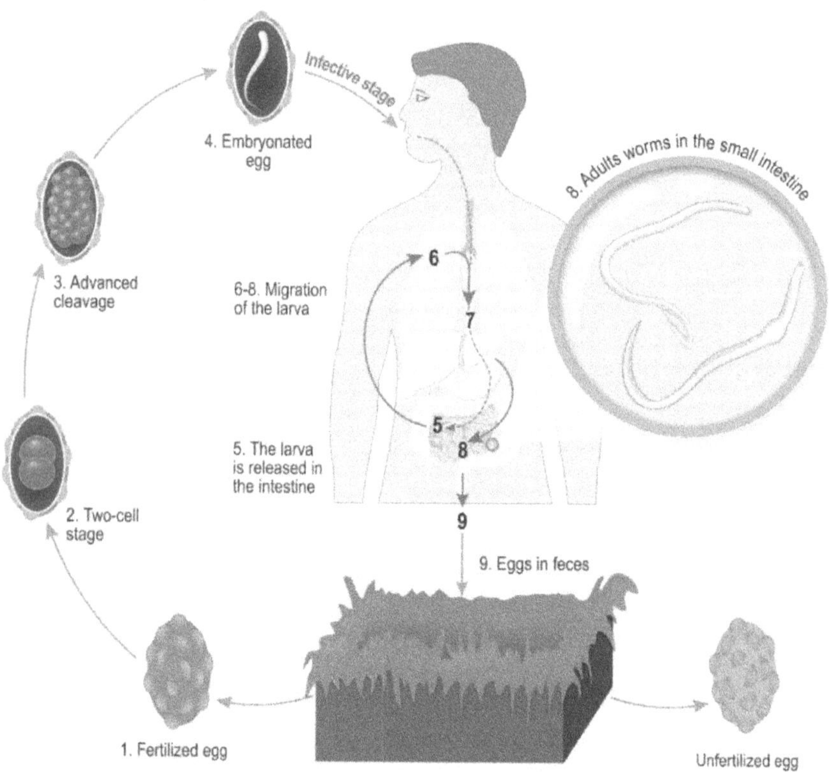

4. Water-related Diseases (Insect Vectors)

These diseases are spread by insects (vectors) that breed in or near water.

> **Malaria:**

- o Water-related disease Malaria is spread by mosquitoes that breed in water. *(Asked in Exam)*
- o Malaria is caused by parasites of the genus *Plasmodium*. It does not require direct contact with water. Instead, it is spread through the bite of an infected female *Anopheles* mosquito. *(Asked in Exam)*

> **Dengue:**

- o Dengue: Requires a mosquito vector for transmission. *(Asked in Exam)*
- o Filariasis: Caused by *Wuchereria bancrofti*, spread by mosquito bites.
- o Trypanosomiasis (Sleeping Sickness): Transmitted by tsetse flies.

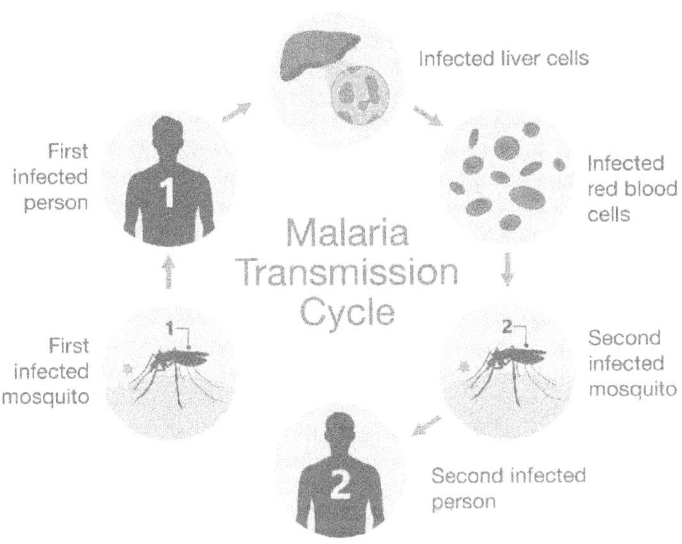

Diseases by Pathogen Type

1. Bacteria:

- ➤ **Cholera** (Vibrio cholerae)
- ➤ **Typhoid** (Salmonella typhi)
- ➤ **Trachoma** (Eye infection)
- ➤ **Acute Diarrhea** (E. coli, Shigella)

2. Viruses:

- ➤ **Hepatitis A & E** (Liver inflammation)
- ➤ **Polio** (Paralysis)
- ➤ **Rotavirus/Norovirus** (Diarrhea)

3. Protozoa (Parasites):

- ➤ **Amebiasis: Caused by *Entamoeba histolytica*, spreads through contaminated food and water.** *(Asked in Exam)*
- ➤ **Giardiasis: Caused by *Giardia lamblia*, spreads via infected water sources.** *(Asked in Exam)*
- ➤ **Cryptosporidiosis:** Caused by *Cryptosporidium*.
- ➤ **Leishmaniasis:** Transmitted by sandflies.
- ➤ **Toxoplasmosis:** Spread by cat feces/undercooked meat.

4. Helminths (Worms):

- ➤ **Schistosomiasis** (Freshwater worms)

> **Hookworm Infection:** Enters through skin contact with contaminated soil.

Chemical Contaminants in Water

Apart from pathogens, water pollution also involves chemical agents:

> Salts are inorganic chemicals that can pollute water. *(Asked in Exam)*
> Pesticides are organic chemicals that can contaminate water. *(Asked in Exam)*
> Radioactive iodine can be a contaminant in water. *(Asked in Exam)*
> Pathogens include fungi which can cause waterborne diseases. *(Asked in Exam)*

Air Pollution: Overview

Definition:

Air pollution occurs when harmful substances, known as pollutants, enter the air and disrupt the natural balance of the atmosphere. These pollutants can be gases, tiny particles, or biological molecules.

Impact:

> **Health:** Breathing polluted air can cause respiratory infections, heart disease, stroke, and lung cancer. It affects the health of babies before birth and is linked to lower IQ and cognitive impairment.
> **Environment:** Leads to climate change, ozone layer depletion, and habitat destruction.
> **Structures:** Damages buildings (e.g., acid rain corrosion).

Classification of Air Pollutants

1. Primary Pollutants:

Emitted directly from a source.

- Examples: Carbon monoxide (CO) from car exhausts, Sulfur dioxide (SO2) from industrial processes.

2. Secondary Pollutants:

Formed when primary pollutants react in the atmosphere.

> **Sulphate, Photochemical smog, and PeroxyAcetyl Nitrate (PAN) are examples of secondary air pollutants.** *(Asked in Exam)*
> **Ground-level Ozone:** Forms when Hydrocarbons & NOx react with sunlight.
> **Acid Rain:** Caused by SO2 & Nox reacting with water.

Particulate Matter (PM)

One of the parameters used to characterize the air quality at a location is PM. Here, the suffix '2.5' refers to the size of suspended particles in certain units (microns). *(Asked in Exam)*

Classification by Size:

- **Coarse Particles: These are larger particles, typically greater than 10 microns in size.** *(Asked in Exam)*
  - Generally not inhaled deeply; less significant indicators of health impacts compared to smaller particles.
- **Respirable Suspended Particulate Matter (RSPM): Typically refers to particulate matter with an aerodynamic diameter of less than 10 microns (PM10).** *(Asked in Exam)*
  - **PM10 is preferred over Total Suspended Particles (TSP) for air quality monitoring studies.** *(Asked in Exam)*
- **Fine Particles (PM_{2.5}): Those SPM whose aerodynamic diameter is less than 2.5 microns.** *(Asked in Exam)*
  - Sources: Combustion, industrial processes, vehicle exhaust.
- **Ultrafine Particles: These are the smallest particles, typically less than 0.1 microns in size.** *(Asked in Exam)*

Modes of Formation:

- **Nucleation Mode: Nucleation mode particles are the finest particulate matter.** *(Asked in Exam)* (< 0.01 microns). Formed from gas-to-particle conversion.
- **Aitken Mode:** 0.01 to 0.1 microns.
- **Accumulation Mode:** 0.1 to 2.5 microns. Remains airborne for a long time.

Health Impact of PM:

- **The most relevant effect of particulate matter in air on human health is the aggravation of respiratory disease.** *(Asked in Exam)*
- **Pathway: Particulate matter enters the body through inhalation, passes into the lungs, moves into the blood, and then reaches the soft tissues of organs.** *(Asked in Exam)*
- **Atmospheric haze is mainly caused by ultra-fine size particulate matters.**

Soot and Black Carbon:

- **Particulate matter, a class of air pollutants, includes Soot, Pollen, Fly ash.** *(Asked in Exam)*
- **Soot particles, also known as black carbon, are toxic substances that contribute to global warming and are capable of penetrating into the deeper regions of the lungs.** *(Asked in Exam)*
- **Black Carbon Aerosols:** Absorb sunlight (warming the atmosphere) and reduce ice/snow reflectivity (accelerating melting).

Major Primary Pollutants

1. Carbon Monoxide (CO):
- ➢ Colorless, odorless, tasteless, and highly toxic.
- ➢ Source: Incomplete combustion of fossil fuels (cars, coal, wood).
- ➢ Mechanism: Carbon monoxide has a very strong affinity towards haemoglobin of the human blood. *(Asked in Exam)*
  - ○ Hemoglobin present in the blood has greater affinity towards carbon monoxide than oxygen. *(Asked in Exam)*
  - ○ It binds to hemoglobin to form Carboxyhemoglobin, reducing oxygen transport.
- ➢ Danger: Carbon monoxide (CO) is a serious asphyxiant: even a short exposure may have fatal health issues. *(Asked in Exam)*

2. Sulfur Dioxide (SO_2):
- ➢ Pungent gas smelling like burnt matches.
- ➢ Source: Sulphur dioxide (SO_2) is a significant air pollutant that primarily comes from human activities. The major man-made sources include the burning of fossil fuels in power plants and industrial processes, particularly those involving the smelting of metal ores. *(Asked in Exam)*
- ➢ Impact: Precursor to acid rain. Taj Mahal is mainly threatened by the deleterious effects of Sulphur dioxide. *(Asked in Exam)*

3. Nitrogen Oxides (NO_x):
- ➢ In air pollution, oxides of nitrogen (NO_x) include Nitric oxide and Nitrogen dioxide. *(Asked in Exam)*
- ➢ Nitric oxide (NO) has the least residence time in the atmosphere. *(Asked in Exam)*
- ➢ Nitrogen oxides (NO_x) is a key ingredient in the formation of photochemical smog. *(Asked in Exam)*

4. Hydrocarbons / BTEX:
- ➢ BTEX stands for Benzene, Toluene, Ethylbenzene, and Xylene.
- ➢ Benzene: Causes leukemia.
- ➢ Toluene: Affects the nervous system.

Major Secondary Pollutants

1. Photochemical Smog:
Also called "Summer Smog." It appears as a brown haze.

- ➢ Formation Requirements: Nitrogen dioxide (NO_2), Volatile Organic Compounds (VOCs), AND Sunlight. *(Asked in Exam)*
- ➢ Sunlight:
  - ○ Sunlight is an essential requirement for the formation of photochemical smog. *(Asked in Exam)*
  - ○ Photochemical smog is more prevalent in the summer season... In winter, conditions are typically less favorable. *(Asked in Exam)*

> ➤ Impacts: Photochemical smog in urban areas is known to cause Respiratory effects, Eye irritation, Nose and throat irritation, and Reduction in visibility. *(Asked in Exam)*

2. Peroxyacyl Nitrates (PANs):

Formed by the oxidation of VOCs and aldehydes in the presence of NO_2 and sunlight.

> ➤ More water-soluble than ozone.
> ➤ **Lachrymators:** Cause eye irritation even at low levels.
> ➤ Mutagenic properties (linked to skin cancer).

3. Ground-Level Ozone (O_3):

> ➤ **Formation:** Reaction between NO_x, VOCs, and sunlight.
> ➤ **Impact:** Irritates eyes, throat, and lungs; worsens asthma and causes COPD. damaging to crops and forests.
> ➤ *Note:* Distinct from the stratospheric ozone layer (which protects us).

4. Acid Rain:

> ➤ Forms when SO_x and NO_x react with water vapor to form sulfuric and nitric acids.
> ➤ **Rain is termed as acid rain when its pH value is Less than 5.6.** *(Asked in Exam)*
> ➤ **Deposition:** Can be Wet (rain, snow) or Dry (acidic particles).

Volatile Organic Compounds (VOCs)

Definition & Characteristics:

VOCs are organic chemicals with high vapor pressure, meaning they evaporate easily at room temperature.

> ➤ Volatile Organic Compounds (VOCs) is an extremely short-lived and unstable air/water pollutant. *(Asked in Exam)*
> ➤ Volatile Organic Compounds (VOCs) include a range of compounds, some of which are known to be carcinogenic. *(Asked in Exam)*
> ➤ Naturally occurring Volatile Organic Compounds (VOCs) generally oxidize to form Carbon Monoxide (CO) and Carbon Dioxide (CO2). *(Asked in Exam)*

Sources of VOCs:

Sources can be categorized into natural and anthropogenic (man-made). Vehicles, Plants, Termites, Power Plants, and Bogs are sources of Volatile Organic Compounds (VOCs). *(Asked in Exam)*

1. **Natural Sources:**

> - Volatile Organic Compounds are emitted from some trees. *(Asked in Exam)*
> - Terpene Volatile Organic Compound (VOC), a kind of air pollutant, is emitted from natural sources such as plants, bogs etc. *(Asked in Exam)*
> - Some tree species emit volatile organic compounds (VOCs) such as isoprene which may contribute to formation of tropospheric ozone. *(Asked in Exam)*
> - *Note on Forests:* While forests help in improving air quality, specific emissions like isoprene can interact with other pollutants. Forests help in improving the air quality of a place. *(Asked in Exam)*

2. **Anthropogenic Sources:**

> - Volatile Organic Compounds (VOCs) are emitted from vehicles. *(Asked in Exam)*
> - Volatile organic compounds air pollutants are produced from room deodorizers. *(Asked in Exam)*
> - Formaldehyde, Benzene, and Toluene: While these compounds can also be classified as volatile organic compounds (VOCs), they are primarily associated with anthropogenic (human-made) sources rather than natural ones. *(Asked in Exam)*
> - Household items: Paints, wood preservatives, aerosol sprays, cleaning products, and dry-cleaned clothing.

SOURCES OF VOCs
VOLATILE ORGANIC COMPOUNDS

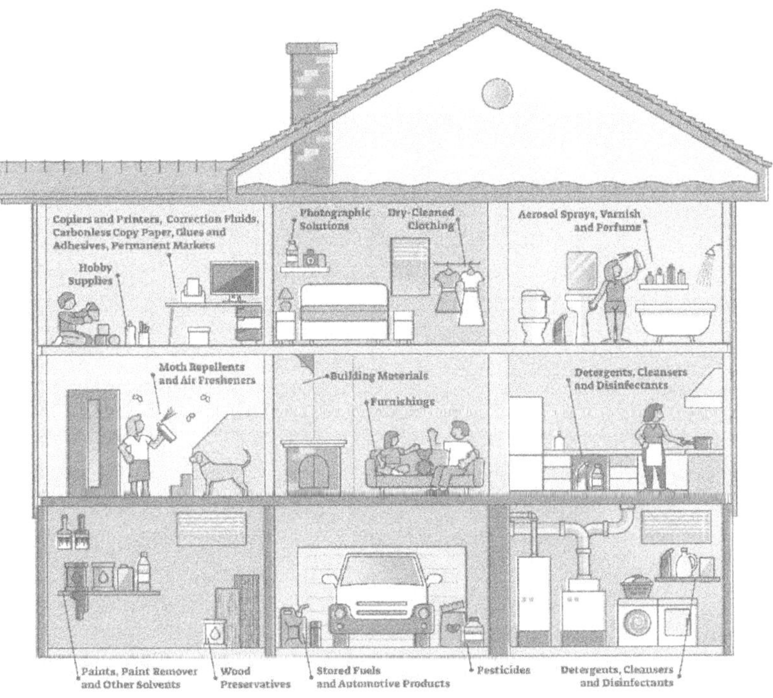

Environmental & Health Impact:

➢ Smog Formation: Anthropogenically emitted VOCs play an important role in the formation of smog. *(Asked in Exam)* specifically photochemical smog. *(Asked in Exam)*

Water Contamination:

➢ Volatile Organic Chemicals (VOCs) are among the most commonly found contaminants in groundwater. *(Asked in Exam)*

➢ Volatile Organic Chemicals (VOCs) are contaminants more commonly found in groundwater than in surface water. *(Asked in Exam)*

➢ *Regulation:* While VOCs can be a concern for drinking water quality, they are not typically one of the primary criterion parameters used universally to determine drinking water quality. *(Asked in Exam)*

Health Risks:

> The Volatile Organic Compounds (VOCs) may cause cancer. *(Asked in Exam)*
> Formaldehyde, widely used in plastics, wood products, insulating materials, glue and fabrics, is a serious allergen. *(Asked in Exam)*

Persistent Organic Pollutants (POPs)

Definition:

The full form of POPs is Persistent Organic Pollutants. *(Asked in Exam)*

These are toxic organic compounds resistant to environmental degradation.

> Persistent Organic Pollutants (POPs) are extremely widespread and occur from tropics to the Arctic and often accumulate in food webs and reach toxic concentrations. *(Asked in Exam)*
> Poly Chlorinated Biphenyls, Dioxins and Furans are examples of Persistent Organic Pollutants (POPs). *(Asked in Exam)*

Key Characteristics:

> **Global Spread:** They travel vast distances via wind and water (Grasshopper effect).
> **Bioaccumulation:** They accumulate in the fatty tissue of living organisms. **Pesticides and Persistent Organic Pollutants (POPs) can be part of bioaccumulation/biomagnification.**
> **Applications: They are widely used as flame retardants and in deodorants. Some chemicals used in making non-stick, waterproof and stain resistant products are categorized as POPs.** *(Asked in Exam)*

Types & Sources:

> The "Dirty Dozen": Includes DDT, dioxins, PCBs, chlordane, aldrin. New additions include PFOS. Dioxins, Poly-Chlorinated Benzenes (PCBs), Organochlorine Pesticides and Furans are examples of Persistent Organic Pollutants (POPs). *(Asked in Exam)*
> Incineration By-products:
>   o Dioxins and Furans are highly toxic substances produced as by-products of solid waste incineration. *(Asked in Exam)*
>   o Dioxins and furans are known for their stability and persistence in the environment. *(Asked in Exam)*
>   o Sources include waste incineration, burning of plastics (PCDDs & PCDFs), and the metallurgical industry.

Health Effects:

> **Acute:** Death, allergies, hypersensitivity.
> **Chronic:** Nervous, endocrine, reproductive damage. **2006 study links POPs to diabetes (Lee et al.).**

> **Developmental:** Disruption of the immune system and developmental changes.

Related Air Pollutants & Concepts

(Important Definitions often tested alongside VOCs)

> Allergens: Allergens are substances that activate the immune system. *(Asked in Exam)*
> Carbon Monoxide (CO): Carbon monoxide (CO) is an asphyxiant. *(Asked in Exam)*
> Nitrogen Dioxide (NO_2): Nitrogen dioxide (NO_2) is associated with respiratory problems and can contribute to conditions like methemoglobinemia ("blue baby" syndrome). *(Asked in Exam)*
> Ozone (O_3): Ozone (O_3) is a potent respiratory irritant and allergen. *(Asked in Exam)*

Indoor Air Quality (IAQ)

Overview:

Indoor air quality (IAQ) refers to the quality of the air within buildings and structures. Poor IAQ due to indoor air pollution can affect the health, comfort, and well-being of occupants. It has been linked to respiratory issues, reduced productivity, and impaired learning in schools.

Indoor Air Pollution in Developing Countries:

> **In the less developed countries of the world, indoor exposure to hazardous air pollutants is much severe.** *(Asked in Exam)*
> **Traditional methods of cooking often involve fuels such as coal, wood, animal dung, kerosene etc.** *(Asked in Exam)*
> This "household air pollution" affects ~3 billion people, mainly women and children.

Common Indoor Air Pollutants:

> Secondhand Tobacco Smoke
> Indoor Combustion pollutants
> Radon, Asbestos Fibers, and Carbon Monoxide
> **Volatile Organic Compounds (VOCs):**
>   o **Concentration of Formaldehyde in indoor environment can be thousand times higher than outdoor environment.** *(Asked in Exam)*
>   o **Formaldehyde is a known carcinogen.** *(Asked in Exam)*
> **Molds and Allergens:**
>   o **Allergens are substances that activate the immune system.** *(Asked in Exam)*

- o **Concentration of allergens in an indoor environment can be thousand times higher than in the air outside.** *(Asked in Exam)*

Sick Building Syndrome (SBS)

Definition:

Sick Building Syndrome (SBS) is a condition of human health due to indoor air pollution. *(Asked in Exam)*

- ➢ **Polluted indoor air causes Sick Building Syndrome (SBS).** *(Asked in Exam)*
- ➢ **Some people suffer from what is called Sick Building Syndrome (SBS).** *(Asked in Exam)*
- ➢ Symptoms include headaches, dizziness, fatigue, and eye/nose/throat irritation. Symptoms typically worsen inside the building and improve upon leaving.

Causes:

SBS is primarily associated with poor indoor air quality due to factors such as:
- ➢ Inadequate ventilation.
- ➢ Chemical contaminants from indoor sources (like adhesives, upholstery, carpeting, copy machines, and cleaning agents). *(Asked in Exam)*
- ➢ Biological contaminants (like mold, bacteria, and pollen). *(Asked in Exam)*
- ➢ Other factors like inadequate temperature, humidity, or lighting. *(Asked in Exam)*

Air Quality Index (AQI)

General Overview:

Air Quality Index (AQI) is used to report to the public an overall assessment of a given day's air quality. *(Asked in Exam)*
- ➢ It measures air pollution and health risks; a higher AQI means greater pollution.
- ➢ The AQI integrates air quality data for more than just two criteria pollutants. It typically includes multiple key pollutants such as particulate matter (PM10 and PM2.5), nitrogen dioxide (NO2), sulfur dioxide (SO2), carbon monoxide (CO), ozone (O3), and sometimes lead (Pb). *(Asked in Exam)*

Pollutants Monitored:

> TSP (Total Suspended Particles) and PM10 (Particulate matters of size 10 microns or less) are types of particulate matter pollutants used in the calculation of Air Quality Index (AQI). *(Asked in Exam)*
> NO2 (Nitrogen dioxide) is included while estimating Air Quality Index (AQI). *(Asked in Exam)*

India's National Air Quality Index (NAQI)

Launched in New Delhi on September 17, 2014, as part of the Swachh Bharat Abhiyan.

AQI Categories:

The NAQI categorizes air quality into six levels: Good, Satisfactory, Moderate, Poor, Severe, and Hazardous.

The 8 Pollutants in NAQI:

The index considers eight pollutants measured based on short-term National Ambient Air Quality Standards (up to 24-hour averaging periods):

1. **PM10** (Particulate Matter $\leq$ 10 microns)
2. **PM2.5** (Particulate Matter $\leq$ 2.5 microns)
3. **NO2** (Nitrogen Dioxide)
4. **SO2** (Sulfur Dioxide) — **Sulphur dioxide pollutants are included in the Air Quality Index in India.** *(Asked in Exam)*
5. **CO** (Carbon Monoxide)
6. **O3** (Ozone)
7. **NH3** (Ammonia)
8. **Pb** (Lead)

Greenhouse Gases (GHGs)

Definition and Mechanism:

Greenhouse gases (GHGs) are special gases in the air that make the Earth's surface warmer. They work like a blanket. Just like a blanket keeps you warm by trapping your body heat, greenhouse gases trap the heat that the Earth gives off after being warmed by the Sun.

1. **Sunlight Warms the Earth:** The Sun shines on the Earth and warms it up.
2. **Earth Gives Off Heat:** The Earth's surface then gives off this heat (thermal radiation).

3. **Greenhouse Gases Trap the Heat: Greenhouse gases primarily absorb infrared radiation from the solar spectrum.** *(Asked in Exam)* They absorb this heat and keep it from escaping back into space, making the Earth warmer.

Without greenhouse gases, the Earth would be freezing -18°C (0°F), but thanks to them, it's a much warmer 15°C (59°F).

- **Greenhouse gases, including water vapor, absorb the earth's thermal radiation and contribute to global warming.** *(Asked in Exam)*
- **Earth's climate was changing even before man appeared on earth.** *(Asked in Exam)*

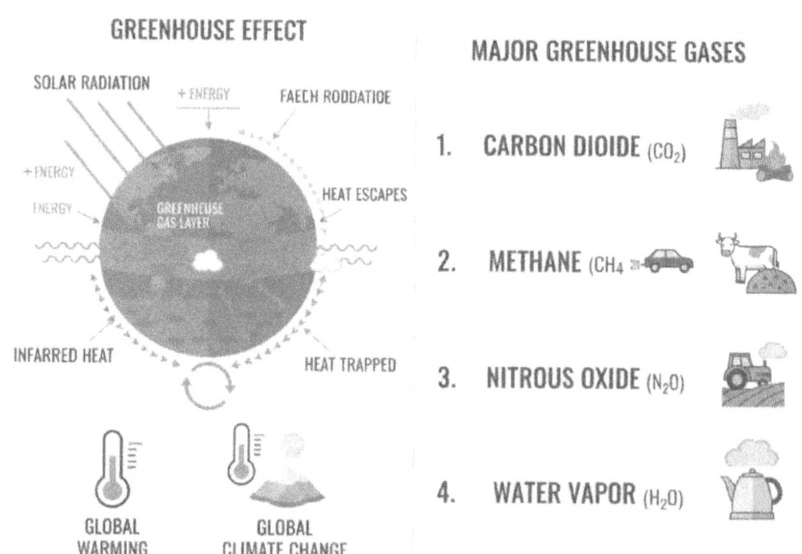

Main Greenhouse Gases

CO2 (Carbon dioxide), H2O (water vapor), CH4 (methane), and O3 (ozone) are Natural GreenHouse Gases (GHGs). *(Asked in Exam)*

1. Water Vapor (H_2O)

- **Naturally occurring, part of the water cycle.**
- Most abundant greenhouse gas; increases with temperature, amplifying warming.
- Traps heat, contributing to climate change but is short-lived and regulated by natural processes.

2. Carbon Dioxide (CO_2)

- **Major contribution to the greenhouse effect comes from carbon dioxide.** *(Asked in Exam)*
- **Carbon dioxide (CO_2) has the maximum contribution to Global Warming.** *(Asked in Exam)*
- Released from burning fossil fuels & deforestation.
- Has a long atmospheric lifetime and accumulates over time.

3. Methane (CH_4)

- Emitted from agriculture, fossil fuel production, and waste.
- **Methane, a greenhouse gas, is emitted from wetlands.** *(Asked in Exam)*
- **Methane (CH_4) is a greenhouse gas that helps in formation of Ozone and is a Volatile Organic Compound (VOC).** *(Asked in Exam)*
- More effective at trapping heat than CO_2 (higher GWP) but has a shorter lifespan.

4. Nitrous Oxide (N_2O)

- Produced from fertilizers & industrial activities.
- **Nitrous oxide (N_2O) has a significantly higher Global Warming Potential (GWP) compared to methane (CH_4), carbon dioxide (CO_2), and carbon monoxide (CO).** *(Asked in Exam)*
- **Nitrogen dioxide is a pollutant that causes aggravation of respiratory disease and atmospheric discolouration.** *(Asked in Exam) (Note: Distinguish between Nitrous Oxide N_2O (GHG) and Nitrogen Dioxide NO_2 (Pollutant)).*

5. Ozone (O_3)

* Forms from reactions with pollutants & sunlight.
* Harmful at ground level (smog), but protects against UV in the stratosphere.

6. Chlorofluorocarbons (CFCs)

* **Chlorofluorocarbons (CFCs) are potent greenhouse gases.** *(Asked in Exam)*
* **Chlorofluorocarbons (CFCs) are stable greenhouse gases that vaporize just below room temperature and can destroy ozone.** *(Asked in Exam)*
* **CFCs have the ability to catalytically destroy ozone in the stratosphere.** *(Asked in Exam)*
* **Discovery of Ozone hole was first made over Antarctic.** *(Asked in Exam)*
* **Chlorofluorocarbon is a non-vehicular pollutant.** *(Asked in Exam)*
* **Status: The concentration of CFCs in the atmosphere has been decreasing due to international efforts to phase out the production and use of these substances under the Montreal Protocol.** *(Asked in Exam)* However, **CFCs already present in the atmosphere will persist for many years.** *(Asked in Exam)*

7. Sulfur Hexafluoride (SF_6)

* Used in electrical insulation & semiconductor industry.
* Strongest greenhouse gas per molecule with an extremely long atmospheric lifetime.

Global Warming Potential (GWP)

Definition:

Global Warming Potential (GWP) is a way to compare how much heat different greenhouse gases trap in the atmosphere over a specific period (usually 100 years). Carbon dioxide (CO_2) is used as the reference gas for Global Warming Potential (GWP) and is assigned a GWP value of 1. *(Asked in Exam)*

Variability:

* **Global warming potential of a molecule of a greenhouse gas over different time spans of decades to 100 years may vary significantly.** *(Asked in Exam)*
* **Some greenhouse gases have shorter lifetimes compared to carbon dioxide.** *(Asked in Exam)*

GWP Rankings *(Asked in Exam):*

- Lowest to Highest GWP:

The gases increase in Global Warming Potential (GWP) in this order: CO_2 < CH_4 < N_2O < CFCs. *(Asked in Exam)*

1. **Carbon dioxide (CO_2):** Baseline, GWP = 1.
2. **Methane (CH_4):** GWP = 28–36.
3. **Nitrous oxide (N_2O):** GWP = 265–298.
4. **Chlorofluorocarbons (CFCs) / HFCs:** GWP = Thousands (e.g., CFC-11 is ~4,660).
5. **Sulfur hexafluoride (SF_6):** GWP = 23,500.

Atmospheric Lifetime

The longevity of gases in the atmosphere varies.
The correct order for decreasing atmospheric lifetimes of these greenhouse gases is: CFC-11 > Nitrous oxide (N_2O) > Methane (CH_4) > Surface ozone (O_3). *(Asked in Exam)*

Global Emissions and Human Activity

Since people started using machines and factories around 1750, emissions have skyrocketed.

- **China is the largest emitter of Greenhouse Gases (GHGs) at present.** *(Asked in Exam)*

Top 10 Countries by GHG Emissions (Largest to Lowest):

1. **China:** Largest emitter, coal-dependent.
2. **USA:** High energy consumption.
3. **India:** Rapidly growing, coal reliance.
4. **Russia:** Oil and gas.
5. **Japan:** Energy-intensive industries.
6. **Germany:** Industrial emissions.
7. **Iran:** Oil and gas production.
8. **South Korea:** Industrial sector.
9. **Saudi Arabia:** Oil extraction.
10. **Indonesia:** Deforestation and peatland.

Mitigation:

- **One of the ways to control greenhouse gas emissions is by encouraging energy efficiency throughout society in our country.** *(Asked in Exam)*
- **Improving energy efficiency has significant environmental benefits.** *(Asked in Exam)*

Impacts of Greenhouse Gases

Global Warming:

- Carbon Dioxide causes about three-quarters of global warming.
- Scientists warn that exceeding a 2.0°C rise could be dangerous.

Sea Level Rise:

- **Thermal expansion of oceans may lead to Sea level rise.** *(Asked in Exam)*
- **Over the past 100 years, the estimated rise of global sea level is by 10-25cm or more. Thermal expansion of ocean waters has the maximum contribution in it.** *(Asked in Exam)*

Ozone Layer: General Overview

Structure & Function:

- **Location:** The ozone layer is located in the **Stratosphere**, 15-35 km above Earth. **Ozone layer which protects us from harmful ultraviolet radiations is situated in Stratosphere.** *(Asked in Exam)*
- **Role:**
  - **Stratospheric ozone is known as 'good ozone'.** *(Asked in Exam)*
  - **Although ozone is a pollutant in the ambient air, but in stratosphere it is valuable because it absorbs harmful UV-Radiations.** *(Asked in Exam)*
  - Protects life by blocking 97-99% of UV rays.

Ozone Types:

1. **Good Ozone (Stratospheric Ozone):** Forms a protective shield against UV radiation.
2. **Bad Ozone (Tropospheric Ozone):**
   - Found in the troposphere, near Earth's surface.

- o **Ozone at the surface level is a serious health hazard and known as pollutant.** *(Asked in Exam)*
- o **Ozone pollutant is considered as surrogate for eye irritation.** *(Asked in Exam)*
- o Contributes to smog and respiratory issues (asthma).

Ground-Level Ozone (Pollutant)

Formation:

- ➢ Tropospheric (ground level) ozone forms when sunlight acts on nitrogen oxides and can also result from downward transfer from the ozone layer. It is a greenhouse gas and a major part of photochemical smog. *(Asked in Exam)*
- ➢ Surface ozone forms mainly due to the interaction of nitrogen oxides, carbon monoxide, and sunlight. *(Asked in Exam)*
- ➢ Tropospheric Ozone has a positive radiative forcing or warming effect in the global climate. *(Asked in Exam)*

Daily Cycle:

- ➢ The tropospheric ozone levels in the afternoon of a hot sunny day are typically higher, not lower. *(Asked in Exam)* This is because intense sunlight drives photochemical reactions.
- ➢ Ground level concentration of ozone decreases at night. *(Asked in Exam)*
- ➢ In the afternoon period, the atmosphere is unstable and its dilution potential is higher as compared to mornings and evenings. *(Asked in Exam)*

Ozone Depletion

Mechanism:

Imagine the ozone layer as a sunscreen. Chemicals like Chlorofluorocarbons (CFCs) break it apart.

- ➢ Process: CFCs reach the stratosphere → Sunlight breaks CFCs releasing Chlorine → Chlorine destroys Ozone.
- ➢ Ultraviolet radiation photolysis the ozone into other components. *(Asked in Exam)*
- ➢ One chlorine radical destroys 100,000 ozone molecules.

Ozone Depleting Substances (ODS):

- ➢ The global environmental issue of Ozone depletion is due to emission of Chlorinated hydrocarbons. *(Asked in Exam)*
- ➢ CFC, Halons, and HCFC are responsible for the destruction of the Ozone layer. *(Asked in Exam)*

> Halocarbons also catalytically destroy stratospheric Ozone. *(Asked in Exam)*
> Emissions from thermal power plants and Excessive use of nitrogen-containing fertilizers also contribute to depletion. *(Asked in Exam)*
> Dioxins is not responsible for the destruction of the Ozone layer. *(Asked in Exam)*

Ozone Hole:

> Ozone hole appears over Antarctica mostly in the month of September. *(Asked in Exam)*
> Polar Stratospheric Clouds are associated with Ozone layer depletion environmental issues. *(Asked in Exam)*

Consequences:

> Thinner ozone layer allows more UV rays to reach Earth.
> Increases skin cancer and cataracts.

Recovery:

> Montreal Protocol banned CFCs, slowing depletion.
> September 16 is International Ozone Preservation Day.
> Nitrous oxide (N_2O) is now the largest ozone-depleting gas.

Related Environmental Concepts (Global Warming & Atmosphere)

Global Warming Potential (GWP):

> The order of Global Warming Potential (GWP) for these atmospheric chemicals is: Carbon dioxide (CO_2) < Methane (CH_4) < Nitrous oxide (N_2O) < Chlorofluorocarbon (CFC). *(Asked in Exam)*
> Halocarbons contribute significantly to global warming. *(Asked in Exam)*

Heat Balance & Atmosphere:

> The atmosphere is essential in maintaining the heat balance of the body. *(Asked in Exam)*
> Gases in the atmosphere absorb infrared radiation from Earth's surface, which is the basic mechanism of the greenhouse effect. *(Asked in Exam)*
> The radiation reflected back to the atmosphere is called albedo. *(Asked in Exam)*

Urban Heat Island Effect:
- ➢ Nighttime temperatures in the central parts of a city are generally higher than those over the surrounding rural areas. *(Asked in Exam)*
- ➢ Radiation losses over the urban areas are less than that over the rural Areas. *(Asked in Exam)*

Methane & Permafrost:
- ➢ Global warming could lead to increased release of the greenhouse gas, Methane. *(Asked in Exam)*
- ➢ There is a large amount of Methane currently frozen in the permafrost in the far northern regions of the world. *(Asked in Exam)*

Water Treatment Note:
- ➢ Chlorine is one of the most commonly used and inexpensive chemical disinfectants for water. *(Asked in Exam)*
- ➢ Optimum Fluoride levels in drinking water help prevent cavities in children. *(Asked in Exam)*

Soil Pollution

Soil pollution refers to the contamination of soil with high concentrations of toxic substances. It is a significant environmental concern due to its many health hazards. For example, exposure to soil with high levels of benzene can increase the risk of developing leukemia.

All soils naturally contain some harmful or toxic compounds. However, in unpolluted soils, the concentrations of these substances are low enough that they do not pose a threat to the surrounding ecosystem. When the concentration of one or more toxic substances becomes high enough to cause harm to living organisms, the soil is considered contaminated.

Causes of Soil Pollution:

Agriculture: Excessive or improper use of pesticides.

Industrial Activity: High levels of industrial operations.

Waste Management: Poor management or inefficient disposal of waste.

Soil Remediation: The process of decontaminating soil, known as soil remediation, is closely linked to the extent of soil pollution. The more contaminated the soil, the more resources are required for its remediation.

Soil pollution is a critical issue that requires careful management and remediation efforts to protect human health and the environment.

Pollutants that Contaminate Soil

Some of the most hazardous soil pollutants are xenobiotics – substances not naturally found in nature and synthesized by humans. The term 'xenobiotic' comes from Greek roots: 'Xenos' (foreigner) and 'Bios' (life). Many xenobiotics are known carcinogens.

Heavy Metals: The presence of heavy metals in soils, such as lead and mercury, in high concentrations can be highly toxic to humans. Some metals that can cause soil pollution include:

- Arsenic
- Mercury
- Lead
- Antimony
- Zinc
- Nickel
- Cadmium
- Selenium
- Beryllium
- Thallium
- Chromium
- Copper

These metals can originate from various sources such as mining activities, agricultural activities, electronic waste (e-waste), and medical waste.

Polycyclic Aromatic Hydrocarbons (PAHs)

PAHs are organic compounds that:

- **Contain only carbon and hydrogen atoms.**
- **Have more than one aromatic ring in their chemical structures.**

Common examples include naphthalene, anthracene, and phenalene. Exposure to PAHs has been linked to several cancers and cardiovascular diseases. Sources of PAH pollution include coke (coal) processing, vehicle emissions, cigarette smoke, and shale oil extraction.

Industrial Waste: The discharge of industrial waste into soils can lead to pollution. Common pollutants from industrial waste include:

> Chlorinated industrial solvents
> Dioxins: Produced from pesticide manufacture and waste incineration.
> Plasticizers/Dispersants
> Polychlorinated biphenyls (PCBs)
> Petroleum hydrocarbons: Benzene and methylbenzene, which are carcinogenic.

Pesticides: Pesticides are substances used to kill or inhibit pests. Common types include:

> **Herbicides**: Kill/control weeds and unwanted plants.
> **Insecticides**: Kill insects.
> **Fungicides**: Kill parasitic fungi or inhibit their growth.

Unintentional diffusion of pesticides into the environment, known as 'pesticide drift,' can lead to soil and water pollution. Important soil contaminants in pesticides include:

> **Herbicides**: Triazines, carbamates, amides, phenyl alkyl acids, aliphatic acids.
> **Insecticides**: Organophosphates, chlorinated hydrocarbons, arsenic-containing compounds, pyrethrum.
> **Fungicides**: Mercury-containing compounds, thiocarbamates, copper sulfate.

These chemicals pose significant health risks to humans, including central nervous system diseases, immune system diseases, cancer, and birth defects.

Processes that Cause Soil Pollution

Soil pollution can be broadly classified into two categories:

> Naturally Caused Soil Pollution
> Anthropogenic Soil Pollution (Caused by Human Activity)
> Natural Pollution of Soil

In rare cases, pollutants can naturally accumulate in soils. This can occur due to differential deposition of soil by the atmosphere or transportation of soil pollutants with precipitation water.

Examples of Natural Soil Pollution: Perchlorate Accumulation: In dry, arid ecosystems, compounds containing the perchlorate anion ($ClO4-$) can accumulate. These can also form in soils containing chlorine and certain metals during thunderstorms.

Anthropogenic Soil Pollution: Almost all cases of soil pollution are caused by human activities. Various processes lead to the contamination of soil, including:

Examples of Anthropogenic Soil Pollution:

- **Demolition of old buildings** contaminates soil with asbestos.
- **Lead-based paints** pollute soil with hazardous lead.
- **Petrol & diesel spills** contaminate soil with hydrocarbons.
- **Metal casting factories** release metallic contaminants.
- **Underground mining** pollutes land with heavy metals.
- **Industrial waste disposal** seeps toxins into soil & groundwater.
- **Chemical pesticides** cause severe soil pollution.
- **Urban sewage** contaminates soil with carcinogens.

Effects on Human Beings

Soil contaminants can exist in solid, liquid, and gaseous phases, which allows them to enter the human body through direct contact with the skin or inhalation of contaminated soil dust.

Short-Term Effects:

- Headaches, nausea, and vomiting
- Coughing, chest pain, and wheezing
- Irritation of the skin and eyes
- Fatigue and weakness

Long-Term Effects:

- **Lead Exposure:** Can cause permanent damage to the nervous system, particularly in children.
- **CNS Depression:** Exposure to certain soil pollutants can depress the central nervous system.
- **Organ Damage:** Damage to vital organs such as the kidneys and liver.
- **Cancer:** Increased risk of developing cancer.
- **Congenital Disorders:** Linked to exposure to petroleum hydrocarbons and industrial solvents.

Effects on Plants and Animals

Soil pollution often reduces the availability of nutrients, causing plant life to struggle. Contaminated soils, especially with inorganic aluminum, can be toxic to plants and increase soil salinity, making it unsuitable for plant growth.

Impact on Plants: Bioaccumulation: Plants grown in polluted soil can accumulate high concentrations of pollutants. When herbivores consume these plants, the pollutants move up the food chain, potentially causing extinction of desirable animal species and diseases in humans.

Impact on Animals: Food Chain Contamination: Pollutants accumulated in plants can transfer to herbivores and further up the food chain, causing health issues in animals and eventually humans.

Effects on the Ecosystem

Soil pollution can significantly impact the ecosystem through various channels:

Air and Water Pollution: Volatile Contaminants: Can be carried into the atmosphere by wind or seep into underground water reserves, contributing to air and water pollution.

Acid Rain: Soil pollutants like ammonia can contribute to acid rain.

Soil Quality: Microorganism Impact: Acidic soils become inhospitable to microorganisms that improve soil texture and help decompose organic matter, thereby degrading soil quality and texture.

Crop Yield: Soil pollution severely affects crop yields. For instance, in China, over 12 million tons of grain are found to be unfit for consumption due to heavy metal contamination, resulting in significant economic losses.

Noise Pollution

Overview:

Noise pollution is the spread of loud, unwanted sounds that disrupt the activities of humans and animals, often causing harm.

> - Exposure to noise pollution adversely affects the physiological health of a person. *(Asked in Exam)*
> - Exposure to noise pollution adversely affects the psychological health of a person. *(Asked in Exam)*

Sources of Noise:

The primary culprits of outdoor noise worldwide are machines, transportation, and various systems of propagation. Poor urban planning can also contribute to noise pollution.

> Average noise levels in heavy traffic zones in major cities in India are generally in 70-95 dBA ranges of noise levels. *(Asked in Exam)*

Understanding Noise Measurement: Pressure, Intensity, and Frequency

Researchers measure noise using three key parameters: pressure, intensity, and frequency.

1. Sound Pressure Level (SPL):

> SPL helps determine how loud a sound is by comparing it to the threshold of hearing.

> **Sound pressure of 20uPa (micropascals) corresponds to a noise of zero decibel.** *(Asked in Exam)* *(Note: Corrected "2j Pa" to the scientific standard 20uPa).*

2. Sound Intensity:

> Measured in Watts per square meter.

> **Two sounds of same intensity but different frequency characteristics may appear to be of different loudness.** *(Asked in Exam)*

3. Frequency:

> Measured in Hertz (Hz). Humans can hear frequencies ranging from 20 Hz to 20,000 Hz.

> **The response of the human ear to noise of different frequencies is not uniform.** *(Asked in Exam)*

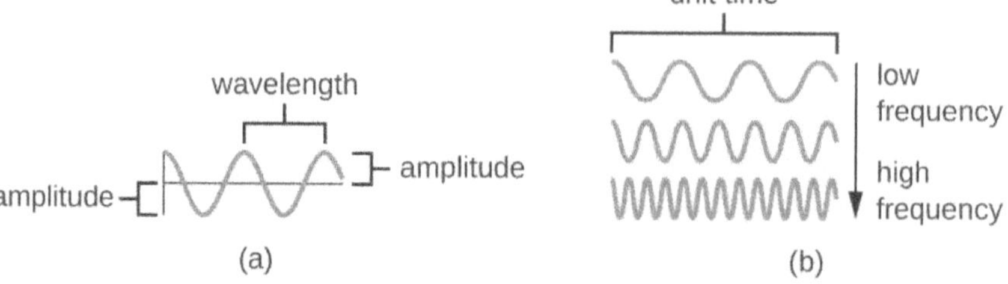

Factors Influencing Impact:

The impact of noise pollution on human health is governed by Intensity of noise, Duration of noise, Sensitivity of human ear, and Frequency range of noise. *(Asked in Exam)*

Decibel (dB) Levels and Regulations

Understanding Decibels:

Noise above 65 dB is classified as pollution by WHO.
The correct sequence of average noise levels in increasing order of their magnitude from different sources: Typical office → Conversational speech → City Street corner → Highway → Aircraft noise during take-off. *(Asked in Exam)*

Noise Standards in India (Regulation and Control Rules, 2000):

> Educational Institutions: According to Noise Pollution (Regulation and Control) Rules in India, noise in educational institutions during night time (10pm-6am) must not exceed 40dB. *(Asked in Exam)*

> Residential Areas: Day time noise standard prescribed for residential areas in India is 55 dB. *(Asked in Exam)*

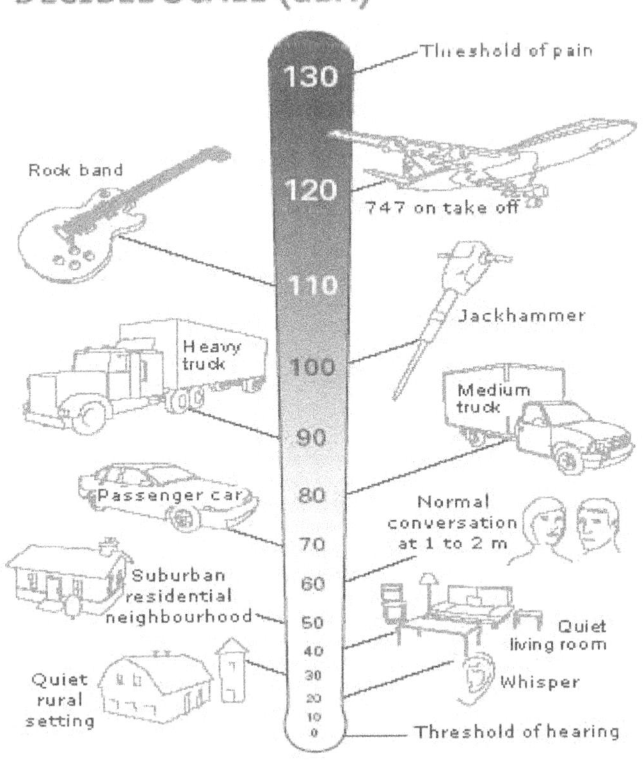

Health Effects of Noise Pollution

Exposure to high levels of noise can have serious health impacts.

> ➢ Exposure to excessive noise pollution can cause Hearing impairment, Insomnia, Rise in blood pressure, and Reduced work efficiency. *(Asked in Exam)*
> ➢ Exposure to noise pollution can cause Sleeplessness, Speech interference, Increase in blood pressure, and Shift in threshold of hearing. *(Asked in Exam)*

Specific Impacts:

> ➢ **Cardiovascular:** High noise levels can lead to cardiovascular problems and hypertension.
> ➢ **Wildlife:** Noise can disrupt predators/prey detection, interference with reproduction and navigation (e.g., in marine invertebrates and mammals).
> ➢ **Real Estate:** Local noise environment impacts property value.

Mitigation

Materials with high surface/mass density act as good noise barriers. *(Asked in Exam)*

Questions

Water Pollution

Q 1. In large parts of Eastern India, the groundwater is contaminated by

1. Arsenic
2. Lead
3. Mercury
4. Nickel

Answer: 1. Arsenic

Q 2. Identify the correct sequence in decreasing order of percentage of total world's water in the following locations:

A. Atmosphere
B. Rivers and streams
C. Ground water
D. Lakes (Fresh water)
E. Ice caps and Glaciers

Choose the correct answer from the options given below:

1. (E), (C), (B), (D), (A)
2. (E), (B), (C), (D), (A)
3. (E), (D), (C), (B), (A)

4. (E), (C), (D), (A), (B)

Answer: 4. (E), (C), (D), (A), (B)

Q 3. Below are given two sets. Set - I mention the types of pollution, while Set - II indicates their source. Match the two sets and select your answer from the code.

Set I (Pollution Type)	Set II (Sources)
a. Air	i. Point and non-point sources such as discharges from industries etc.
b. Land	ii. Industries, thermal power plants and motor vehicles
c. Water	iii. Roadway, aircraft, industrial as well as high intensity sonar.
d. Noise	iv. Over use of chemical fertilizers.

Choose the correct answer from the options given below:

1. (a)–(i), (b)–(ii), (c)–(iii), (d)–(iv)
2. (a)–(ii), (b)–(iv), (c)–(i), (d)–(iii)
3. (a)–(iii), (b)–(i), (c)–(ii), (d)–(iv)
4. (a)–(iv), (b)–(iii), (c)–(ii), (d)–(i)

Answer: 2. (a)–(ii), (b)–(iv), (c)–(i), (d)–(iii)

Q 4. Given below are two statements:

Assertion A: Bottom ash generated into the boilers of the thermal power plants are a major cause of nearby river pollution.

Reason R: The hot water generated from thermal power plants is discharged into the nearby rivers.

In the light of the above statements, choose the correct answer from the options given below:

1. Both A and R are true and R is the correct explanation of A
2. Both A and R are true but R is NOT the correct explanation of A
3. A is true but R is false
4. A is false but R is true

Answer: 2. Both A and R are true but R is NOT the correct explanation of A

Q 5. Recent study showed that, River Ganga will not flow cleaner soon. Which of the following reasons is false?

1. Thinning of flow rate of the river
2. Failure of treatment plants
3. Climatic change
4. Increased sewage

Answer: 3. Climatic change

Q 6. Non-point sources of water pollution are:

A. from specific location
B. diffuse
C. episodic
D. identifiable

E.   difficult to monitor

Choose the correct answer from the options given below:
1.   BCE
2.   ABC
3.   BCD
4.   CDE

Answer: 1. BCE

Q 7. Arrange the following water bodies in increasing order of the quantity of freshwater they hold:
A.   Ice and snow
B.   Freshwater |lakes and reservoirs
C.   Groundwater
D.   Rivers and streams

Choose the correct answer from the options given below:
1.   D, B, C, A
2.   B, C, D, A
3.   B, D, A, C
4.   D, B, A, C

Answer: 1. D, B, C, A

Q 8. Which of the following is the full form of PCB?
1.   Poly Cyclic Benzene
2.   Poly Chlorinated Benzene
3.   Poly Chlorinated Biphenyls
4.   Poly Cyclic Bi phenyls

Answer: 3. Poly Chlorinated Biphenyls

Q 9. Which one of the following has the highest turbidity?
1.   Drinking water
2.   Muddy water
3.   Clear Lake water
4.   Ocean water

Answer: 2. Muddy water

Q 10. Given below are two statements:
Assertion (A): Coral reefs are threatened because of release of sewage in ocean waters near them.
Reason (R): Release of sewage in oceans tends to reduce the clarity of ocean water.
In the light of the above statements, choose the correct answer from the options given below:
(1)   Both (A) and (R) are correct and (R) is the correct explanation of (A)
(2)   Both (A) and (R) are correct but (R) is not the correct explanation of (A)
(3)   (A) is correct but (R) is not correct
(4)   (A) is not correct but (R) is correct

Answer: 1. Both (A) and (R) are correct and (R) is the correct explanation of (A)

Q 11. Given below are two statements:
Statement I: Most of the emerging contaminants of water are Endocrine Disrupting Chemicals (EDCs).
Statement II: Flame retardant additive, found in the environment throughout the globe. are considered to be EDCS.
In the light of the above statements, choose the correct answer from the options given below:
1. Both Statement I and Statement II are true
2. Both Statement I and Statement II are false
3. Statement I is true but Statement II is false
4. Statement I is false but Statement II is true

Answer: 1. Both Statement I and Statement II are true

Q 12. Which of the following can be part of bioaccumulation / biomagnification?
A. Pesticides
B. Volatile Organic Compounds (VOCs)
C. Soot
D. Persistent Organic Pollutants (POPs)

Choose the correct answer from the options given below:
1. AB
2. BC
3. CD
4. AD

Answer: 4. AD

Q 13. Given below are two statements:
Statement I: Biomagnification occurs when the toxic burden of a large number of organisms at higher trophic level is accumulated and concentrated in the organisms at lower trophic level.
Statement II: The effect of toxins are magnified in the environment through food webs.
In the light of the above statements, choose the correct answer from the options given below:
1. Both Statement I and Statement II are true
2. Both Statement I and Statement II are false
3. Statement I is true but Statement II is false
4. Statement I is false but Statement II is true

Answer: 4. Statement I is false but Statement II is true

Q 14. What is the correct sequence of Biomagnification due to contaminated water body?
A. Humans
B. Zooplanktons
C. Bacteria
D. Fish

Choose the correct answer from the options given below:
1. A, C, D, B
2. C, B, D, A
3. A, D, B, C
4. B, C, D, A

Answer: 2. C, B, D, A

Q 15. Given below are two statements:
Statement I: Bioconcentration in humans can occur due to consumption of fish.
Statement II: Bioconcentration is the tendency of hazardous substances to accumulate in human tissues.
In the light of the above statements, choose the correct answer from the options given below:
1. Both Statement I and Statement II are true
2. Both Statement I and Statement II are false
3. Statement I is true but Statement II is false
4. Statement I is false but Statement II is true

Answer: 4. Statement I is false but Statement II is true

Q 16. Given below are two statements:
Statement I: All potential pollutants are synthetic chemicals.
Statement II: Many of the emerging contaminants have been observed to bioaccumulate in wildlife and humans.
In the light of the above statements, choose the correct answer from the options given below:
1. Both Statement I and Statement II are true
2. Both Statement I and Statement II are false
3. Statement I is true but Statement II is false
4. Statement I is false but Statement II is true

Answer: 4. Statement I is false but Statement II is true

Q 17. Which of the following are physical parameters of water quality?
A. Hardness
B. pH
C. Temperature
D. Turbidity
E. TSS

Choose the correct answer from the options given below:
1. CDE
2. ABC
3. BCD
4. ABE

Answer: 1. CDE

Q 18. Given below are two statements:
Statement I: The total solids (dissolved and suspended) in a wastewater sample are the 'materials left after water has evaporated from the sample.

Statement II: The dissolved solids fraction usually includes colloidal particles.
In the light of the above statements, choose the correct answer from the options given below:
    (1) Both Statement I and Statement II are correct
    (2) Both Statement I and Statement II are incorrect
    (3) Statement I is correct but Statement II is incorrect
    (4) Statement I is incorrect but Statement II is correct
Answer: 4. Both Statement I and Statement II are correct

Q 19. Which of the following are chemical parameters of water quality?
    A. pH
    B. Hardness
    C. Turbidity
    D. DO
    E. BOD
Choose the correct answer from the options given below:
    1. ABCD
    2. ABDE
    3. BCDE
    4. ACE
Answer: 2. ABDE

Q 20. Match the column:

List I (Water category)	List II (pH Levels)
A. Normal water	I. <5
B. Rain water	II. >7
C. Acid rain water	III. 5-6
D. Ocean water	IV. 7

Choose the correct answer from the options given below:
    1. A-IV B-I C-III D-II
    2. A-IV B-III C-I D-II
    3. A-IV B-III C-II D-I
    4. A-III B-II C-IV D-I
Answer: 2. A-IV B-III C-I D-II

Q 21. Match the column:

A. BOD	I. Strength of organic matter in water
B. DO	II. Acidic/Basic/Neutral nature of water
C. COD	III. Oxygen consumed by microorganism
D. pH	IV. Amount of oxygen in water

Choose the correct answer from the options given below:
    1. A-III, B-IV, C-II, D-I
    2. A-III, B-IV, C-I, D-II
    3. A-I, B-II, C-III, D-IV
    4. A-I, B-II, C-IV, D-III
Answer: 2. A-III, B-IV, C-I, D-II

Q 22. Given below are two statements:
Assertion (A): Acidity in water with pH level above 5 has detrimental effect on aquatic life.
Reason (R): Water with pH value between 5 to less than 7 is of acidic nature.
In the light of the above statements, choose the correct answer from the options given below:
1. Both (A) and (R) are true and (R) is the correct explanation of (A).
2. Both (A) and (R) are true but (R) is NOT the correct explanation of (A).
3. (A) is true but (R) is false.
4. (A)is false but (R) is true.

Answer: 4. (A)is false but (R) is true.

Q 23. Which of the Following are physical parameters to decide the water quality?
A. pH
B. Temperature
C. Total Suspended Solids (TSS)
D. Hardness
E. Conductivity

Choose the correct answer from the options given below:
1. A, B, C, D only
2. A, B, D, E only
3. C, D, E only
4. B, C, E only

Answer: 4. B, C, E only

Q 24. pH, an important water quality parameter:
A. It is a measure of acidity on water.
B. It is a measure of basicity in water.
C. It can have value only upto 10.
D. It represents the concentration of hydrogen ion.
E. whose value '0' (zero) confirms that water is potable.

Choose the correct answer from the options given below:
1. A, C and E only
2. A, B and D only
3. C, D and E only
4. B, C and E only

Answer: 2. A, B and D only

Q 25. What is the full form of CBOD?
(1) Comparative Biochemical Oxygen Demand
(2) Common Biochemical Oxygen Demand
(3) Carbonaceous Biochemical Oxygen Demand
(4) Classified Biochemical Oxygen Demand

Answer: 3. Carbonaceous Biochemical Oxygen Demand

Q 26. Which of the following statements are true about hardness in water?

(A) It is caused by ions of calcium and magnesium
(B) It is of two types-temporary and permanent
(C) Permanent hardness can easily be removed by heating the water
(D) Hardness causes scales in hot water pipe systems
(E) Hardness decreases the soap consumption

Choose the correct answer from the options given below:

1. ABCD
2. ABD
3. BCDE
4. CDE

Answer: 2. ABD

Q 27. Which of the following is true about hard water?

A. Hardness in water can occur in both surface and underground waters.
B. Hardness increases the cleaning efficiency of water.
C. It is caused by carbonates of magnesium and calcium.
D. Hard water is considered as safe for human consumption.
E. Hard water causes scaling in water distribution systems.

Choose the correct answer from the options given below:

1. ACDE
2. ACE
3. BCDE
4. ABDE

Answer: 1. ACDE

Q 28. Hardness of water is caused by the presence of-

1. Solid particles in the water
2. Pathogens in the water
3. Toxic metals in the water
4. Cations in the water

Answer: 4. Cations in the water

Q 29. Which of the following are characteristics/properties of permanent hardness in water?

(A) Presence of bicarbonates of calcium and magnesium
(B) Presence of sulphates of calcium and magnesium
(C) Forms good lather when comes in contact with soap
(D) Presence of chloride of calcium and magnesium
(E) Can be removed by boiling the water

Choose the correct answer from the options given below:

1. (B), (C) and (D) only
2. (A) and (D) only
3. (A), (B), (D) and (E) only
4. (B) and (D) only

Answer: 4. (B) and (D) only

Q 30. Which of the following contaminants in water can cause adverse human effects such as mental disturbance and impairment of speech, hearing and vision?

1. Arsenic

2. Methyl mercury
3. Lead
4. Nickel and Chromium
Answer: 2. Methyl mercury

Q 31. Lead pollution impacts which of the following parts of the human body most?
1. Heart
2. Brain
3. Eye
4. Skin
Answer: 2. Brain

Q 32. Which of the following represent the nutrient contents of a water body at different levels?
A. Phototropic
B. Eutrophic
C. Mesotrophic
D. Chemotrophic
E. Oligotrophic
Choose the correct answer from the options given below:
1. ACE
2. BCD
3. ABD
4. BCE
Answer: 4. BCE

Q 33. It a water body is healthy and supports no significant biological activity, then its condition is called as
1. Hypotrophic
2. Mesotrophic
3. Eutrophic
4. Oligotrophic
Answer: 4. Oligotrophic

Q 34. When a water body is deficient in nutrients, it is known as-
1. Oligotrophic
2. Eutrophic
3. Mesotrophic
4. Dystrophic
Answer: 1. Oligotrophic

Q 35. Given below are two statements:
Statement I: Rivers and lakes that have low biological productivity are said to be eutrophic.
Statement II: Rivers and lakes that are rich in organisms and organic materials are called oligotrophic.
In the light of the above statements, choose the correct answer from the options given below:

1. Both Statement I and Statement II are correct.
2. Both Statement I and Statement II are incorrect.
3. Statement I is correct but Statement II is incorrect.
4. Statement I is incorrect but Statement II is correct.

Answer: 2. Both Statement I and Statement II are incorrect.

Q 36. Given below are two statements:

Statement I: Rising nutrient levels in a lake change the numbers and types of biota present there.

Statement II: Eutrophic lakes normally have clear water and contain little biomass.

In the light of the above statements, choose the correct answer from the options given below:

1. Both Statement (I) and Statement (II) are correct.
2. Both Statement (I) and Statement (II) are incorrect.
3. Statement (I) is correct but Statement (II) is incorrect
4. Statement (I) is incorrect but Statement (II) is correct

Answer: 3. Statement (I) is correct but Statement (II) is incorrect

Q 37. A Eutrophic lake

A. is rich in nutrients
B. is poor in organic matters
C. has high algal blooms
D. is rich in dissolved oxygen
E. has no issue with survival of fish and other aquatic life

Choose the correct answer from the options given below:

1. ABC
2. CDE
3. AC
4. BD

Answer: 3. AC

Q 38. Given below are two statements:

Statement I: Aquatic weeds are fast growing weeds which can attain very high productivity when cultivated on nutrient rich wastewater such as domestic sewage.

Statement II: Water hyacinth, salvinia and duckweed are some examples of aquatic weeds.

In the light of the above statements, choose the correct answer from the options given below:

1. Both Statement I and Statement II are true
2. Both Statement I and Statement II are false
3. Statement I is true but Statement II is false
4. Statement I is false but Statement II is true

Answer: 1. Both Statement I and Statement II are true

Q 39. What is the full form of NBOD?

1. Neutral Biochemical Oxygen Demand
2. Natural Biochemical Oxygen Demand
3. Normalised Biochemical Oxygen Demand

4. Nitrogenous Biochemical Oxygen Demand
Answer: 4. Nitrogenous Biochemical Oxygen Demand

Q 40. Decreasing dissolved oxygen (DO) level in a water body:
A. Severely threatens the aquatic life
B. is mainly caused by the oxygen demanding wastes
C. indicates the presence of biodegradable organic substances
D. cause undesired taste and colour
E. makes it non- drinkable to human beings
Choose the correct answer from the options given below:
1. A, B, C, D only
2. B, C, D, E only
3. A, C, D, E only
4. A, B, D, E only
Answer: 1. 1. A, B, C, D only

Q 41. Oxygen demanding wastes-
1. Decrease the oxygen level in water.
2. Increase the oxygen level in water.
3. Do not change the oxygen level in water.
4. Increase the temperature of water.
Answer: 1. Decrease the oxygen level in water.

Q 42. Adding organic materials, such as sewage or paper pulp, to water stimulates consumption of these chemicals by decomposers.
1. Carbon dioxide
2. Oxygen
3. Salts
4. Minerals
Answer: 2. Oxygen

Q 43. Given below are two statements:
Statement I: Turbulent and rapidly flowing waters are generally depleted in oxygen.
Statement II: Adding organic materials, such as sewage or paper pulp, to water stimulates activity and oxygen consumption by decomposers.
In the light of the above statements, choose the correct answer from the options given below:
1. Both Statement I and Statement II are Correct
2. Both Statement I and Statement II are Incorrect
3. Statement I is Correct but Statement II is Incorrect
4. Statement I is Incorrect but Statement II is Correct
Answer: 4. Statement I is Incorrect, but Statement II is Correct

---

Q 44. Lower level of Dissolved Oxygen (DO) in water:
A. is bad for human consumption.
B. may have been caused due to the presence of oxygen demanding wastes.
C. threatens the fish and aquatic life.
D. cannot be used for irrigation purposes.

E. may cause undesirable taste and odour.
Choose the correct answer from the options given below:
1. ABC
2. ABD
3. BCE
4. CDE
Answer: 3. BCE

Q 45. Given below are two statements:
Assertion (A): Oxygen-demanding wastes are substances that Oxidized in the receiving body of water.
Reason (R): As bacteria decompose these wastes, they release Oxygen in the water.
In the light of the above statements, choose the correct answer from the options given below:
1. Both A and R are true and R is the correct explanation of A
2. Both A and R are true but R is NOT the correct explanation of A
3. A is true but R is false
4. A is false but R is true
Answer: 3. A is true but R is false

Q 46. Which of the following pairs of elements is most important for the eutrophication process?
(1) Calcium-magnesium
(2) Nitrogen-phosphorus
(3) Nickel-cobalt
(4) Iron-copper
Answer: (2) Nitrogen-phosphorus

Q 47. When a water body gets enriched with nutrients, the process is called as:
1. Oligotrophication
2. Eutrophication
3. Mesotrophication
4. Dystrophication
Answer: 2. Eutrophication

Q 48. Given below are two statements:
Statement I: Cultural eutrophication is caused by increased nutrient input into the water body mainly due to human activities.
Statement II: Cultural eutrophication accelerates the 'aging' of a water body enormously over natural rates.
In the light of the above statements, choose the correct answer from the options given below:
1. Both Statement I and Statement II are correct
2. Both Statement I and Statement II are incorrect
3. Statement I is correct but Statement II is incorrect
4. Statement I is incorrect but Statement II is correct
Answer: 3. Statement I is correct but Statement II is incorrect

Q 49. Eutrophication in a water body leads to which of the following?
A. Bloom of algae
B. Increase in the level of dissolved oxygen (DO)
C. Increase in turbidity and odor of the water body
D. Difficulty in sustaining normal aquatic life
E. Deficiency of nutrients
Choose the correct answer from the options given below:
1. A, B and C only
2. B, C and D only
3. A, C and D only
4. C, D and E only
Answer: 3. A, C and D only

Q 50. Which of the following pollutants is responsible for causing blue baby disease?
1. Mercury
2. Particulate Matter
3. Nitrates
4. Sulphur dioxide
Answer: 3. Nitrates

Q 51. In agricultural regions, groundwater can have significant concentrations of which pollutant?
1. Lead
2. Cadmium
3. Selenium
4. Nitrate
Answer: 4. Nitrate

Q 52. Given below are two statements:
Statement I: Composting is aerobic degradation of organic materials under controlled conditions, yielding a marketable manure.
Statement II: In such composts, concentrations of key nutrients such as nitrogen, phosphorus and potassium are sufficient enough to compete with commercial fertilizers.
In the light of the above statements, choose the correct answer from the options given below:
1. Both Statement (I) and Statement (II) are correct.
2. Both Statement (I) and Statement (II) are incorrect.
3. Statement (I) is correct but Statement (II) is incorrect
4. Statement (I) is incorrect but Statement (II) is correct
Answer: 3. Statement (I) is correct but Statement (II) is incorrect

Q 53. Given below are two statements:
Statement (I): Composting is the aerobic degradation of organic materials by microorganisms mainly under controlled conditions
Statement (II): Both macro and micro-organisms play an important role in the composting process.
In the light of the above statements, choose the correct answer from the options given below:

1. Both Statement (1) and Statement (II) are correct.
2. Both Statement (I) and Statement (II) are incorrect.
3. Statement (l) is correct but Statement (II) is incorrect
4. Statement (l) is incorrect but Statement (II) is correct

Answer: 1. Both Statement (1) and Statement (II) are correct.

Q 54. Given below are two statements:
Statement I: Aerobic digestion of sewage sludge requires lots of energy
Statement II: Aerobic digestion of sewage sludge produces huge amount of methane.
In the light of the above statements, choose the correct answer from the options given below:
1. Both Statement I and Statement II are true
2. Both Statement I and Statement II are false
3. Statement I is true but Statement I is false
4. Statement I is false but Statement II is true

Answer: 3. 3. Statement I is true but Statement I is false

Q 55. Anaerobic digestion of sewage sludge is
A. An effective process for organic solids
B. This process requires lots of energy
C. This process generates methane as an end product
D. Digested sludge is reduced in volume and easily dewatered
E. Very fast process and thus does not require large sized reactors

Choose the correct answer from the options given below:
1. B, C, D and E only
2. A, B and C only
3. A, C, D and E only
4. A, C and D only

Answer: 4. A, C and D only

Q 56. The most important pollutants that cause degradation of water quality in rivers and streams
a)   Bacteria
b)   Nutrients
c)   Metals
d)   Total dissolved solids
e)   Algae

Choose the most appropriate answer from the options given below:
1.   (a), (b) and (c)
2.   (a), (b), (d) and (e)
3.   (a), (b) and (d)
4.   (a), (b), (c), (d) and (e)

Answer: 1. (a), (b) and (c)

Q 57. Identify the correct group of diseases caused by polluted water
1. Cholera, Acute Diarrhoea, Typhoid and Polio
2. Cholera, Typhoid, Enteritis and Tuberculosis
3. Typhoid, Enteritis and Tuberculosis

4. Cholera, Acute Diarrhoea, Typhoid and Tuberculosis

Answer: 1. Cholera, Acute Diarrhoea, Typhoid and Polio

Q 58. Which of the following diseases are due to polluted water?
 (a) Giardia
 (b) Dengue
 (c) Amoebiasis
 (d) Typhoid

Choose the correct answer from the options given below:
 (1) (a), (b) and (d)
 (2) (b), (c) and (d)
 (3) (a), (b), (c) and (d)
 (4) (a), (c) and (d)

Answer: 4. (a), (c) and (d)

Q 59. Match the list:

List I (Water specific diseases)	List II (Examples)
A. Waterborne diseases (Due to ingestion of polluted water)	I. Malaria
B. Water-washed diseases (Due to lack of cleaning water)	II. Schistosomiasis
C. Water-based diseases (Due to contact with polluted water)	III. Typhoid
D. Water-related diseases (Due to habitation of disease-causing parasites in polluted water)	IV. Trachoma

Choose the correct answer from the options:
 1. A-III B-IV C-I D-II
 2. A-III B-IV C-II D-I
 3. A-I B-II C-III D-IV
 4. A-II B-IV C-III D-I

Answer: 2. A-III B-IV C-II D-I

Q 60. Match the column:

A. water borne	I. trachoma
B. water washed	II. malaria
C. water based	III. cholera
D. water related	V. schistosomiasis

Choose the correct answer from the options:
 1. A-II B-I C-II D-IV
 2. A-III B-I C-IV D-II
 3. A-I B-II C-III D-IV
 4. A-I B-IV C-III D-II

Answer: 2. A-III B-I C-IV D-II

Q 61. Which of the following are water borne bacterial diseases?
 A. Cholera
 B. Hepatitis
 C. Typhoid

D. Schistosomiasis
E. Dysentery

Choose the correct answer from the options:
1. ABC
2. BCD
3. ACE
4. ADE

Answer: 3. ACE

Q 62. Match the column:

List I: Water Pollutant Type	List II: example
A. Pathogen	I. Salt
B. Inorganic chemical	II. Iodine
C. Organic chemical	III. Fungi
D. Radioactive material	IV. Pesticide

Choose the correct answer from the options:
1. A-III B-I C-II D-IV
2. A-III B-I C-IV D-II
3. A-IV B-III C-I D-II
4. A-IV B-I C-III D-II

Answer: 2. A-III B-I C-IV D-II

Q 63. Typhoid fever, a waterborne disease is caused by
1. Virus
2. Bacteria
3. Protozoan
4. Helminth

Answer: 2. Bacteria

Q 64. Which one of the following waterborne diseases does not require direct contact with water but a host to spread?
1. Cholera
2. Malaria
3. Trachoma
4. Schistosomiasis

Answer: 2. Malaria

Q 65. Which of the following water borne diseases may be caused by virus, bacteria and protozoa?
1. Cholera
2. Hepatitis
3. Typhoid
4. Diarrhea

Answer: 4. Diarrhea

Q 66. Match the column:

A. Cholera	I. lack of water to maintain cleanliness
B. Trachoma	II. involves water contact but not ingestion
C. Schistosomiasis	III. ingestion of polluted water
D. Dengue	IV. require host

Choose the correct answer from the options:
1. A-ll B-III C-IV D-I
2. A-III B-I C-IV D-II
3. A-III B-I C-II D-IV
4. A-I B-III C-II D-IV

Answer: 3. A-III B-I C-II D-IV

Q 67. Match List I with List II

List I (Pathogens in water)	List II (Disease they cause)
A. Virus	I. Cholera
B. Bacteria	II. Schistosomiasis
C. Protozoa	III. Hepatitis
D. Helminths (Parasitic worm)	IV. Dysentery

Choose the correct answer from the options given below:
1. A - I, B - III, C - IV, D - II
2. A - I, B - III, C - II, D - IV
3. A - III, B - I, C - II, D - IV
4. A - III, B - I, C - IV, D - II

Answer: 4. A - III, B - I, C - IV, D - II

Q 68. Schistosomiasis, a common water contact disease, is spread by which of the following?
1. Giardia
2. E. Coli
3. Cercaria
4. Amoeba

Answer: 3. Cercaria

Air Pollution

Q 69. One of the parameters used to characterise the air quality at a location is PMs. Here, the suffix '2.5' refers to
1. average number of suspected particles in 1.0 cm of air
2. size of suspended particles in certain units
3. concentration of oxides of sulphur and nitrogen
4. concentration of suspended particles in 2.5 m of air

Answer: 2. size of suspended particles in certain units

Q 70. Match the column:

List I (Aerosol particles)	List II (Size)
A. Coarse Particles	(I) < 0.1 microns
B. Respirable Particles	(II) > 10 micron
C. Fine Particles	(III) < 10 micron
D. Ultrafine Particles	(IV) < 2.5 micron

Choose the correct answer from the options given below:
1. A-II B-III C-IV D-I
2. A-II B-III C-I D-IV
3. A-III B-II C-I D-IV
4. A-III B-II C-IV D-I

Answer: 1. A-II B-III C-IV D-I

Q 71. What is the correct sequence of path (from initial to final) of particulate matter exposure to humans?
    A.   Lungs
    B.   Soft tissues of organs
    C.   Blood
    D.   Inhalation
Choose the correct answer from the options given below:
    1.   DABC
    2.   DACB
    3.   ACBD
    4.   ACDB
Answer: 2. DACB

Q 72. Which one of the following is the finest particulate matter?
    1.   Fine mode particles
    2.   Nucleation mode particles
    3.   Aitken mode particles
    4.   Accumulation mode particles
Answer: 2. Nucleation mode particles

Q 73. Statement I: RSPM are those suspended particulate matter (SPM) whose aerodynamic diameter is more than 10 micron.
Statement II: Fine particles are those SPM whose aerodynamic diameter is less than 2.5 micron.
    1.   Both Statement I and Statement II are correct
    2.   Both Statement I and Statement II are incorrect
    3.   Statement I is correct but Statement II is incorrect
    4.   Statement I is incorrect but Statement II is correct
Answer: 4. Statement I is incorrect but Statement II is correct

Q 74. Particulate matter, a class of air pollutants, include.
    A.   Soot
    B.   PAN
    C.   Pollen
    D.   Dioxins
    E.   Fly Ash
Choose the correct answer from the options given below:
    1.   ABC
    2.   ACE
    3.   BCD
    4.   BDE
Answer: 2. ACE

Q 75. Soot particles are:
    A.   are also called black carbon

    B.   are mostly of coarse size range
    C.   are toxic
    D.   contribute in global warming
    E.   can penetrate in to deeper parts of lungs

Choose the correct answer from the options given below:
1. ABCD
2. ABCE
3. ACDE
4. BCDE

Answer: 3. ACDE

Q 76. Given below are two statements:

Assertion (A): PM10 is preferred over Total Suspended Particles (TSP) for air quality monitoring studies.

Reason (R): Particles larger than 10 micron are a better indicator of potential health effects of particulate air pollution.

1. Both (A) and (R) are correct and (R) is the correct explanation of (A)
2. Both (A) and (R) are correct but (R) is not the correct explanation of (A)
3. (A) is correct but (R) is not correct
4. (A) is not correct but (R) is correct

Answer: 3. (A) is correct but (R) is not correct

Q 78. The most relevant effect of particulate matter in air, on human health is:

1. Impaired blood formation
2. Chest tightness
3. Aggravation of respiratory disease
4. Headache and rise in blood pressure level

Answer: 3. Aggravation of respiratory disease

Q 79. Which of the following air pollutants has a very strong affinity towards haemoglobin of the human blood?

1. Carbon monoxide
2. Carbon dioxide
3. Nitric oxide
4. Nitrogen dioxide

Answer: 1. Carbon monoxide

Q 80. Carbon monoxide (CO). an air pollutant when inhaled readily binds with the hemoglobin in the blood stream to form a life-threatening compound known as

1. Hemoglobin
2. Carbo hemoglobin
3. Carbon mono hemoglobin
4. Carboxyhemoglobin Bin

Answer: 4. Carboxyhemoglobin

Q 81. Given below are two statements: One is labelled as Assertion (A) and the other is labelled as Reason (R)

Assertion (A): Carbon monoxide (CO) is a serious asphyxiant: even a short exposure may have fatal health issues.

Reason (R): Hemoglobin present in the blood has greater affinity towards carbon monoxide than oxygen.

In the light of the above statements. choose the most appropriate answer from the options given below:

1. Both (A) and (R) are correct and (R) is the correct explanation of (A)
2. Both (A) and (R) are correct but (R) is NOT the correct explanation of (A)
3. (A) is correct but (R) is not correct
4. (A) is not correct but (R) is correct

Answer: 1. Both (A) and (R) are correct and (R) is the correct explanation of (A)

Q 82. Given below are two statements: One is labelled as Assertion (A) and the other is labelled as Reason (R)

Assertion (A): Carbon monoxide (CO) has a direct greenhouse effect.

Reason (R): Carbon monoxide in atmosphere can form carbon dioxide (CO2) and can also affect the concentration of methane (CH4)

In the light of the above statements. choose the most appropriate answer from the options given below:

1. Both (A) and (R) are true and (R) is the correct explanation of (A).
2. Both (A) and (R) are true but (R) is NOT the correct explanation of (A).
3. (A) is true but (R) is false.
4. (A) is false but (R) is true.

Answer: 4. (A) is false but (R) is true.

Q 83. Which of the following air pollutants causes serious health issues due to its greater affinity for hemoglobin in blood in comparison to oxygen?

1. SO2 (Sulphur dioxide)
2. CO (Carbon Monoxide)
3. CO2 (Carbon dioxide)
4. O3 (Ozone)

Answer: 2. CO (Carbon Monoxide)

Q 84. In the case of which of the following primary pollutants, the man-made contributions to global emissions (million tonnes per year) are more compared to that from natural sources?

1. Sulphur dioxide
2. Nitric oxide
3. Methane
4. Carbon dioxide

Answer: 1. Sulphur dioxide

Q 85. Taj Mahal is mainly threatened by the deleterious effects of

1. Sulphur dioxide
2. Oxygen

3. Chlorine
4. Hydrogen

Answer: 1. Sulphur dioxide

Q 86. Which of the following Pollutants has the least residence time in the atmosphere?
1. Nitric Oxide
2. Nitrous Oxide
3. Chlorofluorocarbons
4. Methane

Answer: 1. Nitric oxide (NO)

Q 87. In air pollution, oxides of nitrogen (NOx) include:
A. Nitric oxide
B. Nitrous oxide
C. Nitrogen dioxide
D. Di-nitrogen trioxide
E. Di-nitrogen penta oxide

Choose the correct answer from the options given below:
1. ABC
2. AC
3. BCD
4. DE

Answer: 2. AC

Q 88. Rain is termed as acid rain when its ph value is
1. 1-3
2. Less than 5.6
3. 5.6-7.0
4. More than 7

Answer: 2. Less than 5.6

Q 89. Which of the following is a key ingredient in the formation of photochemical smog?
1. Carbon dioxide (CO2)
2. Carbon monoxide (CO)
3. Nitrogen oxides (NOx)
4. Sulphur oxides (SOx)

Answer: 3. Nitrogen oxides (NOx)

Q 90. Which of the following are examples of secondary air pollutants?
A. Sulphate
B. Nitric Oxide (NO)
C. Photochemical smog
D. PeroxyAcetyl Nitrate (PAN)
E. Polycyclic Aromatic Hydrocarbons (PAH)

Choose the correct answer from the options given below:

1. ABCD
2. CDE
3. BCD
4. ACD

Answer: 4. ACD

Q 91. Atmospheric haze mainly caused by?

1. Ultra fine size particulate matters
2. Oxides of nitrogen and sulphur
3. Ozone
4. Carbon dioxide and Carbon monoxide

Answer: 1. Ultra fine size particulate matters

Q 92. Which one of the following is an essential requirement for the formation of photochemical smog?

1. Water vapour
2. Sunlight
3. High temperature
4. Snow

Answer: 2. Sunlight

Q 93. Photochemical smog in urban areas is known to cause

A. Respiratory effects
B. Eye irritation
C. Nose and throat irritation
D. Carcinogenic effect
E. Reduction in visibility

Choose the correct answer from the options given below

1. Only (a), (b) and (d)
2. Only (a), (b), (c) and (e)
3. Only (b), (d) and (e)
4. (a), (b), (c), (d) and (e)

Answer: 2. Only (a), (b), (c) and (e)

Q 94. Given below are two statements:

Statement I: Sunlight is a pre-requisite for the formation of photochemical smog in urban areas.

Statement II: Photochemical smog is a recurring phenomenon in winter and summer seasons in urban areas of India.

In the light of the above statements, choose the most appropriate answer from the options given below:

1. Both Statement I and Statement II are true
2. Both Statement I and Statement II are false
3. Statement I is correct but Statement II is false
4. Statement I is incorrect but Statement II is true

Answer: 3. Statement I is correct but Statement II is false

Q 95. Which of the following are essential requirements for the formation of photochemical SMOG?
    A.   Carbon Monoxide(CO)
    B.   Nitrogen dioxide (NO2)
    C.   Carbon dioxide(CO2)
    D.   Volatile Organic Compounds (VOCs)
    E.   Sunlight
Choose the most appropriate answer from the options given below:
    1.   ABD
    2.   ACE
    3.   BCDE
    4.   BDE
Answer: 4. BDE

Q 96. Which of the following are essential components of industrial smog?
    A.   Sulphur Dioxide (SO2)
    B.   Particulate matters
    C.   Fly ash
    D.   Soot
Choose the correct answer from the options given below:
    1.   AB
    2.   ABC
    3.   CD
    4.   ABCD
Answer: 4. ABCD

Q 97. Given below are two statements
Statement I: Classical smog is formed when oxides of nitrogen combine with particulate matter, especially in the summer season.
Statement II: Classical smog reduces atmospheric visibility to a great extent.
In the light of the above statements. choose the most appropriate answer from the options given below:
    1.   Both Statement I and Statement II are true
    2.   Both Statement I and Statement II are false
    3.   Statement I is true but Statement II is false
    4.   Statement I is false but Statement II is true
Answer: 4. Statement I is false but Statement II is true

Q 98. Which of the following are primary aerosols in the atmosphere?
    A.   Sea salt
    B.   Black carbon
    C.   Sulphate
    D.   Nitrate
    E.   Mineral particles
Choose the correct answer from the options given below:

1. ABC
2. BCD
3. ABE
4. CDE

Answer: 3. ABE

Q 99. Identify the primary air pollutant among the following:
1. Ozone
2. Sulphate aerosols
3. Black carbon aerosols
4. Peroxy Acetyl Nitrate (PAN)

Answer: 3. Black carbon aerosols

Q 100. Given below are two statements
Statement (I): Acid rain occurs within, and downwind of areas of major industrial emissions of sulfur dioxide and oxides of nitrogen.
Statement (II): Long range transport of airborne pollutants can be responsible for acid rain in areas far off from industrial missions.
In the light of the above statements. choose the most appropriate answer from the options given below:
1. Both Statement (I) and Statement (II) are correct.
2. Both Statement (I) and Statement (II) are incorrect.
3. Statement (I) is correct but Statement (II) is incorrect
4. Statement (I) is incorrect but Statement (II) is correct

Answer: 1. Both Statement (I) and Statement (II) are correct.

Q 101. Which of the following air pollutants cause acid rain?
ric oxide
rogen dioxide
bon monoxide
phur dioxide
thane
Choose the correct answer from the options given below:
1. A, B, C only
2. A, B, D only
3. B, C, D only
4. C, D, E only

Answer: 2. A, B, D only

Q 102. Which of the following methods would be most appropriate in reducing acid rain and acid deposition problems?
1. Adding lime to the acidic lakes
2. Reducing the use of fossil fuels
3. Promotion of acid-resistant crops
4. Increasing the height of smokestacks

Answer: 2. Reducing the use of fossil fuels

Q 103. Full form of PAN, a type of air pollutant, is
1. Polycyclic Aromatic Nitrate
2. Polycyclic Acetyl Nitrate
3. Peroxy Aromatic Nitrate
4. PeroxyAcetyl Nitrate

Answer: 4. PeroxyAcetyl Nitrate

Q 103. Which of the following are components of BTEX, an air pollutant:
A. Benzene
B. Bisphenol
C. Ethylbenzene
D. Ethylene

Choose the correct answer from the options given below:
1. AB
2. BC
3. AC
4. BD

Answer: 3. AC

Q 104. T of BTEX (Air pollutant) stands for
1. TetraEthyl lead (TEL)
2. Toluene
3. TriNitroToluene (TNT)
4. TriChloroethylene (TCE)

Answer: 2. Toluene

Q 105. Which one of the following is an extremely short-lived and unstable air/water pollutant?
1. SMOG
2. Volatile Organic Compounds (VOCs)
3. Persistent Organic Pollutants (POPs)
4. Polycyclic Aromatic Hydrocarbons (PAHs)

Answer: 2. Volatile Organic Compounds (VOCs)

Q 106. Match the column:

A. Carbon monoxide	**i.** Allergenic
B. Nitrogen dioxide	**ii.** Carcinogenic
C. Volatile Organic Compounds (VOCs)	**iii.** Asphyxiant
D. Ozone (O3)	**iv.** Blue baby-syndrome

Choose the correct answer from the options given below:
1. A-iii B-iv C-ii D-i
2. A-iii B-iv C-i D-ii
3. A-i B-ili C-ii D-iv
4. A-i B-iv C-ii D-iii

Answer: 1. A-iii B-iv C-ii D-i

Q 107. Given below are two statements
Assertion (A): Formaldehyde, widely used in plastics, wood products, insulating materials, glue and fabrics, is a serious allergen
Reason (R): Allergens are substances that activate the immune system.
In the light of the above statements. choose the most appropriate answer from the options given below:
1. Both (A) and (R) are correct and (R) is the correct explanation of (A).
2. Both (A) and (R) are correct but (R) is NOT the correct explanation of (A).
3. (A) is correct but (R) is not correct.
4. (A) is not correct but (R) is correct

Answer: 2. Both (A) and (R) are correct but (R) is NOT the correct explanation of (A).

Q 108. Given below are two statements
Statement (I): Naturally occurring Volatile Organic Compounds (VOCs) generally oxidize to form Carbon Monoxide (CO) and Carbon Dioxide (CO2)
Statement (II): Anthropogenically emitted VOCs play an important role in the formation of smog
In the light of the above statements. choose the most appropriate answer from the options given below:
1. Both Statement I and Statement II are correct
2. Both Statement I and Statement II are incorrect
3. Statement I is correct but Statement II is incorrect
4. Statement I is incorrect but Statement II is correct

Answer: 1. Both Statement I and Statement II are correct

Q 109. Given below are two statements
Statement I: Volatile Organic Compounds (VOCs) are emitted from vehicles.
Statement II: Volatile Organic Compounds are emitted from some trees
In the light of the above statements. choose the most appropriate answer from the options given below:
1. Both Statement I and Statement II are true
2. Both Statement I and Statement II are false
3. Statement I is true but Statement II is false
4. Statement I is false but Statement II is true

Answer: 1. Both Statement I and Statement II are true

Q 110. Which among the following are sources of Volatile Organic Compounds (VOCs)?
A. Vehicles
B. Plants
C. Termites
D. Power Plants
E. Bogs
Choose the correct answer from the options given below:
1. A and D only

2. A, B and D only
3. A, B, D and E only
4. A, B, C, D and E

Answer: 4. A, B, C, D and E

Q 111. Given below are two statements

Statement I: Dioxins and Furans are highly toxic substances produced as by products of solid waste incineration.

Statement II: Dioxins and Furans are very unstable and short lived once they are released in the atmosphere.

Choose the correct answer from the options given below:

1. Both Statement I and Statement II are correct
2. Both Statement I and Statement II are incorrect
3. Statement I is correct but Statement II is incorrect
4. Statement I is incorrect but Statement II is correct

Answer: 3. Statement I is correct but Statement II is incorrect

Q 112. Which of the following Volatile Organic Compound (VOC), a kind of air pollutant, is emitted from natural sources such as plants, bogs etc.?

1. Formaldehyde
2. Benzene
3. Terpene
4. Toluene

Answer: 3. Terpene

Q 113. Given below are two statements

Statement I: Volatile Organic Chemicals (VOCs) are among the most commonly found contaminants in groundwater.

Statement II: The concentration of VOCs in groundwater is much less compared to that in surface waters.

Choose the correct answer from the options given below:

1. Both Statement I and Statement II are true
2. Both Statement I and Statement II are false
3. Statement I is true but Statement II is false
4. Statement I is false but Statement II is true

Explanations:

Answer: 3. Statement I is true but Statement II is false

Q 114. Given below are two statements

Statement I: Volatile Organic Chemicals (VOCs) are contaminants more commonly found in groundwater than in surface water

Statement II: VOCs are one of the criterion parameters to determine drinking water quality

In light of the above statements, choose the correct answer from the options given below

1. Both Statement I and Statement II are true
2. Both Statement I and Statement II are false

3. Statement I is correct but Statement II is false
4. Statement I is incorrect but Statement II is true

Answer: 3. Statement I is correct but Statement II is false

Q 115. Which of the following statements about the Volatile Organic Compounds (VOCs) are correct?

i). They cause acid rain
ii). They may cause cancer
iii). They play an important role in the formation of photochemical smog

Select the correct answer from the options given below:

1. i and ii
2. ii) and iii
3. i) and iii)
4. i), ii) and iii)

Answer: 2. ii) and iii

Q 116. Given below are two statements - one is labelled as Assertion (A) and the other is labelled as Reason (R):

Assertion (A): Forests help in improving the air quality of a place.

Reasons (R): Some tree species emit volatile organic compounds (VOCs) such as isoprene which may contribute to formation of tropospheric ozone.

In the light of the above statements choose the correct option:

1. Both (A) and (R) are true and (R) is the correct explanation of (A)
2. Both (A) and (R) are true but (R) is not the correct explanation of (A)
3. (A) is true, but (R) is false
4. (A) is false. but (R) is true

Answer: 2. Both (A) and (R) are true but (R) is not the correct explanation of (A)

Q 117. Which of the following air pollutants are produced from room deodorizers?

1. Inhalable particulate matter
2. Carbon monoxide
3. Ozone
4. Volatile organic compounds

Answer: 4. Volatile organic compounds

Q 118. Which of the following are examples of Persistent Organic Pollutants (POPs)?

A. Poly Chlorinated Biphenyls
B. Formaldehyde
C. Dioxins
D. Furans

Select the correct answer from the options given below:

1. ABC
2. ACD
3. BCD
4. ABD

Answer: 2. ACD

Q 119. What is the full form of POPs?
1. Persistent Organic Pollutants
2. Persistent Oxygenated Pollutants
3. Polycyclic Organic Pollutants
4. Polymerised Organic Pollutants

Answer: 1. Persistent Organic Pollutants

120. Which of the following are examples of Persistent Organic Pollutants (POPS)?
A. Dioxins
B. Poly-Chlorinated Benzenes (PCBs)
C. Formaldehyde
D. Organo Chlorine Pesticides
E. Furans

Select the correct answer from the options given below:
1. A, C and E only
2. A, B, D and E only
3. B and D only
4. B, C and E only

Answer: 2. A, B, D and E only

Q 121. Which of the following are true about Persistent Organic Pollutants (POPs)?
A. They are extremely widespread and occur from tropics to the Arctic.
B. They often accumulate in food webs and reach toxic concentrations.
C. Volatile Organic Compounds (VOCs) are examples of POPs.
D. They are widely used as flame retardants and in deodorants.
E. Some chemicals used in making non-stick, waterproof and stain resistant products are categorized as POPs.

Select the correct answer from the options given below:
1. ABCD
2. BCDE
3. ABDE
4. ACE

Answer: 3. ABDE

Indoor Air Quality (IAQ)

Q 122. Given below are two statements - one is labelled as Assertion (A) and the other is labelled as Reason (R):
Assertion (A): In the less developed countries of the world indoor exposure to hazardous air pollutants is much severe
Reason (R): Traditional methods of cooking often involve fuels such as coal, wood, animal, dung, kerosene etc.
In the light of the above statements choose the correct option:
1. Both (A) and (R) are correct and (R) is the correct explanation of (A)

   2. Both (A) and (R) are correct but (R) is not the correct explanation of (A)
   3. (A) is correct but (R) is not correct
   4. (A) is not correct but (R) is correct

Answer: 1. Both (A) and (R) are correct and (R) is the correct explanation of (A)

Q 123. Given below are two statements - one is labelled as Assertion (A) and the other is labelled as Reason (R):
Statement I: Air Quality Index (AQI) is used to report to the public an overall assessment of a given day's air quality.
Statement II: Air Quality Index integrates air quality data for any two of the criteria pollutants into a single number that represents the air quality of urban areas.
In the light of the above statements choose the correct option:
   1. Both Statement I and Statement II are correct.
   2. Both Statement I and Statement II are incorrect.
   3. Statement I is correct but Statement II is incorrect.
   4. Statement I is incorrect but Statement II is correct.

Answer: 3. Statement I is correct but Statement II is incorrect.

Q 124. What causes Sick Building Syndrome (SBS)?
   1. corrosion of building
   2. polluted indoor air
   3. Supply of contaminated water in the building
   4. Building in a landslide prone area

Answer: 2. polluted indoor air

Q 125. Given below are two statements - one is labelled as Assertion (A) and the other is labelled as Reason (R):
Statement I: Concentration of Formaldehyde in indoor environment can be thousand times higher than outdoor environment.
Statement II: Formaldehyde is a known carcinogen.
In the light of the above statements choose the correct option:
   1. Both Statement I and Statement II are true
   2. Both Statement I and Statement II are false
   3. Statement I is true but Statement II is false
   4. Statement I is false but Statement II is true

Answer: 1. Both Statement I and Statement II are true

Q 126. Given below are two statements - one is labelled as Assertion (A) and the other is labelled as Reason (R):
Statement I: Some people suffer from what is called Sick Building Syndrome (SBS).
Statement II: SBS is caused due to supply of polluted water in a particular building.
In the light of the above statements choose the correct option:
   1. Both Statement I and Statement II are correct
   2. Both Statement I and Statement II are incorrect
   3. Statement I is correct but Statement II is incorrect

4. Statement I is incorrect but Statement II is correct

Answer: 3. Statement I is correct but Statement II is incorrect

Q 127. Given below are two statements:
Statement I: Allergens are substances that activate the immune system.
Statement II: Concentration of allergens in an indoor environment can be thousand times higher than in the air outside.
In the light of the above statements choose the correct option:
1. Both Statement I and Statement II are true.
2. Both Statement I and Statement II are false.
3. Statement I is true but Statement II is false.
4. Statement I is false but Statement II is true.

Answer: 1. Both Statement I and Statement II are true.

Q 128. Sick Building Syndrome (SBS) is a condition
1. When buildings are very old and about to collapse
2. Of human health due to indoor air pollution
3. Of fear due to deserted building
4. Of building devoid of any modern amenities

Answer: 2. Of human health due to indoor air pollution

Q 129. Which one of the following is included while estimating Air Quality Index (AQI)?
1. N20 Nitrous oxide
2. NO2 Nitrogen dioxide
3. N203 Dinitrogen trioxide
4. N205 Dinitrogen pentoxide

Answer: 2. NO2 Nitrogen dioxide

Q 130. Which of the following types of particulate matter pollutants are used in the calculation of Air Quality Index (AQI)?
(A) TSP (Total Suspended Particles)
(B) PM10 (Particulate matters of size 10 microns or less)
(C) PM2.5 (Particulate matter of size 2.5 microns or less)
(D) PM1 (Particulate matter of size 1 micron or less)
Choose the correct answer from the options given below:
1. (B), (C), and (D) only
2. (B) and (C) only
3. (A) and (B) only
4. (A), (B), and (C) only

Answer: 3. (A) and (B) only

Q 131. Which of the following pollutants is included in the *Air Quality Index in India*?
1. Carbon Dioxide
2. Sulphur dioxide
3. Chlorofluorocarbons

| 4. | Methane |
| **Answer: 2.** Sulphur dioxide |

Greenhouse gases (GHGs)

Q 132. What is the correct sequence of Global Warming Potential (GWP) of following GreenHouse Gases from lowest to highest?

- A. CH4 (Methane)
- B. CO2 (Carbon dioxide)
- C. CFC-11 (Chloro Fluoro carbon -11)
- D. N20 (Nitrous oxide)

Choose the correct answer from the options given below:

1. C, A, B, D
2. A, D, B, C
3. B, A, C, D
4. B, A, D, C

Answer: 4. B, A, D, C

Q 133. Which country is the largest emitter of GreenHouse Gases (GHGs) at present?

1. India
2. China
3. Russia
4. USA

Answer: 2. China

Q 134. Which of the following statements are correct in respect of GreenHouse Gases?

- A. They are generally of light green color
- B. They absorb thermal radiation emitted by the earth.
- C. Water vapor is a greenhouse gas.
- D. Greenhouse gases cause global warming.
- E. Ammonia (NH3) is a greenhouse gas.

Choose the correct answer from the options given below:

1. A, B, C, D Only
2. A, C, E Only
3. B, C, D Only
4. A, B, D, E Only

Answer: 3. B, C, D Only

Q 135. What is the correct increasing order of Global Warming Potential (GWP) of following gases?

- A. Nitrous Oxide (N20)
- B. Carbon dioxide (CO2)
- C. Methane (CH4)
- D. ChlorofluoroCarbon (CFC)

Choose the correct answer from the options given below:

1. ABCD

2. ACBD
3. BACD
4. BCAD

Answer: 4. BCAD

Q 136. Given below are two statements:
Statement I: One of the ways to control greenhouse gas emissions is by encouraging energy efficiency throughout society in our country.
Statement II: Improving energy efficiency has significant environmental benefits.
Choose the correct answer from the options given below:
1. Both Statement I and Statement II are true
2. Both Statement I and Statement II are false
3. Statement I is true but Statement II is false
4. Statement I is false but Statement II is true

Answer: 1. Both Statement I and Statement II are true

Q 137. Identify the correct sequence (decreasing order) of lifetimes of the following greenhouse gases in atmosphere:
A. Methane
B. Nitrous oxide
C. Surface ozone
D. CFC-11

Choose the correct answer from the options given below:
1. (D) > (B) > (A) > (C)
2. (B) > (D) > (C) > (A)
3. (B) > (D) > (A) > (C)
4. (D) > (B) > (C) > (A)

Answer: 1. (D) > (B) > (A) > (C)

Q 138. Given below are two statements: One is labelled as Assertion (A) and the other is labelled as Reason (R)
Assertion (A): Global warming potential of a molecule of a greenhouse gas over different time spans of decades to 100 years may vary significantly.
Reason (R): Some greenhouse gases have shorter life times compared to carbon dioxide.
In the light of the above statements, choose the most appropriate answer from the options given below:
1. Both (A) and (R) are correct and (R) is the correct explanation of (A)
2. Both (A) and (R) are correct but (R) is NOT the correct explanation of (A)
3. (A) is correct but (R) is not correct
4. (A) is not correct but (R) is correct

Answer: 1. Both (A) and (R) are correct and (R) is the correct explanation of (A)

Q 139. Consider the following statements:
(a) Earth would be safer without greenhouse effect
(b) Major contribution to the greenhouse effect comes from carbon dioxide

(c) Earth's climate was changing even before man appeared on earth

Which of the above statements are correct?
1. (a) and (b) only
2. (b) and (c) only
3. (a) and (c) only
4. (a), (b) and (c)

Answer: 2. (b) and (c) only

Q 140. Which of the two following is the correct sequence of greenhouse gases according to their relative global warming potential in increasing order?
1. Nitrous oxide, Methane, Carbon dioxide, Chlorofluorocarbons
2. Carbon dioxide, Methane, Nitrous oxide, Chlorofluorocarbons
3. Methane. Nitrous oxide, Carbon dioxide, Chlorofluorocarbons
4. Carbon dioxide, Nitrous oxide, Methane, Chlorofluorocarbons

Answer: 2. Carbon dioxide, Methane, Nitrous oxide, Chlorofluorocarbons

---

Q 141. Thermal expansion of oceans may lead to
1. Global warming
2. Ozone depletion
3. Melting of glaciers
4. Sea level rise

Answer: 4. Sea level rise

Q 142. Over the past 100 years; the estimated rise of global sea level is by 10-25cm or more. Which one of the following has the maximum contribution in it?
1. Thermal expansion of ocean waters
2. Glacier and ice- cap melting
3. Greenland ice sheet thinning
4. Terrestrial water storage changes due to human activities

Answer: 1. Thermal expansion of ocean waters

Q 143. Which of the following gases has the maximum contribution to Global Warming?
1. Chlorofluorocarbons (CFCs)
2. Methane (CH4)
3. Sulfur Hexafluoride (SF6)
4. Carbon dioxide (CO2)

Answer: 4. Carbon dioxide (CO2)

Q 144. Amongst the following GreenHouse Gases (GHGS). Whose Global Warming Potential (GWP) is considered as 1?
1. Chlorofluorocarbon (CFC)
2. Nitrous Oxide (N20)
3. Carbon dioxide (CO2)
4. Methane (CH4)

Answer: 3. Carbon dioxide (CO2)

Q 145. Methane (CH4):
  A.   is a greenhouse gas
  B.   is a polycyclic Aromatic Hydrocarbon
  C.   is a component in determining Air quality Index (AQI)
  D.   helps in formation of Ozone
  E.   is a Volatile Organic Compound (VOC)

Choose the correct answer from the options given below:
  1.   A B & C only
  2.   A D & E only
  3.   A & E only
  4.   C D & E only

Answer: 2. A D & E only

Q 146. Methane, a greenhouse gas.
  A.   is emitted from
  B.   landfills construction debris
  C.   wetlands le-waste

Choose the correct statements from the options given below?
  1.   (a), (b) and (d)
  2.   (a) and (c) only
  3.   (a), (c) and (d)
  4.   (a) and (d) only

Answer: 2. (a) and (c) only

Q 147. Which of the following pollutants causes aggravation of respiratory disease, and atmospheric discolouration?
  1.   Carbon monoxide
  2.   Lead
  3.   Nitrogen dioxide
  4.   Ozone

Answer: 3. Nitrogen dioxide

Q 148. Which one of the following gases has the maximum Global Warming Potential (GWP).
  1.   Methane (CH4)
  2.   Nitrous Oxide (N2O)
  3.   Carbon dioxide (CO2)
  4.   Carbon Monoxide (CO)

Answer: 2. Nitrous Oxide (N20)

Q 149. Given below are two statements: One is labelled as Assertion (A) and the other is labelled as Reason (R)
Assertion (A): Chlorofluorocarbons (CFCs) are potent greenhouse gas.
Reasons (R): CFCs have the ability to catalytically destroy ozone in the stratosphere.

In the light of the above statements, choose the most appropriate answer from the options given below:

1. Both (A) and (R) are correct and (R) is the correct explanation of (A)
2. Both (A) and (R) are correct but (R) is NOT the correct explanation of (A)
3. (A) is correct but (R) is not correct
4. (A) is not correct but (R) is correct

Answer: 2. Both (A) and (R) are correct but (R) is NOT the correct explanation of (A)

Q 150. Discovery of Ozone hole was first made over-

1. Arctic
2. Equator
3. Antarctic
4. Tropics

Answer: 3. Antarctic

Q 151. Given below are two statements:

Statement I: The concentration Chlorofluorocarbons (CFCs) in the atmosphere has increased in the past few

Statement II: CFCs already present in the atmosphere will persist for many years.

Choose the correct statements from the options given below?

1. Both Statement I and Statement II are true.
2. Both Statement I and Statement II are false.
3. Statement I is true but Statement II is false.
4. Statement I is false but Statement II is true.

Answer: 4. Statement I is false but Statement II is true

Q 152. Chlorofluorocarbons (CFCs), important greenhouse gases.

A. are toxic
B. vaporize just below room temperature
C. are flammable
D. are very stable
E. destroy ozone

Choose the correct statements from the options given below?

1. ABC
2. BCD
3. BDE
4. CDE

Answer: 3. BDE

Q 153. Which of the following is a non-vehicular pollutant?

1. chlorofluorocarbon
2. hydrocarbon
3. carbon-monoxide
4. particulate matter

Answer: 1. Chlorofluorocarbon

Q 154. Which among the following are Natural GreenHouse Gases (GHGs)?
- A. CO2 (carbon dioxide)
- B. H2O (water vapor)
- C. CH4 (methane)
- D. O3 (ozone)
- E. CFC (chlorofluorocarbons)

Choose the correct statements from the options given below?
1. ABCD
2. ACDE
3. BCDE
4. ABCE

Answer: 1. ABCD

Q 155. GreenHouse Gases absorb radiation energy mostly in which of the following regions of the solar spectrum?
1. X-Ray
2. Ultraviolet
3. Infra-red
4. Visible

Answer: 3. Infra-red

Q 156. What is the correct order of Global Warming Potential (GWP) of following atmospheric chemical species?
1. Chlorofluorocarbon (CFC)
2. Methane (CH4)
3. Carbon dioxide (CO2)
4. Nitrous oxide (N20)

Choose the correct statements from the options given below?
1. D>B>C>A
2. C<B<D<A
3. A>B>C>D
4. A<C<D<B

Answer: 2. C<B<D<A

Q 157. Which of the following pollutants is considered as surrogate for eye irritation?
1. Nitrogen dioxide
2. Sulphur dioxide
3. Carbon monoxide
4. Ozone

Answer: 4. Ozone

Q 158. What is the correct increasing order of the contribution to global warming by the following gases?
- A. Methane (CH4)

B.   Carbon Dioxide (CO2)
C.   Nitrous oxide (N20)

Choose the correct statements from the options given below?
1. A, B, C
2. C, A, B
3. B, A, C
4. B, C, A

Answer: 2. C, A, B

Q 159. Given below are two statements:
Statement I: Global warming could lead to increased release of the greenhouse gas, Methane.
Statement II: There is a large amount of Methane currently frozen in the permafrost in the far northern regions of the world.
Choose the correct statements from the options given below?
1. Both Statement I and Statement I are correct
2. Both Statement I and Statement II are incorrect
3. Statement I is correct but Statement II is incorrect
4. Statement I is incorrect but Statement II is correct

Answer: 2. Both Statement I and Statement I are correct

Q 160. Arrange the Global Warming Potential of a molecule of the following greenhouse gases (relative to CO?) in decreasing order:
A. Methane
B. Nitrous Oxide
C. CFC - 12
D. CEC - 11
E. Sulphur hexafluoride (SFO)

Choose the correct answer from the options given below:
(1) E>D>C>B>A
(2) C>E>D>B>A
(3) D>E>C>B>A
(4) E>C>D>B>A

Answer: (4) E>C>D>B>A

Q 161. Given below are two statements:
Statement I: Stratospheric ozone is known as 'good ozone'.
Statement II: Ozone at the surface level is a serious health hazard and known as pollutant.
Choose the correct statements from the options given below?
1. Both Statement I and Statement II are correct
2. Both Statement I and Statement II are incorrect
3. Statement I is correct but Statement II is incorrect
4. Statement I is incorrect but Statement II is correct

Answer: 1. Both Statement I and Statement II are correct

Q 162. Ozone layer which protects us from harmful ultraviolet radiations is situated in:

1. Troposphere
2. Stratosphere
3. Mesosphere
4. Ionosphere

Answer: 2. Stratosphere

Q 163. Although ozone is a pollutant in the ambient air, but in stratosphere it is valuable because it absorbs harmful
1. IR-Radiations
2. X-Rays
3. UV-Radiations
4. Gama- Rays

Answer: 3. UV-Radiations

Q 164. Ozone layer is in-
1. Thermosphere
2. Mesosphere
3. Stratosphere
4. Troposphere

Answer: 3. Stratosphere

Q 165. Given below are two statements:
Statement I: Halocarbons contribute significantly to global warming.
Statement II: Halocarbons also catalytically destroy stratospheric Ozone.
Choose the correct statements from the options given below?
1. Both Statement I and Statement II are true
2. Both Statement I and Statement II are false
3. Statement I is true but Statement II is false
4. Statement I is false but Statement II is true

Answer: 1. Both Statement I and Statement II are true

Q 166. Given below are two statements:
Statement I: Chlorine is one of the most commonly used and inexpensive chemical disinfectants for water.
Statement II: Optimum Fluoride levels in drinking water help prevent cavities in children.
Choose the correct statements from the options given below:
1. Both Statement I and Statement II are correct
2. Both Statement I and Statement II are incorrect
3. Statement I is correct but Statement II is incorrect
4. Statement I is incorrect but Statement II is correct

Answer: 1. Both Statement I and Statement II are correct

Q 167. Ozone hole appears over Antarctica mostly in the month of
1. April
2. March
3. September

4. November

Answer: 3. September

Q 168. Polar Stratospheric Clouds are associated with which of the following environmental issues?
1. Flash floods
2. Acid rain
3. Ozone layer depletion
4. Photochemical smog

Answer: 3. Ozone layer depletion

Q 169. Which of the following are true about tropospheric or ground level ozone?
A. It is called as good ozone
B. It is formed due to downward transfer of ozone from ozone layer
C. It is formed due to the action of sunlight on oxides of nitrogen
D. It is a greenhouse gas
E. It is a key component of photochemical smog

Choose the correct statements from the options given below?
1. BCDE
2. ABC
3. CDE
4. ADE

Answer: 1. BCDE

Q 170. Given below are two statements:
Assertion A: Ground level concentration of ozone decreases at night
Reason R: Ultraviolet radiation photolysis the ozone into other components
Choose the correct statements from the options given below?
1. Both A and R are correct and R is the correct explanation of A
2. Both A and R are correct but R is NOT the correct explanation of A
3. A is correct but R is not correct
4. A is not correct but R is correct

Answer: 2. Both A and R are correct but R is NOT the correct explanation of A

Q 171. Consider the following statements:
(a) The radiation reflected back to the atmosphere is called albedo.
(b) The atmosphere is essential in maintaining the heat balance of the body
(c) The heat and sunlight both pass through the atmosphere.

Which of the statements) given above is/are correct?
1. Only (a)
2. (b) and (c)
3. (a) and (b)
4. (a), (b) and (c)

Answer: 4. (a), (b) and (c)

Q 172. Given below are two statements:

Assertion (A): Night time temperatures in the central parts of a city are generally higher than those over the surrounding rural areas

Reason (R): Radiation losses over the urban areas are less than that over the rural Areas

Choose the correct answer from the options given below:
1. Both (A) and (R) are true and (R) is the correct explanation of (A)
2. Both (A) and (R) are true but (R) is not the correct explanation of (A)
3. (A) is true but (R) is false
4. (A) is false but (R) is true

Answer: 1. Both (A) and (R) are true and (R) is the correct explanation of (A)

Q 173. Which of the following best describes the mechanism of the greenhouse effect in earth's atmosphere?
1. Cosmic radiation from space is absorbed by gases in the atmosphere.
2. Ultraviolet radiation from the sun is absorbed by the Ozone layer in the stratosphere.
3. Infrared radiation from earth's surface is absorbed by gases in the atmosphere.
4. Gamma radiation from the sun is absorbed at ground level by dust particles in the atmosphere.

Answer: 3. Infrared radiation from earth's surface is absorbed by gases in the atmosphere.

Q 174. Which of the following is not responsible for the destruction of the Ozone layer?
1. CFC
2. Halons
3. Dioxins
4. HCFC

Answer: 3. Dioxins

Q 175. Which of the following has a positive radiative forcing or warming effect in the global climate?
1. Tropospheric Ozone
2. Stratospheric Ozone
3. Sulphate Aerosol
4. Sulphur dioxide

Answer: 1. Tropospheric Ozone

Q 176. The global environmental issue of Ozone depletion is due to emission of:
A. Sulphur dioxide
B. Chlorinated hydrocarbons
C. Methane
D. Carbon dioxide

Choose the correct answer from the options given below:
1. (A) and (B) only

2. (B) only
3. (B) and (D) only
4. (A), (B) and (C) only

Answer: 2. (B) only

Q 177. The phenomenon of ozone depletion is caused by
A. Volatile chlorinated hydrocarbons
B. Emissions from thermal power plants
C. Combustion of urban waste
D. Excessive use of nitrogen-containing fertilizers

Choose the correct answer from the options given below:
1. A, B and D only
2. A and D only
3. A, B and C only
4. A. C and D only

Answer: 2. A and D only

Q 178. Given below are two statements - one labelled as Assertion (A) and the other labelled as Reason (R)
Assertion (A): In the afternoon of a hot sunny day during the summer season, the tropospheric ozone levels in a city like Delhi are expected to be lower as compared to morning and evening.
Reasons (R): In the afternoon period, the atmosphere is unstable and its dilution potential is higher as compared to mornings and evenings.
In the light of the above two statements, choose the correct option:
1. Both (A) and (R) are true and (R) is the correct explanation of (A)
2. Both (A) and (R) are true but (R) is not the correct explanation of (A)
3. (A) is true but (R) is false
4. (A) is false but (R) is true

Answer: 4. (A) is false but (R) is true

Q 179. In the formation of surface Ozone, which of the following do play an important role?
A. Oxides of nitrogen
B. Oxides of sulphur
C. Sunlight
D. Carbon monoxide

Choose the correct answer from the code given below:
1. (a), (b), (c)
2. (b), (c), (d)
3. (a), (c), (d)
4. (a), (b), (d)

Answer: 3. (a), (c), (d)

Noise Pollution

Q 180. Given below are two statements:
Statement I: Exposure to noise pollution adversely affects the physiological health of a person.

Statement II: Exposure to noise pollution adversely affects the psychological health of a person.

In the light of the above two statements, choose the correct option:
1. Both Statement I and Statement II are true
2. Both Statement I and Statement II are false
3. Statement I is true but Statement IT is false
4. Statement I is false but Statement II is true

Answer: 1. Both Statement I and Statement II are true

Q 181. Identify the correct sequence of average noise levels in increasing order of their magnitude from different sources.
- A. City street corner
- B. Conversational speech.
- C. Highway
- D. Aircraft noise during take off
- E. Typical office

Choose the correct answer from the code given below:
1. EABCD
2. EBACD
3. BEACD
4. BEADC

Answer: 2. EBACD

Q 182. According to Noise Pollution (Regulation and Control) Rules in India, noise in educational institutions during night time (10pm-6am) must not exceed
1. 35dB
2. 40dB
3. 450B
4. 50dB

Answer: 2. 40dB

Q 183. Given below are two statements:

Statement I: Two sounds of same intensity but different frequency characteristics may
appear to be of different loudness.

Statement II: The response of the human ear to noise of different frequencies is not uniform.

In the light of the above statements, choose the most appropriate answer from the options given below:
1. Both Statement I and Statement II are correct
2. Both Statement I and Statement II are incorrect
3. Statement I is correct but Statement II is incorrect
4. Statement I is incorrect but Statement II is correct

Answer: 1. Both Statement I and Statement II are correct

Q 184. According to Noise Pollution (Regulation and Control) Rules, 2000, the nighttime Noise standard prescribed for Educational Institutions is
1. 55 dB (A)
2. 50 dB (A)
3. 45 dB (A)
4. 40 dB (A)

Answer: 4. 40 dB (A)

Q 185. Day time noise standard prescribed for residential areas in India is
1. 75 dB
2. 65 dB
3. 55 dB
4. 50 dB

Answer: 3. 55 dB

Q 186. The impact of noise pollution on human health is governed by:
A. Intensity of noise
B. Duration of noise
C. Socio-economic status of an individual
D. Sensitivity of human ear
E. Frequency range of noise

Choose your answer from the options given below:
1. (A), (B), (D) AND (E) ONLY
2. (A), (B) AND (C) ONLY
3. (A), (C), (D) AND (E) ONLY
4. (A), (B), (C), (D) AND (E)

Answer: 1. (A), (B), (D) AND (E) ONLY

Q 187. Exposure to excessive noise pollution can cause (A)
A. Hearing impairment
B. Insomnia
C. Rise in blood pressure
D. Respiratory disease
E. Reduced work efficiency

Choose the most appropriate answer from the options given below:
1. (A), (C), (E) only
2. (B), (C) and (E) only
3. (A), (C), (D) only
4. (A), (B), (C) and (E) only

Answer: 4. (A), (B), (C) and (E) only

Q 188. Consider the following statements regarding noise pollution:
(a) Noise levels decrease as we move away from the source of noise
(b) Materials with high surface/mass density act as good noise barriers
(c) Sound pressure of 2j Pa corresponds to a noise of zero decibel

Choose the correct option from those given below:

1. (a) and (b) only
2. (b) and (c) only
3. (a) and (c) only
4. (a), (b) and (c)

Answer: 1. (a) and (b) only

Q 189. Average noise levels in heavy traffic zones in major cities in India are generally in which of the following ranges of noise levels?
1. 31-40 dBA
2. 70-95 dBA
3. 41-50 dBA
4. 110-120 dBA

Answer: 2. 70-95 dBA

Q 190. Exposure to noise pollution can cause
(a) Weakening of immune system
(b) Sleeplessness
(c) Speech interference
(d) Increase in blood pressure
(e) Shift in threshold of hearing
(f) Respiratory problems

Choose the correct option from those given below:
1. (a), (b), (c), (e) and (f)
2. (b), (c), (d), (e) and (f)
3. (b), (c), (d) and (e)
4. (a), (b), (c), (d), (e) and (f)

Answer: 3. (b), (c), (d) and (e)

Last Minute Revisions

Water Pollution

✓ In large parts of Eastern India, the groundwater is contaminated by Arsenic. *(Asked in Exam)*
✓ Correct Sequence in Decreasing Order of Percentage of Total World's Water: Ice caps and Glaciers – Groundwater - Lakes (Freshwater) – Atmosphere - Rivers and Streams. *(Asked in Exam)*
✓ Water Bodies in Increasing Order of Quantity of Freshwater: Rivers and Streams - Freshwater Lakes and Reservoirs – Groundwater - Ice and Snow. *(Asked in Exam)*
✓ Air pollution: industries, power plants, vehicles. *(Asked in Exam)*
✓ Land pollution: excessive chemical fertilizers. *(Asked in Exam)*
✓ Water pollution: industrial discharges and various sources. *(Asked in Exam)*
✓ Noise pollution: roads, aircraft, industry, high-intensity sonar. *(Asked in Exam)*

- ✓ Bottom ash generated into the boilers of the thermal power plants are a major cause of nearby river pollution. *(Asked in Exam)*
- ✓ The hot water generated from thermal power plants is discharged into the nearby rivers. *(Asked in Exam)*
- ✓ The Ganga is unlikely to become cleaner soon due to reduced flow, ineffective treatment plants, and rising sewage levels. *(Asked in Exam)*
- ✓ Thinning of flow rate of the river: This can contribute to pollution by reducing the river's ability to dilute and carry away pollutants. *(Asked in Exam)*
- ✓ Failure of treatment plants: This is a significant reason for the pollution of the river, as untreated or poorly treated wastewater continues to be discharged into the river. *(Asked in Exam)*
- ✓ Increased sewage: This is a major contributor to the river's pollution, as increasing amounts of untreated sewage enter the river. *(Asked in Exam)*
- ✓ Non-point sources of water pollution are diffuse, episodic and difficult to monitor. *(Asked in Exam)*
- ✓ The full form of PCB is Poly Chlorinated Biphenyls. *(Asked in Exam)*
- ✓ Muddy water has the highest turbidity. *(Asked in Exam)*
- ✓ Coral reefs are threatened because of release of sewage in ocean waters near them. *(Asked in Exam)*
- ✓ Release of sewage in oceans tends to reduce the clarity of ocean water. *(Asked in Exam)*
- ✓ Most of the emerging contaminants of water are Endocrine Disrupting Chemicals (EDCs). *(Asked in Exam)*
- ✓ Flame retardant additive, found in the environment throughout the globe, are considered to be EDCS. *(Asked in Exam)*
- ✓ Pesticides and Persistent Organic Pollutants (POPs) can be part of bioaccumulation/biomagnification. *(Asked in Exam)*
- ✓ Biomagnification occurs when the toxic burden of a large number of organisms at higher trophic level is accumulated and concentrated in the organisms at lower trophic level. *(Asked in Exam)*
- ✓ The effect of toxins are magnified in the environment through food webs. *(Asked in Exam)*
- ✓ Biomagnification occurs when toxins become more concentrated as they move up the food chain. The correct sequence starts with the smallest organisms and moves up to the largest. Bacteria - Zooplankton - Fish – Humans. *(Asked in Exam)*
- ✓ Bioconcentration is the tendency of hazardous substances to accumulate in human tissues. *(Asked in Exam)*
- ✓ The correct term for the accumulation of hazardous substances in humans due to the consumption of contaminated fish is biomagnification, not bioconcentration. *(Asked in Exam)*
- ✓ Many of the emerging contaminants have been observed to bioaccumulate in wildlife and humans. *(Asked in Exam)*
- ✓ Not all potential pollutants are synthetic chemicals. Natural substances, such as heavy metals (e.g., mercury, lead), and naturally occurring biological agents (e.g., bacteria, viruses) can also be significant pollutants. *(Asked in Exam)*
- ✓ Temperature, Turbidity and TSS are physical parameters of water quality. *(Asked in Exam)*

- ✓ Temperature, Total Suspended Solids (TSS) and Conductivity are physical parameters to decide the water quality. *(Asked in Exam)*
- ✓ The total solids (dissolved and suspended) in a wastewater sample are the 'materials left after water has evaporated from the sample. *(Asked in Exam)*
- ✓ The dissolved solids fraction usually includes colloidal particles. *(Asked in Exam)*
- ✓ pH, Hardness, DO and BOD are chemical parameters of water quality. *(Asked in Exam)*
- ✓ Normal water typically has a pH level around 7, making it neutral. *(Asked in Exam)*
- ✓ Rainwater tends to be slightly acidic due to dissolved atmospheric gases, with a pH range typically between 5 and 6. *(Asked in Exam)*
- ✓ Acid rainwater is more acidic than normal rainwater, with a pH level below 5, caused by pollutants such as sulfur dioxide and nitrogen oxides. *(Asked in Exam)*
- ✓ Ocean water has a pH level greater than 7, making it alkaline or basic. *(Asked in Exam)*
- ✓ BOD (Biochemical Oxygen Demand) refers to Oxygen consumed by microorganisms *(Asked in Exam)*
- ✓ DO (Dissolved Oxygen) refers to Amount of oxygen in water *(Asked in Exam)*
- ✓ COD (Chemical Oxygen Demand) refers to Strength of organic matter in water *(Asked in Exam)*
- ✓ The full form of CBOD is Carbonaceous Biochemical Oxygen Demand *(Asked in Exam)*
- ✓ pH refers to Acidic/Basic/Neutral nature of water. *(Asked in Exam)*
- ✓ Water with pH value between 5 to less than 7 is of acidic nature. *(Asked in Exam)*
- ✓ pH: An Important Water Quality Parameter *(Asked in Exam)*
- ✓ pH is a measure of acidity in water. *(Asked in Exam)*
- ✓ pH is a measure of basicity in water. *(Asked in Exam)*
- ✓ pH can range from 0 to 14 *(Asked in Exam)*
- ✓ pH represents the concentration of hydrogen ions. *(Asked in Exam)*
- ✓ A pH of 0 indicates highly acidic and dangerous water *(Asked in Exam)*
- ✓ Water with a pH above 5 is not necessarily detrimental to aquatic life. In fact, many aquatic organisms thrive in water with a pH above 5. It is typically water with a pH below 5 that can be harmful to aquatic life. *(Asked in Exam)*
- ✓ Water hardness, due to calcium and magnesium ions, is classified as temporary or permanent. It leads to scale buildup in hot water pipes. *(Asked in Exam)*
- ✓ Hardness in water can occur in both surface and underground waters. *(Asked in Exam)*
- ✓ Hardness in water is caused by carbonates of magnesium and calcium.
- ✓ Hard water is considered as safe for human consumption. *(Asked in Exam)*
- ✓ Hard water causes scaling in water distribution systems. *(Asked in Exam)*
- ✓ Hardness of water is caused by the presence of Cations in the water. *(Asked in Exam)*
- ✓ Permanent hardness in water is caused by calcium and magnesium sulphates or chlorides. *(Asked in Exam)*
- ✓ Methyl mercury in water can cause adverse human effects such as mental disturbance and impairment of speech, hearing and vision. *(Asked in Exam)*
- ✓ Lead exposure can affect various parts of the human body, but it has the most significant and harmful impact on the brain. *(Asked in Exam)*

- ✓ The water body exhibits varying nutrient status at different levels, classified as eutrophic, mesotrophic, or oligotrophic. *(Asked in Exam)*
- ✓ It a water body is healthy and supports no significant biological activity, then its condition is called as Oligotrophic. *(Asked in Exam)*
- ✓ When a water body is deficient in nutrients, it is known as Oligotrophic. *(Asked in Exam)*
- ✓ Eutrophic water bodies are those that have high nutrient levels and high biological productivity, often resulting in excessive growth of algae and other plants. *(Asked in Exam)*
- ✓ Oligotrophic water bodies are those that have low nutrient levels and low biological productivity. *(Asked in Exam)*
- ✓ Rising nutrient levels in a lake change the numbers and types of biota present there. *(Asked in Exam)*
- ✓ Eutrophic lakes typically have high levels of nutrients, leading to high biomass production, especially algae and aquatic plants, which can make the water turbid and reduce clarity. *(Asked in Exam)*
- ✓ A Eutrophic lake is rich in nutrients and has high algal blooms. *(Asked in Exam)*
- ✓ Aquatic weeds are fast growing weeds which can attain very high productivity when cultivated on nutrient rich wastewater such as domestic sewage. *(Asked in Exam)*
- ✓ Water hyacinth, salvinia and duckweed are some examples of aquatic weeds. *(Asked in Exam)*
- ✓ The full form of NBOD is Nitrogenous Biochemical Oxygen Demand. *(Asked in Exam)*
- ✓ A decrease in dissolved oxygen (DO) in water threatens aquatic life, mainly due to oxygen-demanding wastes. These wastes indicate biodegradable organic substances and can cause unwanted taste and color. *(Asked in Exam)*
- ✓ Oxygen demanding wastes decrease the oxygen level in water. *(Asked in Exam)*
- ✓ When organic materials such as sewage or paper pulp are added to water, decomposers (bacteria and other microorganisms) break down the organic matter. This process primarily requires oxygen for aerobic decomposition. *(Asked in Exam)*
- ✓ Adding organic materials, such as sewage or paper pulp, to water stimulates activity and oxygen consumption by decomposers. *(Asked in Exam)*
- ✓ Turbulent and rapidly flowing waters are typically well-oxygenated due to the mixing of water with air, which increases the dissolved oxygen levels. *(Asked in Exam)*
- ✓ Low dissolved oxygen in water, caused by oxygen-demanding wastes, can harm aquatic life and lead to unpleasant taste and odor. *(Asked in Exam)*
- ✓ Oxygen-demanding wastes are substances that Oxidized in the receiving body of water. *(Asked in Exam)*
- ✓ As bacteria decompose oxygen-demanding wastes, they consume oxygen rather than release it. *(Asked in Exam)*
- ✓ Nitrogen-phosphorus is a pair of elements that is most important for the eutrophication process. *(Asked in Exam)*
- ✓ When a water body gets enriched with nutrients, the process is called as Eutrophication. *(Asked in Exam)*
- ✓ Cultural eutrophication is caused by increased nutrient input into the water body mainly due to human activities. *(Asked in Exam)*

- ✓ Cultural eutrophication actually accelerates the aging process of a water body by rapidly increasing the nutrient levels, leading to excessive algal growth, oxygen depletion, and other changes that degrade the water quality much faster than natural processes. *(Asked in Exam)*
- ✓ Eutrophication causes algae blooms, higher turbidity and odors, and makes it harder for aquatic life to thrive. *(Asked in Exam)*
- ✓ Nitrates are responsible for causing blue baby disease. *(Asked in Exam)*
- ✓ In agricultural regions, groundwater can have significant concentrations of Nitrate. *(Asked in Exam)*
- ✓ Composting is aerobic degradation of organic materials under controlled conditions, yielding a marketable manure. *(Asked in Exam)*
- ✓ While compost does contain important nutrients like nitrogen, phosphorus, and potassium, the concentrations of these nutrients in compost are generally lower than those found in commercial chemical fertilizers. *(Asked in Exam)*
- ✓ Composting is the aerobic degradation of organic materials by microorganisms mainly under controlled conditions. *(Asked in Exam)*
- ✓ Both macro and micro-organisms play an important role in the composting process. *(Asked in Exam)*
- ✓ Aerobic digestion of sewage sludge requires lots of energy. *(Asked in Exam)*
- ✓ Aerobic digestion primarily produces carbon dioxide and water, not methane. Methane is produced in anaerobic digestion, where the process occurs in the absence of oxygen. *(Asked in Exam)*
- ✓ Anaerobic digestion of sewage sludge is an efficient method for treating organic solids. This process produces methane as a byproduct, and results in digested sludge that has a reduced volume and can be dewatered with greater ease. *(Asked in Exam)*
- ✓ Bacteria, nutrients, and metals are the primary pollutants responsible for lowering the water quality in rivers and streams. *(Asked in Exam)*
- ✓ Cholera, Acute Diarrhoea, Typhoid and Polio diseases caused by polluted water. *(Asked in Exam)*
- ✓ Giardia, Amoebiasis and Typhoid diseases are due to polluted water. *(Asked in Exam)*
- ✓ Waterborne diseases (Ingested polluted water) cause Typhoid (Salmonella typhi in contaminated water). *(Asked in Exam)*
- ✓ Water-washed diseases (Lack of clean water) cause Trachoma (Poor hygiene causes repeated eye infections). *(Asked in Exam)*
- ✓ Water-based diseases (Contact with polluted water) cause Schistosomiasis (Caused by waterborne parasites). *(Asked in Exam)*
- ✓ DWater-related diseases (Parasite habitat in water) cause Malaria (Mosquitoes breed in stagnant water). *(Asked in Exam)*
- ✓ Water-borne diseases Cholera is caused by drinking water contaminated with cholera bacteria. *(Asked in Exam)*
- ✓ Water-washed disease Trachoma is related to lack of water for personal hygiene. *(Asked in Exam)*
- ✓ Water-based disease Schistosomiasis results from contact with contaminated water. *(Asked in Exam)*
- ✓ Water-related disease Malaria is spread by mosquitoes that breed in water. *(Asked in Exam)*
- ✓ Pathogens include fungi which can cause waterborne diseases. *(Asked in Exam)*

✓ Salts are inorganic chemicals that can pollute water. *(Asked in Exam)*
✓ Pesticides are organic chemicals that can contaminate water. *(Asked in Exam)*
✓ Radioactive iodine can be a contaminant in water. *(Asked in Exam)*
✓ Typhoid fever, a waterborne disease is caused by Bacteria. *(Asked in Exam)*
✓ Malaria is caused by parasites of the genus Plasmodium. It does not require direct contact with water. Instead, it is spread through the bite of an infected female Anopheles mosquito, which serves as the host for the parasite. *(Asked in Exam)*
✓ Diarrhea: Diarrhea can be caused by a variety of pathogens, including viruses, bacteria, and protozoa. *(Asked in Exam)*
✓ Viruses: Examples include rotavirus and norovirus. *(Asked in Exam)*
✓ Bacteria: Examples include Escherichia coli (E. coli), Salmonella, and Shigella. *(Asked in Exam)*
✓ Protozoa: Examples include Giardia lamblia and Entamoeba histolytica. *(Asked in Exam)*
✓ Cholera: Transmission occurs via ingestion of contaminated water. *(Asked in Exam)*
✓ Trachoma: Associated with inadequate personal hygiene and insufficient water for cleaning. *(Asked in Exam)*
✓ Schistosomiasis: Spread through skin contact with polluted water, not through ingestion. *(Asked in Exam)*
✓ Dengue: Requires a mosquito vector for transmission. *(Asked in Exam)*
✓ Hepatitis, particularly hepatitis A, is caused by a virus and spread through contaminated water. *(Asked in Exam)*
✓ Cholera is caused by the bacterium Vibrio cholerae. *(Asked in Exam)*
✓ Dysentery can be caused by protozoa such as Entamoeba histolytica. *(Asked in Exam)*
✓ Schistosomiasis is caused by parasitic worms (helminths). *(Asked in Exam)*
✓ Schistosomiasis, a common water contact disease, is spread by Cercaria. *(Asked in Exam)*

Air Pollution

✓ One of the parameters used to characterise the air quality at a location is PMs. Here, the suffix '2.5' refers to size of suspended particles in certain units. *(Asked in Exam)*
✓ Coarse Particles: These are larger particles, typically greater than 10 microns in size. *(Asked in Exam)*
✓ Respirable Particles: These particles are small enough to be inhaled into the respiratory system, typically less than 10 microns in size. *(Asked in Exam)*
✓ Fine Particles: These are smaller particles, typically less than 2.5 microns in size. *(Asked in Exam)*
✓ Ultrafine Particles: These are the smallest particles, typically less than 0.1 microns in size. *(Asked in Exam)*
✓ Particulate matter enters the body through inhalation, passes into the lungs, moves into the blood, and then reaches the soft tissues of organs. *(Asked in Exam)*
✓ Nucleation mode particles are the finest particulate matter. *(Asked in Exam)*
✓ Fine particles are those SPM whose aerodynamic diameter is less than 2.5 micron. *(Asked in Exam)*

- ✓ RSPM (Respirable Suspended Particulate Matter) typically refers to particulate matter with an aerodynamic diameter of less than 10 microns, not more. *(Asked in Exam)*
- ✓ Particulate matter, a class of air pollutants, include Soot, Pollen, Fly and Ash. *(Asked in Exam)*
- ✓ Soot particles, also known as black carbon, are toxic substances that contribute to global warming and are capable of penetrating into the deeper regions of the lungs. *(Asked in Exam)*
- ✓ PM10 is preferred over Total Suspended Particles (TSP) for air quality monitoring studies. *(Asked in Exam)*
- ✓ Particles larger than 10 microns are generally not inhaled deeply into the lungs and thus are less significant indicators of health impacts compared to smaller particles (PM10 and PM2.5 *(Asked in Exam)*
- ✓ The most relevant effect of particulate matter in air, on human health is Aggravation of respiratory disease. *(Asked in Exam)*
- ✓ Carbon monoxide has a very strong affinity towards haemoglobin of the human blood. *(Asked in Exam)*
- ✓ Carbon monoxide (CO). an air pollutant when inhaled readily binds with the hemoglobin in the blood stream to form a life-threatening compound known as Carboxyhemoglobin. *(Asked in Exam)*
- ✓ Carbon monoxide (CO) is a serious asphyxiant: even a short exposure may have fatal health issues. *(Asked in Exam)*
- ✓ Hemoglobin present in the blood has greater affinity towards carbon monoxide than oxygen. *(Asked in Exam)*
- ✓ CO (Carbon Monoxide) causes serious health issues due to its greater affinity for hemoglobin in blood in comparison to oxygen. *(Asked in Exam)*
- ✓ Sulphur dioxide (SO_2) is a significant air pollutant that primarily comes from human activities. The major man-made sources include the burning of fossil fuels in power plants and industrial processes, particularly those involving the smelting of metal ores. *(Asked in Exam)*
- ✓ Taj Mahal is mainly threatened by the deleterious effects of Sulphur dioxide. *(Asked in Exam)*
- ✓ Nitric oxide (NO) has the least residence time in the atmosphere. *(Asked in Exam)*
- ✓ In air pollution, oxides of nitrogen (NOx) include Nitric oxide and Nitrogen dioxide. *(Asked in Exam)*
- ✓ Rain is termed as acid rain when its ph value is Less than 5.6. *(Asked in Exam)*
- ✓ Nitrogen oxides (NOx) is a key ingredient in the formation of photochemical smog. *(Asked in Exam)*
- ✓ Sulphate, Photochemical smog and PeroxyAcetyl Nitrate (PAN) are examples of secondary air pollutants. *(Asked in Exam)*
- ✓ Atmospheric haze mainly caused by Ultra fine size particulate matters
- ✓ Sunlight is an essential requirement for the formation of photochemical smog. *(Asked in Exam)*
- ✓ Photochemical smog in urban areas is known to cause Respiratory effects, Eye irritation, Nose and throat irritation and Reduction in visibility. *(Asked in Exam)*
- ✓ Sunlight is a pre-requisite for the formation of photochemical smog in urban areas. *(Asked in Exam)*

- ✓ Photochemical smog is more prevalent in the summer season when there is abundant sunlight to drive the photochemical reactions. In winter, conditions are typically less favorable for the formation of photochemical smog due to lower temperatures and reduced sunlight. *(Asked in Exam)*
- ✓ Nitrogen dioxide (NO2), Volatile Organic Compounds (VOCs) AND Sunlight. *(Asked in Exam)*
- ✓ are essential requirements for the formation of photochemical SMOG. *(Asked in Exam)*
- ✓ Sulphur Dioxide (SO2), Particulate matters, Fly ash and Soot are essential components of industrial smog. *(Asked in Exam)*
- ✓ Classical smog reduces atmospheric visibility to a great extent. *(Asked in Exam)*
- ✓ Classical smog, also known as London smog or winter smog, is primarily formed by the combination of sulfur dioxide (SO_2) and particulate matter under cool and humid conditions. *(Asked in Exam)*
- ✓ Sea salt, Black carbon and Mineral particles are primary aerosols in the atmosphere. *(Asked in Exam)*
- ✓ Black carbon aerosols is the primary air pollutant. *(Asked in Exam)*
- ✓ Acid rain occurs within, and downwind of areas of major industrial emissions of sulfur dioxide and oxides of nitrogen. *(Asked in Exam)*
- ✓ Long range transport of airborne pollutants can be responsible for acid rain in areas far off from industrial missions. *(Asked in Exam)*
- ✓ Nitric oxide, Nitrogen dioxide and Sulphur dioxide are the air pollutants cause acid rain. *(Asked in Exam)*
- ✓ Reducing the use of fossil fuels would be most appropriate in reducing acid rain and acid deposition problems. *(Asked in Exam)*
- ✓ Full form of PAN, a type of air pollutant, is PeroxyAcetyl Nitrate (PAN).
- ✓ PeroxyAcetyl Nitrate (PAN) is a significant secondary pollutant found in photochemical smog. It is formed by the reaction of volatile organic compounds (VOCs) and nitrogen oxides (NOx) in the presence of sunlight. *(Asked in Exam)*
- ✓ Benzene and Ethylbenzene are components of BTEX, an air pollutant. *(Asked in Exam)*
- ✓ T of BTEX (Air pollutant) stands for Toluene. *(Asked in Exam)*
- ✓ Volatile Organic Compounds (VOCs) is an extremely short-lived and unstable air/water pollutant. *(Asked in Exam)*
- ✓ Carbon monoxide (CO) is an asphyxiant. *(Asked in Exam)*
- ✓ Nitrogen dioxide (NO2) is associated with respiratory problems and can contribute to conditions like methemoglobinemia ("blue baby" syndrome). *(Asked in Exam)*
- ✓ Volatile Organic Compounds (VOCs) include a range of compounds, some of which are known to be carcinogenic. *(Asked in Exam)*
- ✓ Ozone (O3) is a potent respiratory irritant and allergen. *(Asked in Exam)*
- ✓ Formaldehyde, widely used in plastics, wood products, insulating materials, glue and fabrics, is a serious allergen. *(Asked in Exam)*
- ✓ Allergens are substances that activate the immune system. *(Asked in Exam)*
- ✓ Naturally occurring Volatile Organic Compounds (VOCs) generally oxidize to form Carbon Monoxide (CO) and Carbon Dioxide (CO2). *(Asked in Exam)*
- ✓ Anthropogenically emitted VOCs play an important role in the formation of smog. *(Asked in Exam)*

- Volatile Organic Compounds (VOCs) are emitted from vehicles. *(Asked in Exam)*
- Volatile Organic Compounds are emitted from some trees. *(Asked in Exam)*
- Vehicles, Plants, Termites, Power Plants and Bogs are sources of Volatile Organic Compounds (VOCs). *(Asked in Exam)*
- Dioxins and Furans are highly toxic substances produced as by products of solid waste incineration. *(Asked in Exam)*
- Dioxins and furans are known for their stability and persistence in the environment. *(Asked in Exam)*
- Terpene Volatile Organic Compound (VOC), a kind of air pollutant, is emitted from natural sources such as plants, bogs etc. *(Asked in Exam)*
- Volatile Organic Chemicals (VOCs) are among the most commonly found contaminants in groundwater. *(Asked in Exam)*
- Formaldehyde, Benzene, and Toluene: While these compounds can also be classified as volatile organic compounds (VOCs), they are primarily associated with anthropogenic (human-made) sources rather than natural ones. *(Asked in Exam)*
- Volatile Organic Chemicals (VOCs) are contaminants more commonly found in groundwater than in surface water. *(Asked in Exam)*
- While VOCs can be a concern for drinking water quality, they are not typically one of the primary criterion parameters used universally to determine drinking water quality. *(Asked in Exam)*
- The Volatile Organic Compounds (VOCs) may cause cancer and can play an important role in the formation of photochemical smog. *(Asked in Exam)*
- Forests help in improving the air quality of a place. *(Asked in Exam)*
- Some tree species emit volatile organic compounds (VOCs) such as isoprene which may contribute to formation of tropospheric ozone. *(Asked in Exam)*
- Volatile organic compounds air pollutants are produced from room deodorizers. *(Asked in Exam)*
- Poly Chlorinated Biphenyls, Dioxins and Furans are examples of Persistent Organic Pollutants (POPs). *(Asked in Exam)*
- The full form of POPs is Persistent Organic Pollutants. *(Asked in Exam)*
- Dioxins, Poly-Chlorinated Benzenes (PCBs), Organo Chlorine Pesticides and Furansare are examples of Persistent Organic Pollutants (POPS). *(Asked in Exam)*
- Persistent Organic Pollutants (POPs) are extremely widespread and occur from tropics to the Arctic and often accumulate in food webs and reach toxic concentrations. They are widely used as flame retardants and in deodorants. Some chemicals used in making non-stick, waterproof and stain resistant products are categorized as POPs. *(Asked in Exam)*
- In the less developed countries of the world indoor exposure to hazardous air pollutants is much severe. *(Asked in Exam)*
- Traditional methods of cooking often involve fuels such as coal, wood, animal, dung, kerosene etc. *(Asked in Exam)*
- Air Quality Index (AQI) is used to report to the public an overall assessment of a given day's air quality. *(Asked in Exam)*
- The AQI integrates air quality data for more than just two criteria pollutants. It typically includes multiple key pollutants such as particulate matter

(PM10 and PM2.5), nitrogen dioxide (NO2), sulfur dioxide (SO2), carbon monoxide (CO), ozone (O3), and sometimes lead (Pb). *(Asked in Exam)*

✓ Polluted indoor air causes Sick Building Syndrome (SBS). *(Asked in Exam)*

✓ Concentration of Formaldehyde in indoor environment can be thousand times higher than outdoor environment. *(Asked in Exam)*

✓ Formaldehyde is a known carcinogen. *(Asked in Exam)*

✓ Some people suffer from what is called Sick Building Syndrome (SBS). *(Asked in Exam)*

✓ SBS is primarily associated with poor indoor air quality due to factors such as inadequate ventilation, chemical contaminants from indoor sources (like adhesives, upholstery, carpeting, copy machines, and cleaning agents), biological contaminants (like mold, bacteria, and pollen), and other factors like inadequate temperature, humidity, or lighting. *(Asked in Exam)*

✓ Allergens are substances that activate the immune system. *(Asked in Exam)*

✓ Concentration of allergens in an indoor environment can be thousand times higher than in the air outside. *(Asked in Exam)*

✓ Sick Building Syndrome (SBS) is a condition of human health due to indoor air pollution. *(Asked in Exam)*

✓ NO2 Nitrogen dioxide is included while estimating Air Quality Index (AQI). *(Asked in Exam)*

✓ TSP (Total Suspended Particles) and PM10 (Particulate matters of size 10 microns or less) are types of particulate matter pollutants are used in the calculation of Air Quality Index (AQI). *(Asked in Exam)*

✓ Sulphur dioxide pollutants are included in the Air Quality Index in India. *(Asked in Exam)*

✓ The correct order of Global Warming Potential (GWP) for these greenhouse gases, from the lowest to the highest, is: CO_2 (Carbon Dioxide), CH_4 (Methane), N_2O (Nitrous Oxide), and CFC-11 (Chloro Fluoro Carbon-11). *(Asked in Exam)*

✓ China is the largest emitter of Greenhouse Gases (GHGs) at present. *(Asked in Exam)*

✓ Greenhouse gases, including water vapor, absorb the earth's thermal radiation and contribute to global warming. *(Asked in Exam)*

✓ The gases increase in Global Warming Potential (GWP) in this order: CO2 < CH4 < N2O < CFCs. *(Asked in Exam)*

✓ One of the ways to control greenhouse gas emissions is by encouraging energy efficiency throughout society in our country. *(Asked in Exam)*

✓ Improving energy efficiency has significant environmental benefits. *(Asked in Exam)*

✓ The correct order for decreasing atmospheric lifetimes of these greenhouse gases is: CFC-11 (Chlorofluorocarbon-11), nitrous oxide (N2O), methane (CH4), and surface ozone (O3). *(Asked in Exam)*

✓ Global warming potential of a molecule of a greenhouse gas over different time spans of decades to 100 years may vary significantly. *(Asked in Exam)*

✓ Some greenhouse gases have shorter life times compared to carbon dioxide. *(Asked in Exam)*

✓ Major contribution to the greenhouse effect comes from carbon dioxide. *(Asked in Exam)*

✓ Earth's climate was changing even before man appeared on earth. *(Asked in Exam)*

- **Greenhouse gases listed by increasing global warming potential (GWP):** Carbon dioxide (CO2) has a baseline GWP of 1. Next is methane (CH4), which ranges from 28 to 36 times greater than CO2 over a 100-year period. Following that is nitrous oxide (N2O), with a GWP of 298. Finally, chlorofluorocarbons (CFCs) have GWPs that can be thousands to tens of thousands times higher than CO2. *(Asked in Exam)*
- Thermal expansion of oceans may lead to Sea level rise. *(Asked in Exam)*
- Over the past 100 years; the estimated rise of global sea level is by 10-25cm or more. Thermal expansion of ocean waters has the maximum contribution in it. *(Asked in Exam)*
- Carbon dioxide (CO2) has the maximum contribution to Global Warming. *(Asked in Exam)*
- Carbon dioxide (CO2) is used as the reference gas for Global Warming Potential (GWP) and is assigned a GWP value of 1. *(Asked in Exam)*
- Methane (CH4) is a greenhouse gas that helps in formation of Ozone and is a Volatile Organic Compound (VOC). *(Asked in Exam)*
- Methane, a greenhouse gas is emitted from wetlands le-waste.
- Nitrogen dioxide is a pollutant causes aggravation of respiratory disease, and atmospheric discolouration. *(Asked in Exam)*
- Nitrous oxide (N2O) has a significantly higher Global Warming Potential (GWP) compared to methane (CH4), carbon dioxide (CO2), and carbon monoxide (CO). *(Asked in Exam)*
- Chlorofluorocarbons (CFCs) are potent greenhouse gas. *(Asked in Exam)*
- CFCs have the ability to catalytically destroy ozone in the stratosphere. *(Asked in Exam)*
- Discovery of Ozone hole was first made over Antarctic. *(Asked in Exam)*
- CFCs already present in the atmosphere will persist for many years. *(Asked in Exam)*
- The concentration of CFCs in the atmosphere has been decreasing due to international efforts to phase out the production and use of these substances under the Montreal Protocol. *(Asked in Exam)*
- Chlorofluorocarbons (CFCs) are stable greenhouse gases that vaporize just below room temperature and can destroy ozone. *(Asked in Exam)*
- Chlorofluorocarbon is a non-vehicular pollutant. *(Asked in Exam)*
- CO2 (carbon dioxide), H2O (water vapor), CH4 (methane) and O3 (ozone) are Natural GreenHouse Gases (GHGs). *(Asked in Exam)*
- Greenhouse gases primarily absorb infrared radiation from the solar spectrum. *(Asked in Exam)*
- The order of Global Warming Potential (GWP) for these atmospheric chemicals is: Carbon dioxide (CO2), Methane (CH4), Nitrous oxide (N2O), Chlorofluorocarbon (CFC). *(Asked in Exam)*
- Ozone pollutant is considered as surrogate for eye irritation. *(Asked in Exam)*
- Global warming could lead to increased release of the greenhouse gas, Methane. *(Asked in Exam)*
- There is a large amount of Methane currently frozen in the permafrost in the far northern regions of the world. *(Asked in Exam)*
- Stratospheric ozone is known as 'good ozone'. *(Asked in Exam)*
- Ozone at the surface level is a serious health hazard and known as pollutant. *(Asked in Exam)*

- ✓ Ozone layer which protects us from harmful ultraviolet radiations is situated in Stratosphere. *(Asked in Exam)*
- ✓ Although ozone is a pollutant in the ambient air, but in stratosphere it is valuable because it absorbs harmful UV-Radiations. *(Asked in Exam)*
- ✓ Ozone layer is in Stratosphere. *(Asked in Exam)*
- ✓ Halocarbons contribute significantly to global warming. *(Asked in Exam)*
- ✓ Halocarbons also catalytically destroy stratospheric Ozone. *(Asked in Exam)*
- ✓ Chlorine is one of the most commonly used and inexpensive chemical disinfectants for water. *(Asked in Exam)*
- ✓ Optimum Fluoride levels in drinking water help prevent cavities in children. *(Asked in Exam)*
- ✓ Ozone hole appears over Antarctica mostly in the month of September. *(Asked in Exam)*
- ✓ Polar Stratospheric Clouds are associated with Ozone layer depletion environmental issues. *(Asked in Exam)*
- ✓ Tropospheric (ground level) ozone forms when sunlight acts on nitrogen oxides and can also result from downward transfer from the ozone layer. It is a greenhouse gas and a major part of photochemical smog. *(Asked in Exam)*
- ✓ Ground level concentration of ozone decreases at night. *(Asked in Exam)*
- ✓ Ultraviolet radiation photolysis the ozone into other components. *(Asked in Exam)*
- ✓ The radiation reflected back to the atmosphere is called albedo. *(Asked in Exam)*
- ✓ The atmosphere is essential in maintaining the heat balance of the body. *(Asked in Exam)*
- ✓ The heat and sunlight both pass through the atmosphere. *(Asked in Exam)*
- ✓ Nighttime temperatures in the central parts of a city are generally higher than those over the surrounding rural areas. *(Asked in Exam)*
- ✓ Radiation losses over the urban areas are less than that over the rural Areas. *(Asked in Exam)*
- ✓ Gases in the atmosphere absorb infrared radiation from Earth's surface, which is the basic mechanism of the greenhouse effect. *(Asked in Exam)*
- ✓ Dioxins is not responsible for the destruction of the Ozone layer. *(Asked in Exam)*
- ✓ CFC, Halons and HCFC are responsible for the destruction of the Ozone layer. *(Asked in Exam)*
- ✓ Tropospheric Ozone has a positive radiative forcing or warming effect in the global climate. *(Asked in Exam)*
- ✓ The global environmental issue of Ozone depletion is due to emission of Chlorinated hydrocarbons. *(Asked in Exam)*
- ✓ The phenomenon of ozone depletion is caused by Emissions from thermal power plants and Excessive use of nitrogen-containing fertilizers. *(Asked in Exam)*
- ✓ In the afternoon period, the atmosphere is unstable and its dilution potential is higher as compared to mornings and evenings. *(Asked in Exam)*
- ✓ The tropospheric ozone levels in the afternoon of a hot sunny day are typically higher, not lower. This is because the intense sunlight in the afternoon leads to photochemical reactions that produce ozone. *(Asked in Exam)*

✓ Surface ozone forms mainly due to the interaction of nitrogen oxides, carbon monoxide, and sunlight. *(Asked in Exam)*

Noise Pollution

- ✓ Exposure to noise pollution adversely affects the physiological health of a person. *(Asked in Exam)*
- ✓ Exposure to noise pollution adversely affects the psychological health of a person. *(Asked in Exam)*
- ✓ The correct sequence of average noise levels in increasing order of their magnitude from different sources: Typical office →Conversational speech →City Street corner →Highway →Aircraft noise during take-off. *(Asked in Exam)*
- ✓ According to Noise Pollution (Regulation and Control) Rules in India, noise in educational institutions during night time (10pm-6am) must not exceed 40dB. *(Asked in Exam)*
- ✓ Two sounds of same intensity but different frequency characteristics may appear to be of different loudness. *(Asked in Exam)*
- ✓ The response of the human ear to noise of different frequencies is not uniform. *(Asked in Exam)*
- ✓ According to Noise Pollution (Regulation and Control) Rules, 2000, the night time Noise standard prescribed for Educational Institutions is 40 dB (A). *(Asked in Exam)*
- ✓ Day time noise standard prescribed for residential areas in India is 55 dB. *(Asked in Exam)*
- ✓ The impact of noise pollution on human health is governed by Intensity of noise, Duration of noise, Sensitivity of human ear and Frequency range of noise. *(Asked in Exam)*
- ✓ Exposure to excessive noise pollution can cause Hearing impairment, Insomnia, Rise in blood pressure and Reduced work efficiency. *(Asked in Exam)*
- ✓ Materials with high surface/mass density act as good noise barriers. *(Asked in Exam)*
- ✓ Sound pressure of 2j Pa corresponds to a noise of zero decibel. *(Asked in Exam)*
- ✓ Average noise levels in heavy traffic zones in major cities in India are generally in 70-95 dBA ranges of noise levels. *(Asked in Exam)*
- ✓ Exposure to noise pollution can cause Sleeplessness, Speech interference, Increase in blood pressure and Shift in threshold of hearing. *(Asked in Exam)*

Chapter 3

Waste (solid, liquid, biomedical, hazardous, electronic and Nuclear Waste)

Waste (solid, liquid, biomedical, hazardous, electronic)

Definition of Waste: Waste, or wastes, refer to any unwanted or unusable materials. These are substances discarded after primary use or deemed worthless, defective, and of no use. In contrast, a by-product is a joint product of relatively minor economic value. A waste product can become a by-product, joint product, or resource if an invention raises its value above zero.

Examples of Waste:

- ➢ **Municipal Solid Waste:** Household trash/refuse.
- ➢ **Hazardous Waste**: Dangerous materials requiring special disposal.
- ➢ **Wastewater:** Includes sewage (bodily wastes like feces and urine) and surface runoff.
- ➢ **Radioactive Waste:** Materials that emit radiation.

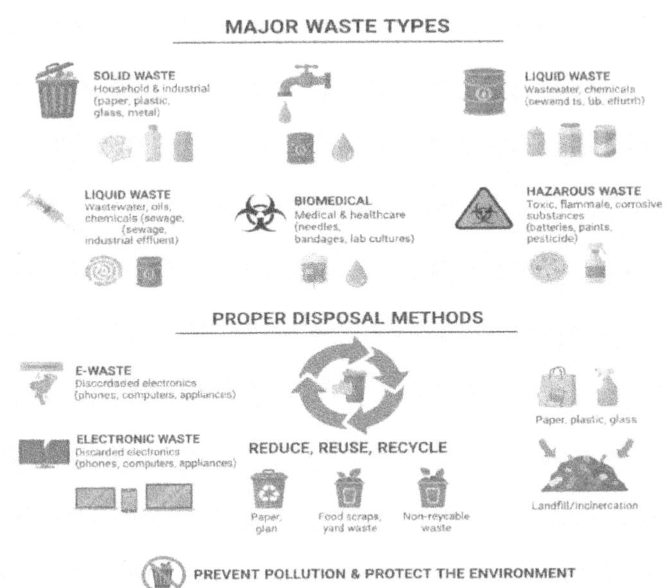

Historical Context: Since the industrial revolution, waste has been a significant problem. Technology and automation have profoundly impacted the environment, leading to the accumulation of non-biodegradable plastics and ozone-destroying CFCs. Understanding how waste accumulation affects the planet is crucial.

Sources and Types of Waste: Waste generation can be identified by recognizing the different types of waste produced daily. Here's a brief overview:

Solid Wastes:

- Unwanted substances discarded by human society.
- Include urban wastes, industrial wastes, agricultural wastes, biomedical wastes, and radioactive wastes.

Liquid Wastes:

- Generated from washing, flushing, or manufacturing processes in industries.
- Examples include wastewater from households and industrial effluents.

Gaseous Wastes:

- Released in the form of gases from automobiles, factories, or fossil fuel combustion.
- These wastes mix with the atmosphere and can cause events like smog and acid rain.

Waste management is a critical issue that needs addressing to mitigate its impact on the environment. By understanding the sources and types of waste, we can develop better strategies for managing and reducing waste, ultimately leading to a cleaner and healthier planet.

Sources of Wastes

Waste generation is an integral part of daily human life. Wastes can be generated from various sources, each contributing differently to the overall waste management challenge.

Household and Public Waste

Everyday trash or garbage from households, schools, offices, marketplaces, restaurants, and other public places. Common items include:

- Food debris
- Used plastic bags
- Soda cans and plastic water bottles
- Broken furniture

> Broken home appliances
> Clothing

Medical or Clinical Waste

Produced by healthcare facilities such as hospitals, clinics, surgical theaters, veterinary hospitals, and labs. Examples include:

> Surgical items
> Pharmaceuticals
> Blood and body parts
> Wound dressing materials
> Needles and syringes

Agricultural Waste

Generated by agricultural activities including horticulture, livestock breeding, market gardens, and seedling nurseries. Examples include:

> Empty pesticide containers
> Old silage wrap
> Out-of-date medicines and wormers
> Used tires
> Surplus milk
> Cocoa pods and corn husks

Industrial Waste:

Released from manufacturing and processing industries such as chemical plants, cement factories, power plants, textile industries, food processing industries, and petroleum industries. Examples include:

> Chemical by-products
> Industrial sludge
> Scrap metals
> Packaging materials

Construction and Demolition Waste

Produced from the construction and demolition of buildings and infrastructure. Examples include:

> Concrete debris
> Wood
> Huge package boxes
> Plastics from building materials
> Demolition rubble

Commercial Waste

Generated from commercial enterprises in modern cities, industries, and automobiles. Examples include:

- ➢ Food items
- ➢ Disposable medical items
- ➢ Textiles

Mining Waste

Generated from mining activities that disturb the land and atmosphere. Examples include:

- ➢ Overburden material
- ➢ Mine tailings (waste left after extracting ore)
- ➢ Harmful gases released by blasting

Radioactive Waste:

Produced from nuclear reactors, mining of radioactive substances, and atomic explosions.

Electronic Waste

Commonly known as e-waste, e-scrap, or waste electrical and electronic equipment (WEEE). Examples include:

- ➢ DVD and music players
- ➢ TV, Telephones, and computers
- ➢ Vacuum cleaners
- ➢ Other obsolete electrical items
- ➢ Contains harmful substances like lead, mercury, and cadmium

Nuclear Energy

Overview:

Nuclear energy is produced by nuclear fission or fusion. It releases energy from atomic nuclei. Fission splits atoms, while fusion combines them. It is primarily used for electricity, medicine, and research. While it is a low-carbon source, it produces radioactive waste.

Status in Energy Mix:

- ➢ **In many countries, including India, the share of renewable energy (which includes solar, wind, hydro, and biomass) in the energy mix is higher than that of nuclear energy.** *(Asked in Exam)*
- ➢ **Nuclear sources of energy in electricity generation in India at present is the least.** *(Asked in Exam)*

Nuclear Power Plants:

A nuclear power plant uses nuclear fission to generate heat. This heat converts water into steam for turbines, which drive generators to produce electricity.

- ➢ **A nuclear power reactor is a system designed to sustain a fission chain reaction and extract useful energy.** *(Asked in Exam)*

> ➤ **Light Water Reactors (LWR) are nuclear reactors that use ordinary water (H_2O) as a moderator.** *(Asked in Exam)*
> ➤ **Light water nuclear reactors use Ordinary water H_2O.** *(Asked in Exam)*

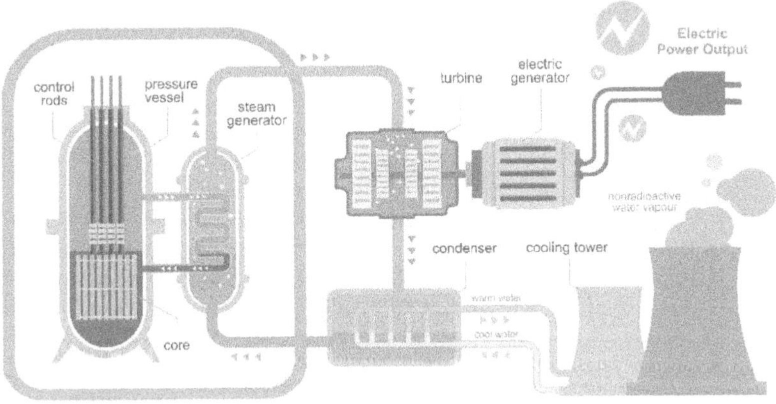

Nuclear Fuel:

> ➤ **Uranium-235: U-235 (Uranium-235) is a fissile isotope of uranium, meaning it can sustain a nuclear chain reaction.** *(Asked in Exam)*
> ➤ **Plutonium-239: Plutonium – 239 is fissile.** *(Asked in Exam)*
> ➤ **Enrichment: Enrichment increases the U-235 concentration in natural uranium.** *(Asked in Exam)*

Reactor Dynamics:

> ➤ **Moderators: The substance that slows down the neutrons to have a controlled chain reaction during nuclear energy production is called a Moderator.** *(Asked in Exam)*
> ➤ **Thermal Reactors: Thermal reactors produce energy by fission of the Uranium-235 (235), Uranium-233 (233), and Plutonium-239 nuclear fuels.** *(Asked in Exam)*

Breeder Reactors

General Overview:

Breeder reactors generate more fissile material than they consume. They use uranium-238 or thorium to create new fuel and convert non-fissile isotopes into fissile ones like plutonium-239.

- ➢ **Breeder reactors produce more fissile material than they consume.** *(Asked in Exam)*
- ➢ **In a breeder reactor, the amount of fissile material produced is more than the amount of fissile material consumed. Breeder reactors are specifically designed to generate more fissile material than they use, thereby "breeding" fuel.** *(Asked in Exam)*
- ➢ **A nuclear breeder reactor produces more fissile material than it consumes.** *(Asked in Exam)*

Technical Characteristics:

- ➢ **Conversion Ratio: For breeding operations, the conversion ratio (fissile material produced/fissile material consumed) should be more than one.** *(Asked in Exam)*
- ➢ **Neutrons & Moderators: Breeder reactors typically use fast neutrons to convert fertile material into fissile material. Slow (thermal) neutrons are not suitable for breeding because they do not effectively convert fertile material. Therefore, moderators, which slow down neutrons, are not used in breeder reactors.** *(Asked in Exam)*

Types and Examples:

- ➢ **Types: Breeder reactors are the two types (Fast and Slow) of breeder reactors.** *(Asked in Exam)*
  - ○ *Fast Breeder Reactors (FBRs):* Use fast neutrons, no moderator.
  - ○ *Thermal Breeder Reactors:* Use a moderator, convert thorium-232 to uranium-233.
  - ○ *Liquid Metal Fast Breeder Reactors (LMFBRs):* Cooled by liquid sodium for high efficiency.
- ➢ **Example: In India, Kalpakkam (Chennai) Nuclear Power Plant is an example of a breeder reactor.** *(Asked in Exam)*

Advantages & Risks:

- ➢ *Advantages:* More efficient fuel use; generates less nuclear waste than conventional reactors; extends fuel supply.
- ➢ *Risks:* High construction costs; liquid sodium coolant is reactive; proliferation concerns.

Nuclear Waste Management

Radioactive Waste:

Radioactive waste is a type of hazardous waste containing radioactive material resulting from nuclear medicine, research, power generation, and weapons reprocessing.

Categories:

1. **Low-Level Waste (LLW):** Paper, rags, tools with short-lived radioactivity.
2. **Intermediate-Level Waste (ILW):** Requires shielding.
3. **High-Level Waste (HLW):** Highly radioactive, generates decay heat, needs cooling.

Depleted Uranium:

- ➢ **Waste uranium from the nuclear reactors is called Depleted uranium.** *(Asked in Exam)*
- ➢ Remains radioactive for thousands of years and can be repurposed for military or industry.

Disposition and Storage:

- ➢ **Salt Formations: Salt mines are better suited for dumping of nuclear waste.** *(Asked in Exam)* They are stable, self-sealing, have low permeability, and conduct heat well.
- ➢ **Nuclear Reprocessing:** 96% of spent fuel is recycled. Waste is often vitrified into glass-like ceramics for deep storage.

Nuclear Disasters

Fukushima disaster, Chernobyl disaster, and Three-mile Island incident belong to the category of nuclear disasters. *(Asked in Exam)*

1. **Chornobyl (1986):** Explosion in Ukraine; massive radiation release; worst in history.
2. **Three Mile Island (1979):** Partial meltdown in Pennsylvania, USA; strict regulations followed.
3. **Fukushima (2011):** Triggered by earthquake/tsunami; loss of cooling led to meltdowns.

Health Dangers and Toxicology

Exposure Pathways:

- ➢ Inhalation, Dermal, and Ingestion are pathways for toxicants to enter into our body. *(Asked in Exam)*

Toxicological Concepts:

- ➢ Toxicodynamics: Toxicodynamics refers to the effects of chemicals on the body, including the mechanisms by which they cause harm at the cellular or organ level. *(Asked in Exam)*
- ➢ Toxicokinetics: Toxicokinetics refers to the processes of absorption, distribution, metabolism, and excretion (ADME) of chemicals in the body. *(Asked in Exam)*

Acute vs. Chronic Effects:

Acute:
> ➤ Acute toxic effects are typically immediate and short-term, resulting from a single exposure to a high dose of a toxin. They are not usually long-lasting or irreversible, though they can be severe and sometimes fatal. *(Asked in Exam)*
> ➤ Acute health effects are caused due to short-term exposure to a chemical. These effects appear rapidly after exposure. *(Asked in Exam)*

Chronic:
> ➤ Chronic toxic effects result from single dose of very high toxic substance or continuous exposure of sub-lethal dose. *(Asked in Exam)*
> ➤ Chronic health effects occur when an individual is exposed to a chemical for a prolonged period. *(Asked in Exam)*
> ➤ Chronic toxicity caused by hazardous wastes is often difficult to determine because it usually results from long-term, low-level exposure, making it hard to link specific health effects directly to the exposure. *(Asked in Exam)*
> ➤ Chronic effects typically do not appear immediately after exposure. Instead, they develop over a longer period, often after repeated or continuous exposure to a hazardous substance. *(Asked in Exam)*

Organ-Specific Toxicity:

Toxic chemicals often injure organs as well as organ systems. *(Asked in Exam)*
> ➤ **Kidneys: Nephrotoxic affects the kidney.** *(Asked in Exam)*
> ➤ **Blood: Hematotoxic affects the blood.** *(Asked in Exam)*
> ➤ **Lungs: Pulmonotoxic affects the lungs.** *(Asked in Exam)*
> ➤ **Liver: Hepatotoxic affects the liver.** *(Asked in Exam)*
> > ○ *Correction Note:* **Hepatotoxins are chemicals that can damage the liver, not the kidneys. Chemicals that damage the kidneys are referred to as nephrotoxins.** *(Asked in Exam)*

Questions

Nuclear Energy and Nuclear Waste

Q 1. Which of the following elements is fissile?
1. Thorium - 232
2. Plutonium - 239
3. Uranium - 237
4. Uranium - 238

Answer: 2. Plutonium - 239

Q 2. Waste uranium from the nuclear reactors is called as
1. Euriched uranium

> 2. Depleted uranium
> 3. Fertile uranium
> 4. Fissile uranium

Answer: 2. Depleted uranium

Q 3. Thermal reactors produce energy by fission of the following nuclear fuels

A. Uranium-235 (235)
B. Uranium-233 (233)
C. Uranium-238 (238)
D. Thorium-232 (232Th)
E. Plutonium-239 (239Pu)

Choose the correct answer from the options given below:

1. A. B, C and E only
2. A, B, C. D and E
3. A, B, D and E only
4. A, B and E only

Answer: 4. A, B and E only

Q 4. Which one of the following isotopes of Uranium is fissile material and can be used for nuclear reactions?

1. U-234
2. U-235
3. U-236
4. U-238

Answer: 2. U-235

Q 5. Given below are two statements:

Statement I: Chronic toxic effects result from single dose of very high toxic substance or continuous exposure of sub lethal dose.

Statement II: Acute toxic effects are long lasting and irreversible mainly caused due to prolonged exposure to toxins and survival rate is very low.

In the light of the above statements, choose the correct answer from the options given below:

1. Both Statement I and Statement II are true
2. Both Statement I and Statement II are false
3. Statement I is correct but Statement II is false
4. Statement I is incorrect but Statement II is true

Answer: 3. Statement I is correct but Statement II is false

Q 6. Which of the following disasters belongs to the category of nuclear disasters?

A. Fukushima disaster
B. Chernobyl disaster
C. Three-mile Island incident
D. The love canal disaster

Choose your answer from the options given below:

1. (a), (b) and (c)

   2.   (a), (b) and (d)
   3.   (a), (c) and (d)
   4.   (b), (c) and (d)

Answer: 1. (a), (b) and (c)

Q 7. Which of the following are true about breeder reactors?

  A.   They produce more fissile material than they consume.
  B.   There are no breeder reactors in India.
  C.   There are two types (fast and Slow) of breeder reactors.
  D.   For breeding operations, the conversion ratio (fissile material produced/fissile material consumed) should be more than one.
  E.   Breeder reactors produce more nuclear waste than conventional ones.

Choose the correct answer from the options given below:

   1.   ACD
   2.   ABD
   3.   BCE
   4.   ACDE

Answer: 1. ACD

Q 8. Light water nuclear reactors use the following moderator:

   1.   Ordinary water H20
   2.   Graphite
   3.   Heavy water D20
   4.   Pressurized water

Answer: 1. Ordinary water H20

Q 9. Given below are two statements:

Statement I: In a breeder reactor more fissile material is produced than it is consumed.

Statement II: In a breeder reactor, breeding works best with slow neutrons and hence moderators are required.

In the light of the above statements, choose the correct answer from the options given below:

   1.   Both Statement I and Statement II are true.
   2.   Both Statement I and Statement II are false.
   3.   Statement I is true but Statement II is false.
   4.   Statement I is false but Statement II is true.

Answer: 3. Statement I is true but Statement II is false.

Q 10. Given below are two statements:

Statement I: In a breeder reactor the amount of fissile material consumed is more than the amount of fissile material produced.

Statement II: In India, Kalpakkam (Chennai) Nuclear Power Plant is an example of a breeder reactor.

In the light of the above statements, choose the correct answer from the options given below:

   1.   Both Statement I and Statement II are true
   2.   Both Statement I and Statement II are false

3. Statement I is true but Statement II is false
4. Statement I is false but Statement II is true

Answer: 4. Statement I is false but Statement II is true

Q 11. Given below are two statements:

Statement I: A nuclear breeder reactor produces more fissile material than it consumes.

Statement II: Present share of nuclear energy in the energy mix of the country is more than that of renewable energy.

In the light of the above statements, choose the correct answer from the options given below:

1. Both Statement I and Statement II are correct
2. Both Statement I and Statement II are incorrect
3. Statement I is correct but Statement II is incorrect
4. Statement I is incorrect but Statement II is correct

Answer: 3. Statement I is correct but Statement II is incorrect

Q 12. Given below are two statements:

Statement I: A nuclear power reactor is a system designed to sustain a fission chain reaction and extract useful energy.

statement II: Light water reactors use ordinary water as the moderator.

In the light of the above statements, choose the correct answer from the options given below:

1. Both Statement I) and Statement (II) are correct.
2. Both Statement (1) and Statement (II) are incorrect.
3. Statement (I) is correct but Statement (II) is incorrect
4. Statement I) is incorrect but Statement (II) is correct

Answer: 1. Both Statement I) and Statement (II) are correct.

Q 13. Through the enrichment process, concentration of which uranium isotope is increased in the natural uranium?

1. U-234
2. U-235
3. U-238
4. U-239

Answer: 2. U-235

Q 14. Light Water Reactors (LWR) are nuclear reactors

1. Which use heavy water as a coolant
2. Which use graphite rod as moderator
3. Which use ordinary water as moderator
4. Which use steam as moderator

Answer: 3. Which use ordinary water as moderator

Q 15. The substance that slows down the neutrons to have controlled chain reaction during nuclear energy production is called as-

1. Controller
2. Inhibitor
3. Moderator
4. Reducer

Answer: 3. Moderator

Q 16. Amongst the following, which is better suited for dumping of nuclear waste?

1. Salt mines
2. Deserts
3. Forests
4. Oceans

Answer: 1. Salt mines

Q 17. The share of which of the following sources of energy in electricity generation in India at present is the least?

1. Thermal
2. Hydro
3. Solar and Wind
4. Nuclear

Answer: 4. Nuclear

Q 18. Match the lists

List I (Types of toxicants)	List II (Affected Organ)
A. Nephrotoxic	I. Lungs
B. Hematotoxic	II. Kidney
C. Pulmonotoxic	III. Liver
D. Hepatotoxic	IV. Blood

Choose the correct answer from the options given below:

1. A-II, B-IV, C-I, D-III
2. A-II, B-IV, C-III, D-I
3. A-I, B-II, C-III, D-IV
4. A-III, B-I, C-IV, D-II

Answer: 1. A-II, B-IV, C-I, D-III

Q 19. Given below are two statements:

Statement I: Acute health effects are caused due to prolonged exposure to a chemical.

Statement II: Chronic health effects occur when an individual is exposed for a very short period.

In the light of the above statements, choose the correct answer from the options given below:

1. Both Statement I and Statement II are true
2. Both Statement I and Statement II are false
3. Statement I is true but Statement II is false
4. Statement I is false but Statement II is true

Answer: 2. Both Statement I and Statement II are false

Q 20. Which of the following are pathways for toxicants to enter into our body?
   A. Inhalation
   B. Absorption
   C. Dermal
   D. Ingestion
   E. Extraction
Choose the correct answer from the options given below:
   1. ACD
   2. AE
   3. BCD
   4. CDE
Answer: 1. ACD

Q 21. Given below are two statements:
Statement I: Toxicodynamics refers to the distribution of chemicals in the body.
Statement II: Toxicokinetics refers to the process by which chemicals produce effects in the body.
In the light of the above statements, choose the correct answer from the options given below:
   1. Both Statement I and Statement II are true
   2. Both Statement I and Statement II are false
   3. Statement I is true but Statement II is false
   4. Statement I is false but Statement II is true
Explanations:
Answer: 2. Both Statement I and Statement II are false

Q 22. Given below are two statements:
Statement I: Chronic toxicity caused due to hazardous wastes is not difficult to determine.
Statement II: Chronic effects may be seen immediately after the exposure.
In the light of the above statements, choose the correct answer from the options given below:
   1. Both Statement I and Statement II are correct
   2. Both Statement I and Statement II are incorrect
   3. Statement I is correct but Statement II is incorrect
   4. Statement I is incorrect but Statement II is correct
Answer: 2. Both Statement I and Statement II are incorrect

Q 23. Given below are two statements:
Statement I: Toxic chemicals often injure organs as well as organ systems
Statement II: Hepatotoxins are chemicals that can damage kidneys

> **In the light of the above statements, choose the correct answer from the options given below:**
> 1. Both Statement I and Statement II are true
> 2. Both Statement I and Statement II are false
> 3. Statement I is true but Statement II is false
> 4. Statement I is false but Statement II is true
>
> **Answer: 3.** Statement I is true but Statement II is false

Last Minute Revisions

Nuclear Waste

- ✓ Plutonium – 239 is fissile. *(Asked in Exam)*
- ✓ Waste uranium from the nuclear reactors is called as Depleted uranium. *(Asked in Exam)*
- ✓ Thermal reactors produce energy by fission of the Uranium-235 (235), Uranium-233 (233) and Plutonium-239 (239Pu) nuclear fuels. *(Asked in Exam)*
- ✓ U-235 (Uranium-235) is a fissile isotope of uranium, meaning it can sustain a nuclear chain reaction. *(Asked in Exam)*
- ✓ Chronic toxic effects result from single dose of very high toxic substance or continuous exposure of sub lethal dose. *(Asked in Exam)*
- ✓ Acute toxic effects are typically immediate and short-term, resulting from a single exposure to a high dose of a toxin. They are not usually long-lasting or irreversible, though they can be severe and sometimes fatal. *(Asked in Exam)*
- ✓ Fukushima disaster, Chernobyl disaster and Three-mile Island incident belongs to the category of nuclear disasters. *(Asked in Exam)*
- ✓ Breeder reactors produce more fissile material than they consume. *(Asked in Exam)*
- ✓ Breeder reactors are the two types (fast and Slow) of breeder reactors. *(Asked in Exam)*
- ✓ In a breeder reactor more fissile material is produced than it is consumed. *(Asked in Exam)*
- ✓ Breeder reactors typically use fast neutrons to convert fertile material into fissile material. Slow (thermal) neutrons are not suitable for breeding because they do not effectively convert fertile material. Therefore, moderators, which slow down neutrons, are not used in breeder reactors. *(Asked in Exam)*
- ✓ For breeding operations, the conversion ratio (fissile material produced/fissile material consumed) should be more than one. *(Asked in Exam)*
- ✓ In India, Kalpakkam (Chennai) Nuclear Power Plant is an example of a breeder reactor. *(Asked in Exam)*
- ✓ Light water nuclear reactors use Ordinary water H_2O. *(Asked in Exam)*
- ✓ In a breeder reactor, the amount of fissile material produced is more than the amount of fissile material consumed. Breeder reactors are specifically designed to generate more fissile material than they use, thereby "breeding" fuel. *(Asked in Exam)*

- ✓ A nuclear breeder reactor produces more fissile material than it consumes. *(Asked in Exam)*
- ✓ In many countries, including India, the share of renewable energy (which includes solar, wind, hydro, and biomass) in the energy mix is higher than that of nuclear energy. *(Asked in Exam)*
- ✓ A nuclear power reactor is a system designed to sustain a fission chain reaction and extract useful energy. *(Asked in Exam)*
- ✓ Light water reactors use ordinary water as the moderator. *(Asked in Exam)*
- ✓ Enrichment increases the U-235 concentration in natural uranium. *(Asked in Exam)*
- ✓ Light Water Reactors (LWR) are nuclear reactors use ordinary water as moderator. *(Asked in Exam)*
- ✓ The substance that slows down the neutrons to have controlled chain reaction during nuclear energy production is called as Moderator. *(Asked in Exam)*
- ✓ Salt mines are better suited for dumping of nuclear waste. *(Asked in Exam)*
- ✓ Nuclear sources of energy in electricity generation in India at present is the least. *(Asked in Exam)*
- ✓ Nephrotoxic affects the kidney. *(Asked in Exam)*
- ✓ Hematotoxic affects the blood. *(Asked in Exam)*
- ✓ Pulmonotoxic affects the lungs. *(Asked in Exam)*
- ✓ Hepatotoxic affects the liver. *(Asked in Exam)*
- ✓ Acute health effects are caused due to short-term exposure to a chemical. These effects appear rapidly after exposure. *(Asked in Exam)*
- ✓ Chronic health effects occur when an individual is exposed to a chemical for a prolonged period. *(Asked in Exam)*
- ✓ Inhalation, Dermal and Ingestion are pathways for toxicants to enter into our body. *(Asked in Exam)*
- ✓ Toxicodynamics refers to the effects of chemicals on the body, including the mechanisms by which they cause harm at the cellular or organ level. *(Asked in Exam)*
- ✓ Toxicokinetics refers to the processes of absorption, distribution, metabolism, and excretion (ADME) of chemicals in the body. *(Asked in Exam)*
- ✓ Chronic toxicity caused by hazardous wastes is often difficult to determine because it usually results from long-term, low-level exposure, making it hard to link specific health effects directly to the exposure. *(Asked in Exam)*
- ✓ Chronic effects typically do not appear immediately after exposure. Instead, they develop over a longer period, often after repeated or continuous exposure to a hazardous substance. Acute effects are those that occur soon after exposure, while chronic effects take time to manifest. *(Asked in Exam)*
- ✓ Toxic chemicals often injure organs as well as organ systems. *(Asked in Exam)*
- ✓ Hepatotoxins are chemicals that can damage the liver, not the kidneys. Chemicals that damage the kidneys are referred to as nephrotoxins. *(Asked in Exam)*

Chapter 4

Natural and energy resources: Solar, Wind, Soil, Hydro, Geothermal, Biomass, Nuclear and Forests

Natural Resources

Definition and Importance: Natural resources are materials or substances that occur in nature and can be used for economic gain or human benefit with minimal modifications. These resources are essential for various purposes including commercial and industrial use, aesthetic value, scientific interest, and cultural significance. Examples of natural resources include sunlight, atmosphere, water, land, minerals, vegetation, and wildlife.

Types and Classifications: Natural resources are an integral part of Earth's natural heritage and are often protected in nature reserves to preserve biodiversity and geodiversity. These resources can be classified in several ways:

Renewable Resources: Resources that can be replenished naturally over time, such as sunlight, wind, and biomass.

Non-Renewable Resources: Resources that cannot be replenished once they are depleted, such as fossil fuels (coal, oil, and natural gas), minerals, and metals.

Examples of Natural Resources:

> **Freshwater**: Essential for drinking, agriculture, and industry.
> **Air**: Vital for all aerobic life forms.
> **Living Organisms:** Fish, forests, and wildlife.
> **Extracted Resources:** Metal ores, rare-earth elements, petroleum, timber, and most forms of energy.

Economic and Political Implications: The allocation and extraction of natural resources are often central to economic and political conflicts. Scarcity and overconsumption can lead to confrontations within and between countries. Resource extraction has also been linked to human rights violations and significant environmental damage.

Sustainable Management and Development: The Sustainable Development Goals (SDGs) and other international agendas emphasize the need for sustainable resource extraction. Efforts are being made to develop economic models that reduce reliance on resource extraction. These models, such as the circular economy, focus on reuse, recycling, and the sustainable management of renewable resources. The goal is to create a balance between resource use and environmental conservation, ensuring that natural resources are available for future generations.

In summary, natural resources are vital for human survival and economic development. However, their management requires careful consideration to avoid depletion and environmental degradation, ensuring sustainability for future generations.

Hydropower

Water, being about 800 times denser than air, can generate substantial amounts of energy even from a slow-flowing stream or moderate sea swell. Water can generate electricity with a conversion efficiency of about 90%, the highest rate among renewable energy sources. There are various forms of water energy:

Large Hydroelectric Dams and Reservoirs: Historically, hydroelectric power has been generated by constructing large dams and reservoirs. Examples include the Three Gorges Dam in China and the Itaipu Dam built by Brazil and Paraguay.

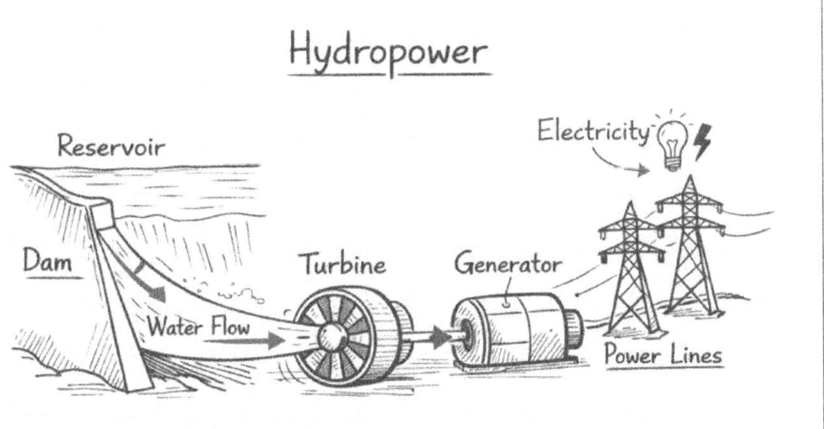

Small Hydro Systems: These installations typically produce up to 50 MW of power and are often used on small rivers or as low-impact developments on larger rivers. China leads the world in hydroelectricity production with more than 45,000 small hydro installations.

Run-of-the-River Hydroelectricity: These plants derive energy from rivers without creating large reservoirs. Water is conveyed along the side of the river valley using channels, pipes, or tunnels until it is high above the valley floor, then allowed to fall through a penstock to drive a turbine. These plants can still produce large amounts of electricity, such as the Chief Joseph Dam on the Columbia River in the United States. However, many run-of-the-river plants are micro or pico hydro plants.

Advantages and Challenges

Flexibility: Hydropower is highly flexible and can complement wind and solar power.

As of 2021, the global renewable hydropower capacity was 1,360 GW. However, only a third of the world's estimated hydroelectric potential of 14,000 TWh/year has been developed.

Challenges: New hydropower projects often face opposition from local communities due to their large impact, including the relocation of communities and flooding of wildlife habitats and farming land. High costs and long lead times due to the permission process, including environmental and risk assessments, and the lack of environmental and social acceptance, are primary challenges for new developments.

Repowering and Upgrading: It is popular to repower old dams to increase their efficiency and capacity and improve their responsiveness on the grid. For example, existing dams like the Russell Dam, built in 1985, may be updated with "pump back" facilities for pumped-storage, useful for peak loads or to support intermittent wind and solar power.

Economic and Environmental Considerations

Value of Dispatchable Power: Dispatchable power (power that can be turned on or off as needed) is more valuable than variable renewable energy (VRE) sources like wind and solar.

Countries with large hydroelectric developments, such as Canada and Norway, are investing billions to expand their grids to trade with neighboring countries that have limited hydro resources.

Water energy, through various forms of hydropower, plays a crucial role in renewable energy production. While large-scale projects have been the traditional focus, small and run-of-the-river systems offer significant potential with lower environmental impacts. Addressing challenges such as community opposition, high costs, and long lead times is essential for the continued expansion and optimization of hydropower.

India's Hydroelectric Power: Current Status and Challenges

Global Standing and Capacity: India is ranked 5th globally for installed hydroelectric power capacity. As of 31 March 2020:

> **Installed Utility-Scale Hydroelectric Capacity:**

- 46,000 MW (12.3% of total utility power generation capacity).
- ➤ **Smaller Hydroelectric Units:**
  - Total capacity of 4,683 MW (1.3% of total utility power generation capacity).
- ➤ **Total Hydroelectric Potential:**
  - Estimated at 148,700 MW at a 60% load factor.

Historical Context: The hydroelectric power plants at Darjeeling (1898) and Shivanasamudra (1902) were among the first in Asia, marking India's early involvement in global hydroelectric power development. India also imports surplus hydroelectric power from Bhutan.

Categories of Hydropower

- ➤ **Small Hydropower:**
  - Facilities with nameplate capacities up to 25 MW,
  - Managed by the Ministry of New and Renewable Energy (MNRE).
- ➤ **Large Hydropower:**
  - Facilities above 25 MW,
  - Managed by the Ministry of Power.
- ➤ **Largest Hydroelectric Plant:**
  - Koyna Hydroelectric Project
  - With a capacity of 1,960 MW.

Recent Performance and Challenges

In the fiscal year 2019–20:

- ➤ **Total Hydroelectric Power Generated:**
  - 156 TWh (excluding small hydro).
- ➤ **Average Capacity Factor:** 38.71%.

However, in the fiscal year ending March 31, 2024:

- ➤ **Decline in Hydroelectric Output:**
  - A 16.3% drop, the largest decline in 38 years, due to low rainfall.
- ➤ **Hydroelectricity's Share of Total Power Generation:**
  - Fell to a historic low of 8.3%.
- ➤ **Hydroelectric Generation:**
  - Reached a five-year low of 146 billion kWh.
- ➤ **Increased Reliance on Coal:**
  - Due to the shortfall in hydroelectric power.
- ➤ **Influence of Weather Patterns:**
  - Lightest rainfall since 2018,
  - Potentially influenced by the El Niño weather pattern.

Implications and Future Outlook: The decline in hydroelectric power generation highlights the vulnerabilities and challenges posed by erratic weather patterns. This has led to a diminished role for hydroelectric power in India's energy mix and increased reliance on coal. The reliability of hydroelectric power is being questioned, emphasizing the need for a diversified and resilient energy strategy to accommodate changing environmental conditions and ensure sustainable energy supply.

In conclusion, while India has significant hydroelectric potential and historical prominence in this sector, recent challenges underscore the need for adaptive strategies to cope with climate variability and ensure a stable energy future.

Wind Power

Definition and Basics:

Wind power is the use of wind energy to generate useful work.1 Historically, it was utilized by sails, windmills, and windpumps. Today, wind power is primarily used to generate electricity using wind turbines, which are generally grouped into wind farms and connected to the electrical grid.

- **Wind farms are large concentrations of wind generators producing electricity.** *(Asked in Exam)*
- **Wind Farms are often installed in rows, create noise pollution, can be installed on land or offshore, and contribute electricity to the power grid.** *(Asked in Exam)*
- **Wind energy does not have a high energy density compared to other sources of energy like fossil fuels.**

WIND POWER:
CLEAN RENEWABLE ENERGY

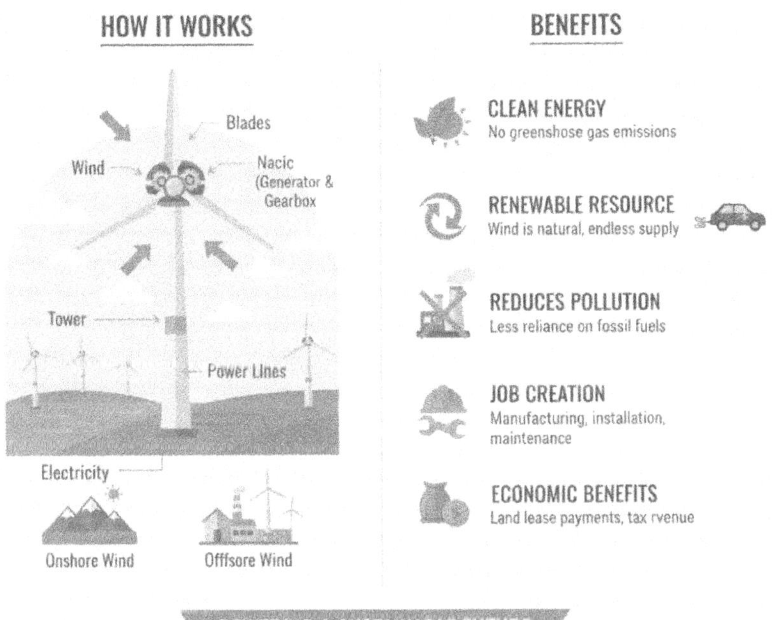

Current Status and Global Leaders:

In 2022, wind power supplied over 2000 TWh of electricity, accounting for over 7% of global electricity and about 2% of world energy. With approximately 100 GW added during 2021, global installed wind power capacity exceeded 800 GW. As of now, China is the leading country in wind energy-based electricity production. *(Asked in Exam)*

Advantages and Challenges:

Wind power is a sustainable and renewable energy source with a much smaller environmental impact compared to burning fossil fuels. However, there are inherent challenges:

- **Intermittency: Wind energy is an intermittent source of energy.** *(Asked in Exam)* Wind speed variability affects energy production, requiring energy storage or other dispatchable generation sources to ensure a reliable electricity supply.

Types of Wind Farms and Locations:

> **Onshore Wind Farms:** These have a greater visual impact on the landscape compared to most other power stations per unit of energy produced.
> **Offshore Wind Farms:** These have less visual impact and higher capacity factors but are generally more expensive. Offshore wind power currently accounts for about 10% of new installations.
> **Location Potential:** Regions in the higher northern and southern latitudes have the highest potential for wind power. **Coastlines are considered as high potential areas for wind energy generation.** *(Asked in Exam)* Additionally, **ocean water can be utilized as a coolant during wind energy production.** *(Asked in Exam)*

Cost and Efficiency:

Wind power is one of the lowest-cost electricity sources per unit of energy produced. In many locations, new onshore wind farms are cheaper than new coal or gas plants. Wind power generation is often higher at night and in winter when solar power output is low, making wind and solar power combinations suitable for many countries.

Impact on Environment and Landscape

Wind power offers a sustainable alternative to fossil fuels with significantly lower environmental impacts. However, specific environmental concerns exist for different energy sources:

Comparative Environmental Impacts of Energy Sources:

> **Thermal Energy is associated with the emission of greenhouse gases.** *(Asked in Exam)*
> **Hydroelectric power leads to a loss of riparian vegetation.** *(Asked in Exam)*
> **Photovoltaic energy involves the production of toxic wastes.** *(Asked in Exam)*
> **Wind Energy is hazardous for birds and bats.** *(Asked in Exam)*

Specific Impacts of Wind Power:

1. Wildlife Concerns:

> Habitat loss & fragmentation affect ecosystems.
> Bird & bat mortality from turbine collisions. **Wind Energy is hazardous for birds and bats.** *(Asked in Exam)*
> However, statistics show fewer bird deaths than fossil fuel plants.

2. Visual & Land Use Impact:

> Wind farms have a significant visual presence.
> Large land area needed due to turbine spacing.
> Energy sprawl allows agriculture between turbines.

> ➤ May impact tourism in scenic landscapes.

3. Turbine Blade Disposal:

> ➤ Fiberglass blades last ~20 years before disposal.
> ➤ Recycling efforts include repurposing for bridges.
> ➤ New blades designed for full recyclability.

4. Noise & Health Impact:

> ➤ Noise levels at 300m are ~45 dB, similar to a fridge.
> ➤ No scientific evidence linking turbines to health issues.

Key Concepts and Terms:

> ➤ **Wind Turbine:** Converts wind kinetic energy into mechanical power.
> ➤ **Windmill:** Uses sails on a rotating shaft to tap wind energy.
> ➤ **Offshore Wind Power:** Generates electricity from wind farms in water. Higher wind speeds at sea increase power output.
> ➤ **Intermittency:** Wind speed variability affects energy production.

Conclusion:

Wind power plays a crucial role in the transition to renewable energy, offering a sustainable alternative to fossil fuels. Despite challenges such as intermittency and higher costs for offshore installations, wind power remains a cost-effective and environmentally friendly energy source.

Wind Energy in India: Overview and Key Facts

Importance of Wind Energy: Wind energy is a crucial renewable energy source in India, contributing significantly to the country's energy mix. India is home to some of the largest operational onshore wind farms, playing a vital role in meeting the country's renewable energy goals.

Largest Wind Power Plants in India

Wind Power Plant	Megawatt (MW)	Location
Muppandal wind farm	1500	Tamil Nadu, Kanyakumari
Jaisalmer Wind Park	1064	Rajasthan, Jaisalmer
Brahmanvel wind farm	528	Maharashtra, Dhule
Dhalgaon wind farm	278	Maharashtra, Sangli
Vankusawade Wind Park	259	Maharashtra, Satara District
Vaspet	144	Maharashtra, Vaspet
Tuljapur	126	Maharashtra, Osmanabad

Beluguppa Wind Park	100.8	Andhra Pradesh, Beluguppa
Mamatkheda Wind Park	100.5	Madhya Pradesh, Mamatkheda
Anantapur Wind Park	100	Andhra Pradesh, Nimbagallu

Key Wind Power Plants in India:

> - **Muppandal Wind Farm**: Developed by Tamil Nadu Energy Development Agency, it is the largest operational onshore wind farm in India.
> - **Jaisalmer Wind Park**: Located in Rajasthan, developed by Suzlon Energy, it is the second-largest operational onshore wind farm in India.
> - **Vankusawade Wind Park**: Located in Maharashtra's Satara District, it is a significant wind farm on a high mountain plateau.

Wind Power Potential and Policies in India

Potential: India has an estimated wind power potential of 148,700 MW. Western states like Gujarat, Maharashtra, Karnataka, Tamil Nadu, and Andhra Pradesh have stable and strong wind flow, making them ideal for wind energy projects.

Top States for Installed Capacity:

Tamil Nadu: Largest installed wind power capacity, contributing 28% to its electricity generation in 2018.

Gujarat: Second-largest installed capacity, contributing 19%.

Maharashtra, **Karnataka**, and **Rajasthan**: Follow in terms of installed wind power capacity.

Policies:

> - **National Wind Power Policy**: Framework for developing wind energy.
> - **National Offshore Wind Energy Policy**: Launched in October 2015 to develop offshore wind energy.
> - **Solar-Wind Hybrid Policy**: Issued in May 2018 to promote large grid-connected wind-solar hybrid systems for optimal resource utilization and grid stability.

Global Context

India's Muppandal wind farm and Jaisalmer Wind Park are among the top 10 largest wind power plants in the world.

Wind Power Plant	Megawatt (MW)	Location
Gansu	7,965	China
Alta	1,548	United States of America (USA)
Muppandal wind farm	1,500	Tamil Nadu, Kanyakumari
Jaisalmer Wind Park	1,064	Rajasthan, Jaisalmer

Los Vientos Wind Farm	912	United States of America (USA)
Shepherds Flat	845	United States of America (USA)
Meadow Lake Wind Farm	801	United States of America (USA)
Roscoe	782	United States of America (USA)
Horse Hollow	736	United States of America (USA)
Tehachapi Pass Wind Farm	705	United States of America (USA)

Wind energy is a vital part of India's renewable energy strategy. With substantial potential and supportive policies, India aims to expand its wind energy capacity, contributing to global efforts in combating climate change and promoting sustainable development.

Solar Energy

Overview:

Solar power involves converting sunlight into electricity, either directly using photovoltaics (PV) or indirectly using concentrated solar power. Energy can be harnessed from the Sun and animal excreta. *(Asked in Exam)*

From the energy security perspective, solar energy is considered the most secure renewable energy source. *(Asked in Exam)*

Solar Energy through Photovoltaics (PV)

Solar Panels:

Devices that convert sunlight into electricity using photovoltaic (PV) cells.

- ➤ **DC Output: Photovoltaic (PV) cells produce Direct Current (DC), not Alternating Current (AC).** *(Asked in Exam)*
- ➤ **Grid Integration: Increasingly, photovoltaic panels are being used to supplement electrical energy from the power grid.** *(Asked in Exam)*
- ➤ **Arrays: A photovoltaic array is a combination of solar panels.** *(Asked in Exam)*

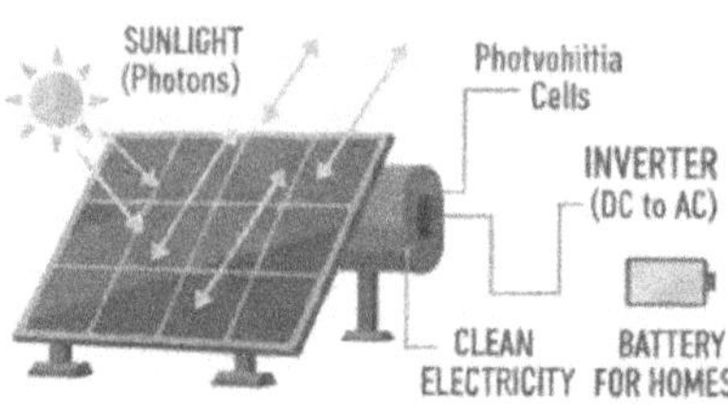

Types of Solar Cells:

1. **Crystalline Silicon Cells:**
   - Dominant in photovoltaic technology; efficient and durable.
   - **Silicon is widely used in solar cell fabrication.** *(Asked in Exam)*
   - **Photovoltaic cells are often made up of crystal silicon.** *(Asked in Exam)*
2. **Amorphous Silicon Cells:**
   - Made of inexpensive silicon without crystal properties.
   - **Photovoltaic cells are also made up of inexpensive amorphous silicon, which is like ordinary glass and has no crystal properties.** *(Asked in Exam)*
3. **Photoelectrochemical (PEC) Cells:**
   - **Photo ElectroChemical (PEC) solar cells are based on a hybrid structure of inorganic semiconductors and an electrolyte.** *(Asked in Exam)*
   - Convert the electric potential from the photoelectric effect directly into chemical energy, eliminating the need for battery storage.

Efficiency Challenges:

- **Photovoltaic cells are exposed directly to the sun; therefore, as temperature rises, leakage across the cell increases.** *(Asked in Exam)*

Solar Energy through Concentrated Methods & Thermal Energy

Solar Collectors:

Devices that collect and/or concentrate solar radiation. Primarily used for active solar heating, allowing for the heating of water or air.

1. **Flat Plate Collectors:**
   - A heat exchanger that converts radiant solar energy into heat energy.
   - **Flat plate collectors are examples of the simplest and most economic solar collectors.** *(Asked in Exam)*
   - **Solar flat plate collectors essentially work on the principle of the Greenhouse Effect.** *(Asked in Exam)*
   - **Black absorber plate radiates infrared radiations.** *(Asked in Exam)*
2. **Concentrating Collectors (STECs):**
   - **Solar Thermal Energy Collectors (STECs) are available in both flat plate and concentrating configurations. These systems are capable of reaching temperatures exceeding one thousand degrees Celsius and are utilised for electricity generation.** *(Asked in Exam)*
   - **Some of the solar concentrating collectors essentially use flat plate collectors.** *(Asked in Exam)*
   - **In concentrating type solar collector, temperature can be raised up to 500°C.** *(Asked in Exam)*
   - **The parabolic dish collector, a type of STEC, can achieve temperatures up to 2000°C.** *(Asked in Exam)*

Solar Ponds:

A large solar energy collector that looks like a pond. It uses a large, salty lake as a flat plate collector to absorb and store energy from the sun in the warm, lower layers of the pond.

- **Solar ponds store solar thermal energy by creating a salt gradient.** *(Asked in Exam)*
- **Concept of salt gradient is utilized to store the heat energy in Solar ponds.** *(Asked in Exam)*
- **Solar ponds store solar energy in the form of heat because solar ponds contain water with a definite gradient of salt concentration.** *(Asked in Exam)*

Applications of Solar Energy

1. **Electricity Generation:** Solar panels generate electricity for residential, commercial, and industrial use.
2. **Water Heating:** Solar collectors and flat plate collectors are used for heating water.
3. **Water Desalination (Solar Still):**

- o A device that uses solar energy to desalinate impure water, like brackish or saline water.
  - o **'Solar water still' is a device to convert saline water to potable water using solar energy.** *(Asked in Exam)*
  - o **'Solar Water Still' is a device to produce potable water by using solar energy.** *(Asked in Exam)*
4. **Heating:** Solar ponds and collectors can be used for space heating and industrial processes.

Solar Power in India: Current Status and Key Developments
Installed Capacity and Global Standing:

As of 31 May 2024, India's installed solar power capacity was 84.28 GW AC, making it the third-largest producer of solar power globally.

Government Initiatives:

- ➢ **National Solar Mission:** The Government of India aims to achieve a total installed solar capacity of 20 GW by 2022 (original target), prioritizing solar energy to meet the country's energy demands.
- ➢ **Solar Parks:** India has established nearly 42 solar parks. The **Gujarat Hybrid Renewable Energy Park** is a notable example, set to generate 30 GW AC power from solar panels and wind turbines.

International Initiatives:

- ➢ **International Solar Alliance (ISA):** Proposed by India and headquartered in India, ISA aims to promote solar energy globally.
- ➢ **One Sun One World One Grid:** Aims to harness solar power on a global scale.
- ➢ **World Solar Bank:** Supports global solar energy projects.

Major Solar Power Parks in India:

India has more than 40 major solar power plants, each generating at least 10 MW of power. Below is a list of the 10 major solar power parks:

- ➢ Bhadla Solar Park, Rajasthan
- ➢ Pavagada Solar Park, Karnataka
- ➢ Kurnool Ultra Mega Solar Park, Andhra Pradesh
- ➢ NP Kunta, Andhra Pradesh
- ➢ Rewa Ultra Mega Solar, Madhya Pradesh
- ➢ Charanka Solar Park, Gujarat
- ➢ Kamuthi Solar Power Project, Tamil Nadu
- ➢ Ananthapuramu – II, Andhra Pradesh
- ➢ Galiveedu Solar Park, Andhra Pradesh
- ➢ Mandsaur Solar Farm, Madhya Pradesh

Geothermal Energy

Definition: Geothermal energy is thermal energy extracted from the Earth's crust, combining heat from the planet's formation and radioactive decay. This energy has been used for centuries for various purposes such as heating and electricity generation.

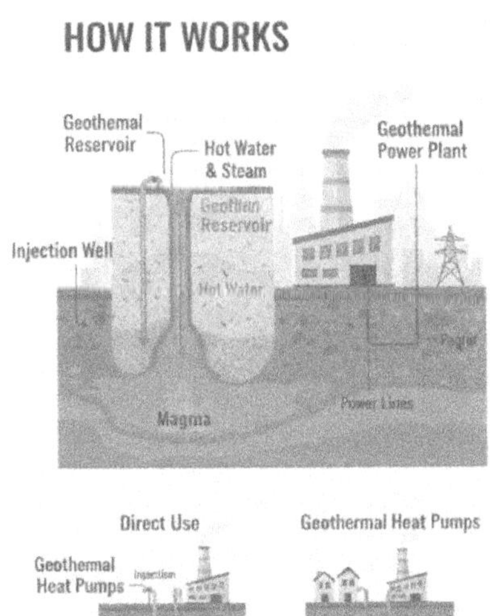

Historical Context

Ancient Uses:

Geothermal Heating: Used since Paleolithic times for bathing in hot springs and since Roman times for space heating.

Geothermal Power: Generation of electricity from geothermal energy has been used since the 20th century.

Advantages of Geothermal Energy

> **Power Stability**

- - ○ **Constant Power Production**: Unaffected by **weather conditions**, unlike wind & solar.
    - ○ **Reliable Energy Source**: Provides **stable electricity** 24/7.
  - ➤ **Resource Availability**
    - ○ **Sufficient Resources**: Ample geothermal potential **near tectonic boundaries**.
    - ○ **Long-Term Viability**: Earth's heat is a **renewable & sustainable** energy source.
  - ➤ **Economic Benefits**
    - ○ **Cost-Effective**: Power generation **became 25% cheaper** in past decades.
    - ○ **Low Energy Cost**: Modern plants produce power **at ~0.05/kWh**.

Global Geothermal Power Capacity

- ➤ **Installed Capacity:** As of 2019, there were 13,900 MW of geothermal power available worldwide.
- ➤ **Additional Uses:** An additional 28 GW provided heat for district heating, space heating, spas, industrial processes, desalination, and agricultural applications.
- ➤ **Employment:** The industry employed about one hundred thousand people in 2019.

Geothermal Power Generation

Types of Geothermal Power Plants:

- ➤ **Dry Steam Plants:** Use steam directly from geothermal reservoirs to turn turbines and generate electricity.
- ➤ **Flash Steam Plants:** Pull high-pressure hot water from the ground and convert it to steam to drive turbines.
- ➤ **Binary Cycle Plants:** Transfer heat from geothermal hot water to another liquid that boils at a lower temperature than water, which then turns the turbines.
- ➤ **Global Presence:** As of 2010, geothermal electricity was generated in 26 countries. As of 2019, worldwide geothermal power capacity was 15.4 GW, with the United States contributing 3.68 GW.
- ➤ **Significant Contributors: Countries with High Geothermal Energy Utilization:**
  - ➤ Iceland
  - ➤ El Salvador
  - ➤ Kenya
  - ➤ The Philippines
  - ➤ New Zealand

Environmental Impact:

Renewable Resource: Geothermal energy is considered renewable because heat extraction rates are negligible compared to the Earth's heat content.

Low Emissions: The greenhouse gas emissions of geothermal electric stations average 45 grams of carbon dioxide per kilowatt-hour of electricity, which is less than 5% of the emissions from coal-fired plants.

Geothermal energy is a reliable and sustainable source of power and heat, with a long history of use and significant potential for future expansion. It provides a constant supply of energy, has low greenhouse gas emissions, and is cost-effective, making it an essential component of the global renewable energy mix. With ongoing technological advancements and increasing capacity, geothermal energy will continue to play a crucial role in meeting the world's energy needs sustainably.

Thermal Power in India

- ➢ **General Overview**
    - ○ **Largest contributor** to India's electricity generation.
    - ○ **Coal-based power** dominates the thermal sector.
    - ○ **Accounts for ~75%** of total power production.
    - ○ **Gas-based plants** supplement power supply.
    - ○ **Diesel-based plants** have minimal contribution.
- ➢ **Advantages & Challenges**
    - ○ **Reliable energy source** for base load demand.
    - ○ **Cost-effective** compared to renewable sources.
    - ○ **High carbon emissions** contribute to pollution.
    - ○ **Requires large water supply** for cooling.
    - ○ **Coal dependency** leads to environmental concerns.
- ➢ **Major Thermal Power Plants**
    - ○ **Vindhyachal Super Thermal Power Station** (Madhya Pradesh) – **4,760 MW**.
    - ○ **Mundra Thermal Power Station** (Gujarat) – **4,620 MW**.
    - ○ **Talcher Super Thermal Power Station** (Odisha) – **3,000 MW**.
    - ○ **Sipat Thermal Power Station** (Chhattisgarh) – **2,980 MW**.
    - ○ **Korba Super Thermal Power Station** (Chhattisgarh) – **2,600 MW**.

Breakdown of India's Electricity Production (as of recent data):

- ➢ **Thermal Power (~75%) Thermal Energy contributes maximum to India's total electricity production.** *(Asked in Exam)*
    - ○ **Coal (~55%)** – The largest contributor to electricity generation.
    - ○ **Gas (~7%)** – Used for peaking power supply.
    - ○ **Diesel (<1%)** – Minimal contribution.
- ➢ **Renewable Energy (~22%)**
    - ○ **Solar & Wind (~15%)** – Rapidly growing.
    - ○ **Hydropower (~12%)** – Major source of renewable energy.
- ➢ **Nuclear Power (~3%)**
    - ○ Plays a small but stable role in energy production.

Biomass Energy

What is Biomass?

Biomass is organic material derived from plants and animals. It includes things like wood, wood leftovers, energy crops, agricultural waste like straw, and organic waste from homes and industries. Wood and its residues are the biggest sources of biomass energy today. Wood can be burned directly or processed into pellet fuel or other types of fuel. Other plants like maize, switchgrass, miscanthus, and bamboo can also be used as fuel.

BIOMASS ENERGY

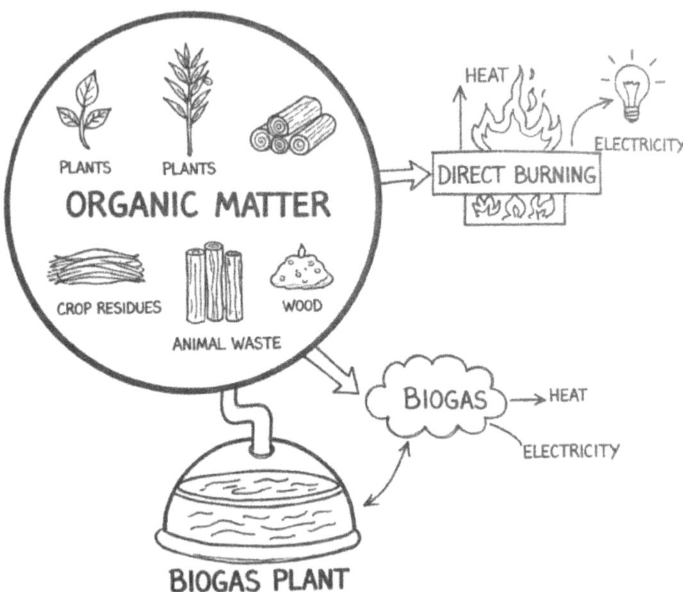

Biomass fuels have the potential to form a sustainable carbon-neutral energy source because they produce as much carbon dioxide on combustion as they consume when they grow. *(Asked in Exam)* However, in terms of energy density, **Biomass has the lowest energy content per unit mass.** *(Asked in Exam)*

Types of Waste Used in Biomass Energy

The main types of waste used for biomass energy are:
- ➢ **Wood Waste:** Leftovers from logging and wood processing.
- ➢ **Agricultural Waste:** Crop leftovers like straw.
- ➢ **Municipal Solid Waste:** Organic waste from households. **Even when solid waste is buried in landfills, it can still provide energy because buried waste produces natural gas which can be captured and burned.** *(Asked in Exam)*
- ➢ **Manufacturing Waste:** Organic waste from industries.

Energy Crops:

Energy crops are fast-growing, low-cost, and low-maintenance plants cultivated specifically for renewable bioenergy production. These crops are processed into fuels such as biofuel, biodiesel, or biogas.
Energy crops are fast-growing plants and can be converted into gaseous and liquid fuel. They generally have high calorific value. *(Asked in Exam)*

Conversion and Upgrading Methods
Raw biomass can be turned into better fuels using different methods:

1. Producer Gas (Gasification):
- ➤ **Producer Gas is the result of the conversion of solid biomass into gaseous fuels. It can be used as fuel in internal combustion engines. Hydrogen and methane present in Producer Gas determine its heating value.** *(Asked in Exam)*

2. Bio-Oil (Pyrolysis):
- ➤ Pyrolysis is a technology used to convert biomass into an intermediate liquid product called Bio-Oil.
- ➤ **Pyrolysis produces bio-oil with minimal waste, and the resulting liquid can replace heating oil.** *(Asked in Exam)*

3. Biodiesel:
- ➤ Biodiesel is a renewable, biodegradable fuel produced domestically. Biodiesel can be created from vegetable oils and animal fats. *(Asked in Exam)*
- ➤ It offers an eco-friendly alternative to traditional diesel, though with some differences: Biodiesel has a higher viscosity compared to petroleum diesel. This higher viscosity can affect the flow characteristics of the fuel in engines. *(Asked in Exam)*

4. Biogas:
- ➤ Biogas is a renewable fuel produced through the anaerobic digestion of organic matter, such as food or animal waste.
- ➤ **Calorific Value:** The energy content of biogas is determined by its methane percentage. With a high methane content of around 60%, biogas has a significant calorific value.

Carbon Neutrality and Climate Impact

Carbon neutrality involves balancing carbon emissions with carbon absorption in carbon sinks.
- ➤ Energy produced from biomass is considered 'carbon neutral'. *(Asked in Exam)*
- ➤ Biomass is considered as carbon neutral because the amount of carbon they emit is equal to the amount of carbon they have consumed during their lifetime. *(Asked in Exam)*

> Energy production from biomass has traditionally been considered carbon neutral because carbon dioxide emissions from combustion of biomass are sequestered by growing biomass. *(Asked in Exam)*
> Consequently, Carbon dioxide emissions from bioenergy production has traditionally been excluded from most emission inventories and climate impact studies. *(Asked in Exam)*

However, it is important to note:

> **Biomass adds CO2 to the atmosphere.** *(Asked in Exam)* Burning wood releases carbon dioxide, but this is balanced if new trees are planted.
> **Carbon dioxide emissions associated with the production of bioenergy are significantly less compared to those from combustion of fossil fuels.** *(Asked in Exam)*

Advantages, Challenges, and Economic Viability

> Cost: A source of renewable power which can be developed with minimum cost is Biomass power. *(Asked in Exam)* Biomass power plants often have lower initial costs compared to wind and tidal energy.
> Land Use: The biggest hindrance in using biomass as a major energy source is large amounts of land required to grow energy crops. *(Asked in Exam)* Sustainable land use is crucial for viability.
> Environmental Side Effects (Eutrophication): The use of agricultural resources can impact water bodies. An over-fertile lake experiences excessive nutrient enrichment, particularly from nitrates and phosphates, leading to eutrophication. This process results in: Quality of fishes produced is impaired, Increased algal growth (algal blooms), Oxygen depletion, and Poor water quality. *(Asked in Exam)*

Comparison with Natural Gas:

While discussing cleaner fuels, it is worth noting: Natural gas is a very attractive eco-friendly fuel because it produces fewer pollutants and less carbon dioxide per unit energy than any other fossil fuel on combustion. *(Asked in Exam)*

Nuclear Power

What is Nuclear Power?

Nuclear power uses nuclear reactions to produce electricity. It primarily comes from:

> **Nuclear Fission:** Splitting of uranium and plutonium atoms in nuclear power plants.
> **Nuclear Decay:** Used in niche applications like space probes.
> **Nuclear Fusion:** Still in the research phase for electricity generation.

How Do Nuclear Power Plants Work?

Thermal Reactors: Most plants use enriched uranium in a once-through fuel cycle.

Fuel Cycle: Fuel is removed after about three years when it can no longer sustain a chain reaction, then cooled in spent fuel pools before long-term storage. Uranium, specifically uranium-235 (U-235), is the most widely used fuel in nuclear power plants for nuclear fission due to its easily split atoms, which release significant energy. This energy heats water to produce steam that drives turbines, generating electricity. Plutonium-239 (Pu-239) is also used in some reactors, but U-235 remains the primary choice for its efficiency and effectiveness in sustaining a chain reaction.

Waste Management: Spent fuel is high-level radioactive waste and must be isolated for hundreds of thousands of years, although new technologies like fast reactors could reduce this time.

Reprocessing and Plutonium: Some countries reprocess spent fuel to extract fissile and fertile elements for new fuel, although this is more expensive and poses proliferation risks due to plutonium-239.

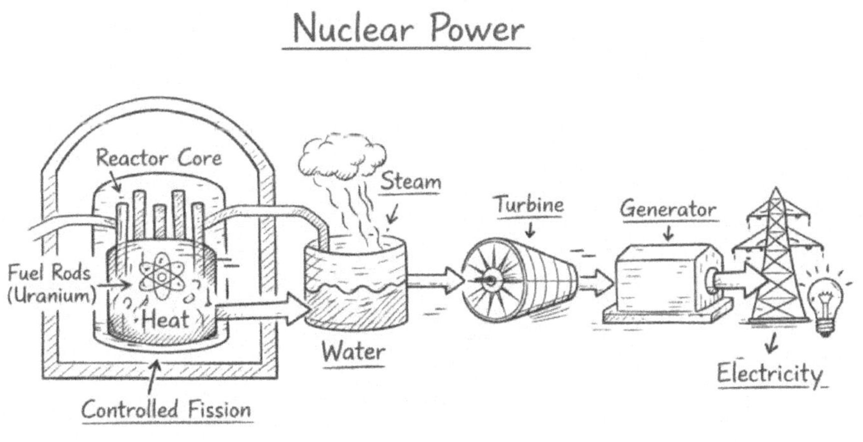

Historical Development

> - **1950s: First nuclear power plant built.**
> - **1970s-1990s: Global installed nuclear capacity grew to 300 GW by 1990.**

Accidents: The Three Mile Island (1979) and Chernobyl (1986) disasters increased regulation and public opposition.

Nuclear Disasters:

Chornobyl Disaster: On April 26, 1986, an explosion at reactor No. 4 of the Chornobyl Nuclear Power Plant near Pripyat in the Ukrainian SSR, close to the Byelorussian SSR border, resulted in one of the worst nuclear disasters in history. The explosion released massive amounts of radioactive material into the environment, leading to widespread contamination and long-term health impacts.

Three Mile Island Accident: On March 28, 1979, at 4 a.m., a partial meltdown occurred at the Unit 2 reactor of the Three Mile Island Nuclear Generating Station on the Susquehanna River in Londonderry Township, Pennsylvania, near Harrisburg. The accident released radioactive gases and iodine into the environment, raising concerns about nuclear safety in the United States.

Fukushima Nuclear Accident: On March 11, 2011, a major nuclear accident occurred at the Fukushima Daiichi Nuclear Power Plant in Okuma, Fukushima, Japan. Triggered by a massive earthquake and subsequent tsunami, the disaster led to reactor meltdowns, hydrogen explosions, and the release of radioactive materials, causing significant environmental and health concerns.

Current Status

- ➢ **Capacity:**
    - ○ As of 2022, global nuclear capacity was 390 GW,
    - ○ Supplying about 10% of global electricity.
- ➢ **Reactors:**
    - ○ 410 civilian reactors worldwide as of August 2023,
    - ○ With more under construction and planned.
- ➢ **United States:**
    - ○ Largest fleet, generating nearly 800 TWh/year with a 92% capacity factor.

Fission Process: Fission is a type of chain reaction where neutrons released during fission cause additional fission in at least one more nucleus, which then releases more neutrons, continuing the cycle.

Controlled Fission Process in Reactors: In nuclear reactors, a moderator is used to slow down neutrons from their fast speeds to facilitate a sustained chain reaction. In water-cooled reactors, water serves both as the coolant and the moderator.

Breeder Reactors: A breeder reactor is a type of nuclear reactor that generates more fissile material than it consumes. Unlike conventional reactors that use uranium-235, breeder reactors can use more abundant isotopes like uranium-238.

Breeder Reactors in India: India plans to set up six Fast Breeder Reactor units, with the first two units located in Kalpakkam, Tamil Nadu. Sites for the remaining units are being identified, and all six units are expected to be operational by 2039.

Advantages of Nuclear Power

> - **Low Fatality Rate:** Fewer fatalities per unit of energy compared to coal, petroleum, natural gas, and hydroelectricity.
> - **Low Carbon Emissions:** Emits no greenhouse gases and has lower life-cycle carbon emissions than common renewables.
> - **High Capacity Factor:** Average global capacity factor is 89%, indicating efficient and reliable energy production.

Challenges and Opposition

> - **Safety Concerns:** Risks of accidents, as evidenced by Fukushima in 2011.
> - **Waste Management:** Long-term storage of radioactive waste.
> - **Cost and Deployment:** High construction costs and slow deployment compared to other renewable energy sources.

Nuclear Power in India

Nuclear power is **the fifth-largest source of electricity in India**, following coal, gas, hydroelectricity, and wind power. As of November 2020, **India operates 23 nuclear reactors** across 8 nuclear power plants, with a combined installed capacity of 7,380 MW. In the fiscal year 2020-21, **nuclear power generated 43 TWh,** accounting for 3.11% of India's total power generation (1,382 TWh). An additional 10 reactors, with a combined capacity of 8,000 MW, are currently under construction.

In October 2010, India planned to reach a nuclear power capacity of 63 GW by 2032. However, the 2011 Fukushima nuclear disaster sparked numerous anti-nuclear protests, notably **against the Jaitapur Nuclear Power Project in Maharashtra and the Kudankulam Nuclear Power Plant in Tamil Nadu.** A proposed large nuclear plant near Haripur was denied permission by the Government of West Bengal, and a Public Interest Litigation (PIL) was filed against the government's civil nuclear program at the Supreme Court.

Historically, India's nuclear power plants have experienced low capacity factors, with a lifetime weighted energy availability factor of 66.1% as of 2021. However, there has been improvement, with an availability factor of 74.4% from 2019 to 2021, despite challenges like nuclear fuel shortages.

India is also advancing thorium-based fuel technologies, aiming to design and develop a prototype atomic reactor using thorium and low-enriched uranium, which is a key component of India's three-stage nuclear power program.

List of Nuclear Power Plants in India:

- Tarapur Atomic Power Station (TAPS), Maharashtra
- Rajasthan Atomic Power Station (RAPS), Rajasthan
- Madras Atomic Power Station (MAPS), Tamil Nadu
- Narora Atomic Power Station (NAPS), Uttar Pradesh
- Kakrapar Atomic Power Station (KAPS), Gujarat
- Kaiga Generating Station (KGS), Karnataka
- Kudankulam Nuclear Power Plant (KKNPP), Tamil Nadu
- Prototype Fast Breeder Reactor (PFBR), Tamil Nadu (under construction)
- Jaitapur Nuclear Power Project, Maharashtra (proposed)
- Gorakhpur Haryana Anu Vidyut Pariyojana (GHAVP), Haryana (under construction)

On December 5th, 2025, India–Russia nuclear cooperation marked another major milestone when Russia's state-owned nuclear corporation, Rosatom, delivered the first consignment of nuclear fuel for the initial loading of Kudankulam Nuclear Power Plant's Unit-3 in Tamil Nadu. The delivery coincided with President Vladimir Putin's visit to New Delhi, highlighting the strategic importance of the partnership. The fuel assemblies, produced by the Novosibirsk Chemical Concentrates Plant, arrived via a cargo flight operated by Rosatom's Nuclear Fuel Division. In total, seven shipments from Russia are planned to supply the full reactor core and reserve fuel under a 2024 contract, which guarantees lifetime fuel supply for both the Third and Fourth VVER-1000 reactors. With six reactors planned and a total capacity of six thousand megawatts, Kudankulam remains India's largest and most significant nuclear power project, symbolizing deep and ongoing Indo-Russian collaboration in the nuclear energy sector.

Energy Forestry

Energy forestry involves growing fast-growing tree or woody shrub species specifically for biomass or biofuel used in heating or power generation. There are two main types:

- **Short Rotation Coppice (SRC):**
  - **Species**: Poplar, Willow, Eucalyptus
  - **Growth Cycle**: 2 to 5 years before harvest
- **Short Rotation Forestry (SRF):**
  - **Species**: Alder, Ash, Birch, Eucalyptus, Poplar, Sycamore
  - **Growth Cycle:** 8 to 20 years before harvest

Advantages of Energy Forestry:

- ➢ **Carbon Neutrality**:
  - ○ Trees absorb nearly the same amount of carbon dioxide while growing as they release when burned,
  - ○ Making them more sustainable compared to fossil fuels.
- ➢ **Efficiency**:
  - ○ Wood is a highly efficient source of bioenergy in terms of energy released per unit of carbon emitted.
- ➢ **Harvest Flexibility:**
  - ○ Trees don't need to be harvested annually;
  - ○ Harvest can be delayed based on market conditions.
- ➢ **Versatility**:
  - ○ Wood products have multiple end-uses.

Environmental Benefits:

- ➢ **Bank Stabilisation:** Helps prevent soil erosion.
- ➢ **Phytoremediation**: Cleans and improves soil quality.
- ➢ **Water Quality:** Experiments in Sweden show willow plantations improve soil and water quality compared to conventional crops.
- ➢ **Multifunctional Systems**: Can meet bioenergy demands while increasing biodiversity, reducing soil erosion, enhancing pollination, and mitigating flooding.

Yield: Potential yields can reach up to 11 oven dry tonnes per hectare annually, although actual yields in commercial plantations, such as in Scandinavia, may be lower.

Energy forestry offers a sustainable and flexible alternative to fossil fuels, with significant environmental benefits and the ability to adapt to market and ecological conditions.

Questions

Natural Resources: Hydropower and Wind Power
Q 1. Which of the following are true about wind farms?

A. They are often installed in rows
B. They create noise pollution
C. They can be installed on land or offshore
D. They are non-renewable energy sources
E. They contribute electricity to power grid

Choose the correct answer from the options given below:

1. ABCD
2. ABCE
3. ADE
4. BDE

Answer: 2. ABCE

Q 2. Wind farms?
1. Places where winds blow at a speed of more than 5 m/s.
2. Potential places of wind energy generation.
3. Places where winds help in good farming practices.
4. Large concentrations of wind generators producing electricity.

Answer: 4. Large concentrations of wind generators producing electricity.

Q 3. Given below are two statements:
Statement I: Wind energy has high energy density.
Statement II: Wind energy is an intermittent source of energy.
In the light of the above statements, choose the most appropriate answer from the options given below
1. Both Statement I and Statement II are correct.
2. Both Statement I and Statement II are incorrect.
3. Statement I is correct but Statement II is incorrect.
4. Statement I is incorrect but Statement II is correct.

Answer: 4. Statement I is incorrect but Statement II is correct.

Q 4. Wind energy
A. is an intermittent energy
B. is extremely useful at remote and isolated places
C. does not depend upon weather
D. is a clean energy
E. does not have any environmental impact at all

Choose the correct answer from the options given below:
1. ABC
2. ABD
3. BCD
4. CDE

Answer: 2. ABD

Q 5. Match the column:

A. Wind Energy	I. Emission of GreenHouse Gases
B. Thermal Energy	II. Loss of riparian vegetation
C. Hydroelectric Energy	III. Hazardous for birds and bats
D. Photovoltaic energy	IV. Production of toxic wastes

Choose the correct answer from the options given below:
1. A-IV, B-III, C-II, D-I
2. A-IV, B-II, C-I, D-III
3. A-III, B-I, C-IV, D-II
4. A-III, B-I, C-II, D-IV

Answer: 4. A-III, B-I, C-II, D-IV

Q 6. Given below are two statements:

Assertion A: Coastlines are considered as high potential areas for wind energy generation.
Reason R: Ocean water can be utilized as coolant during wind energy production

1. Both A and R are correct and R is the correct explanation of A
2. Both A and R are correct but R is NOT the correct explanation of A
3. A is correct but R is not correct
4. A is not correct but R is correct

In the light of the above statements, choose the most appropriate answer from the options given below

Answer: 2. Both A and R are correct but R is NOT the correct explanation of A

Q 7. As of now, which of the following is a leading country in wind energy-based electricity
1. India
2. France
3. China
4. Denmark

Answer: 3. China

Q 8. Which of the following types of energy sources employ direct energy conversion processes to produce electricity?
1. Biomass
2. Geothermal
3. Wind
4. Nuclear

Answer: 3. Wind

Natural Resources: Solar Energy

Q 9. Energy can be harnessed from the following sources
A. Sun
B. Sea
C. Animal excreta
D. Soil

Choose the correct answer from the options given below:
1. ABC
2. BCD
3. ADC
4. ABD

Answer: 1. ABC

Q 10. Which of the following are true about Solar Thermal Energy Collectors (STEC)?
A. The Basic Unit of STEC is a solar cell.
B. STECs may be Flat plate or concentrating type.
C. Temperature in STECs may rise over a thousand degrees centigrade.
D. STECs can produce electricity.

E. Parabolic dish collector is an example of STEC where temperature can go up to 2000°C.

Choose the most appropriate answer from the options given below

A. AD
B. BCDE
C. ABCE
D. ABCDE

Answer: 2. BCDE

Q 11. Concept of salt gradient is utilized to store the heat energy in which of the following solar energy collecting systems?

1. Solar thermal collectors
2. Solar cells
3. Solar ponds
4. Solar kilns

Answer: 3. Solar ponds

Q 12. Given below are two statements:

Statement I: Photovoltaic cells produce Alternating current (a.c.).

Statement II: Photovoltaic cells are exposed directly to the sun, therefore as temperature rises leakage across the cell increases.

In the light of the above statements, choose the most appropriate answer from the options given below

1. Both Statement (I) and Statement (II) are correct.
2. Both Statement (I) and Statement (II) are incorrect.
3. Statement (I) is correct but Statement (II) is incorrect
4. Statement (I) is incorrect but Statement (II) is correct

Answer: 4. Statement (I) is incorrect but Statement (II) is correct

Q 13. Given below are two statements:

Statement I: Increasingly, photovoltaic panels are being used to supplement electrical energy from the power grid.

Statement II: The compatibility of photovoltaic panels with the power grid is also because it produces Direct Current (DC).

In the light of the above statements, choose the most appropriate answer from the options given below

1. Both Statement (I) and Statement (II) are correct.
2. Both Statement (I) and Statement (II) are incorrect.
3. Statement (I) is correct but Statement (II) is incorrect
4. Statement (I) is incorrect but Statement (II) is correct

Answer: 3. Statement (I) is correct but Statement (II) is incorrect

Q 14. Given below are two statements:

Assertion A: In concentrating type solar collector temperature can be raised upto 500°C.

Reason R: In concentrating type solar collectors, the magnitudes of collector area and absorber area are numerically same.

In the light of the above statements, choose the most appropriate answer from the options given below

1. Both A and R are correct and R s the correct explanation of A

2.   Both A and R are correct but R is not the correct explanation of A
3.   A is correct but R is not correct
4.   A is not correct but R is correct

Answer: 3. A is correct but R is not correct

Q 15. A photovoltaic array is:
1.   a single solar cell
2.   a single solar module
3.   a single solar panel
4.   combination of solar panels

Answer: 4. combination of solar panels

Q 16. Photo ElectroChemical (PEC) solar cells are based on
1.   Only inorganic semiconductors
2.   Only organic semiconductors
3.   Only crystal silicon semiconductor
4.   Hybrid structure of inorganic semiconductors and an electrolyte

Answer: 4. Hybrid structure of inorganic semiconductors and an electrolyte

Q 17. Given below are two statements:
Statement I: Flat plate collectors are examples of simplest and most economic solar collectors.
Statement II: Some of the solar concentrating collectors essentially use flat plate collectors.
In the light of the above statements, choose the most appropriate answer from the options given below
1.   Both Statement I and Statement I are true.
2.   Both Statement I and Statement II are false.
3.   Statement I is true but Statement II is false.
4.   Statement I is false but Statement II is true.

Answer: 1. Both Statement I and Statement I are true.

Q 18. Solar ponds store solar thermal energy by?
1.   Photovoltaic cells
2.   Creating salt gradient
3.   Using solar thermal collectors
4.   Covering major portion of pond by plastic sheets

Answer: 2. Creating salt gradient

Q 19. Given below are two statements:
Statement I: Increasingly. photovoltaic panels are being used to supplement electrical energy from the power grid.
Statement II: One issue with grid-connected photovoltaics is that PV cells produce Alternating Current (AC) whereas power grids use Direct Current (DC)
In the light of the above statements, choose the most appropriate answer from the options given below
1.   Both Statement I and Statement II are true
2.   Both Statement I and Statement II are false
3.   Statement I is true but Statement II is false
4.   Statement I is false but Statement II is true

Answer: 3. Statement I is true but Statement II is false

Q 20. Given below are two statements:
Statement I: Photovoltaic cells are often made up of crystal silicon
Statement II: Photovoltaic cells are also made up of inexpensive amorphous silicon, which is like ordinary glass and has no crystal properties.
In the light of the above statements, choose the most appropriate answer from the options given below
1. Both Statement I and Statement II are true
2. Both Statement I and Statement II are false
3. Statement I is true but Statement II is false
4. Statement I is false but Statement II is true

Answer: 1. Both Statement I and Statement II are true

Q 21. 'Solar water still' is a device to
1. Pump water using solar energy
2. Convert saline water to potable water using solar energy
3. Heat water using solar energy
4. Generate electricity using solar energy

Answer: 2. Convert saline water to potable water using solar energy

Q 22. Given below are two statements:
Statement I: Solar flat plate collectors essentially work on the principle of GreenHouse Effect.
Statement II: Black absorber plate radiates infrared radiations.
In the light of the above statements, choose the most appropriate answer from the options given below
1. Both Statement I and Statement II are true
2. Both Statement I and Statement II are false
3. Statement I is true but Statement II is false
4. Statement 1 is false but Statement II is true

Answer: 1. Both Statement I and Statement II are true

Q 23. From the energy security perspective, which of the following energy sources is considered most secure for
1. Geothermal
2. Solar
3. Wind
4. Hydro

Answer: 2. Solar

Q 24. 'Solar Water Still' is a device to
1. Produce potable water by using solar energy
2. Pump water by using solar energy
3. Generate electricity by using solar energy
4. Produce heat using solar energy

Answer: 1. Produce potable water by using solar energy

Q 25. Given below are two statements: One is labelled as Assertion (A) and the other is labelled as Reason (R):

Assertion (A): Solar ponds, store solar energy in the form of heat.
Reason (R): Solar ponds contain water with a definite gradient of salt concentration.
In the light of the above statements, choose the most appropriate answer from the options given below -
1. Both (A) and (R) are correct and (R) is the correct explanation of (A)
2. Both (A) and (R) are correct but (R) is NOT the correct explanation of (A)
3. (A), is correct but (R) is not correct
4. (A), is not correct but (R) is correct

Q 26. Which of the following materials is widely used in solar cell fabrication?
1. Nubi dium
2. Nickel
3. Silicon
4. Chromium

Answer: 3. Silicon

Natural Resources: Soil, Geothermal, Biomass, Nuclear and Energy Forestry.

Q 26. Which of the following are true about Producer Gas?
A. It is the result of conversion of solid biomass into gaseous fuels.
B. It is done at a lower temperature.
C. It can be used as fuel in internal combustion engines.
D. It is produced in the complete absence of oxygen.
E. Hydrogen and methane present in Producer Gas determine its heating value.

Choose the correct answer from the options given below:
1. ABC
2. BD
3. CDE
4. ACE

Answer: 4. ACE

Q 27. Given below are two statements: One is labelled as Assertion (A) and the other is labelled as Reason (R):
Assertion (A): Even when a solid waste is buried in landfills, it can still provide energy.
Reason (R): Buried waste produces natural gas which can be captured and burned
In the light of the above statements, choose the most appropriate answer from the options given below -
1. Both (A) and (R) are correct and (R) is the correct explanation of (A).
2. Both (A) and (R) are correct but (R) is NOT the correct explanation of (A).
3. (A) is correct but (R) is not correct.
4. (A) is not correct but (R) is correct.

Answer: 1. Both (A) and (R) are correct and (R) is the correct explanation of (A).

Q 28. Given below are two statements:
Statement I: Biodiesel can be created from vegetable oils and animal fats.
Statement II: Biodiesel viscosity is significantly lower than that of petroleum diesel.
In the light of the above statements, choose the most appropriate answer from the options given below -
1. Both Statement I and Statement II are correct
2. Both Statement I and Statement II are incorrect
3. Statement I is correct but Statement II is incorrect
4. Statement I is incorrect but Statement II is correct

Answer: 3. Statement I is correct but Statement II is incorrect

Q 29. Pyrolysis-
A. is a biochemical conversion process
B. is useful for production of bio-oil
C. yields minimum waste
D. liquid is a good substitute of heating oil
E. can produce Ethanol

Choose the correct answer from the options given below:
1. ABCD
2. BCD
3. BCDE
4. ADE

Answer: 2. BCD

Q 30. Which one of the following energy sources has the lowest energy content per unit mass?
1. Coal
2. Biomass
3. Hydrogen
4. Natural Gas

Answer: 2. Biomass

Q 31. Given below are two statements:
Assertion (A): Energy produced from biomass is considered 'carbon neutral'.
Reason (B): Biomass does not add CO_2 to the atmosphere.
Choose the correct answer from the options given below:
1. Both A and R are true and R is the correct explanation of A
2. Both A and R are true but R is NOT the correct explanation of A
3. A is true but R is false
4. A is false but R is true

Answer: 3. A is true but R is false

Q 32. Given below are two statements: One is labelled as Assertion (A) and the other is labelled as Reason (R):
Assertion A: Biomass is considered as carbon neutral.

Reason R: The amount of carbon they emit is equal to the amount of carbon they have consumed during their lifetime.

In the light of the above statements, choose the most appropriate answer from the options given below -
1. Both A and R are true and R is the correct explanation of A
2. Both A and R are true but R is NOT the correct explanation of A
3. A is true but R is false
4. A is false but R is true

Answer: 1. Both A and R are true and R is the correct explanation of A

Q 33. Which of the following statements are correct in this context of energy crops?
A. They are fast-growing plants
B. They require specific season to grow
C. They necessarily require fertile land to grow
D. They can be converted into gaseous and liquid fuel
E. They generally have high calorific value

Choose the correct answer from the options given below:
1. A, D and E only
2. A, B, C and D only
3. B, C, D and E only
4. C, D and E only

Answer: 1. A, D and E only

Q 34. Which of the following is true about an over fertile lake?
1. Nitrate level decreases
2. Depletion in algal productivity
3. Oxygen level increases
4. Quality of fishes produced is impaired

Answer: 4. Quality of fishes produced is impaired

Q 35. Given below are two statements: One is labelled as Assertion (A) and the other is labelled as Reason (R).

Assertion (A): Energy production from biomass has traditionally been considered carbon neutral.

Reason (R): Carbon dioxide emissions from combustion of biomass are sequestered by growing biomass

In the light of the above statements, choose the correct answer from the options given below:
1. Both (A) and (R) are true and (R) is the correct explanation of (A)
2. Both (A) and (R) are true but (R) is not the correct explanation of (A)
3. (A) is true but (R) is false
4. (A) is false but (R) is true

Answer: 1. Both (A) and (R) are true and (R) is the correct explanation of (A)

Q 36. Given below are two statements: One is labelled as Assertion (A) and the other is labelled as Reason (R):

Assertion (A): Carbon dioxide emissions from bioenergy. Production has traditionally been excluded from most emission inventories and climate impact studies.

Reason (R): Carbon dioxide emissions associated with production of bioenergy are significantly less compared to those from combustion of fossil fuels.

In the light of the above statements, choose the correct answer from the options given below:
1. Both (A) and (R) are true and (R) is the correct explanation of (A)
2. Both (A) and (R) are true but (R) is NOT the correct explanation of (A)
3. (A) is true but (R) is false
4. (A) is false but (R) is true

Answer: 2. Both (A) and (R) are true but (R) is NOT the correct explanation of (A)

Q 37. Biomass fuels have the potential to form a sustainable carbon-neutral energy source because they
1. Produce carbon dioxide on combustion as much as they consume when they grow
2. Produce less amount of carbon dioxide on combustion compared to the amount they use during their growth
3. Have carbon content same as fossil fuels
4. Do not produce hazardous emissions on combustion

Answer: 1. Produce carbon dioxide on combustion as much as they consume when they grow.

Q 38. A source of renewable power which can be developed with minimum cost is:
1. Windmills
2. Tidal power
3. Geothermal energy
4. Biomass power

Answer: 4. Biomass power

Q 39. The biggest hindrance in using biomass as a major energy source is:
1. Technology not well developed for commercialisation.
2. Energy yield of low level.
3. Large amounts of land required to grow energy crops.
4. Air pollution due to combustion.

Answer: 3. Large amounts of land required to grow energy crops.

Q 40. Given below are two statements: One is labelled as Assertion (A) and the other is labelled as Reason (R):
Assertion (A): Natural gas is a very attractive eco-friendly fuel.
Reason (R): It Produces fewer pollutants and less carbon dioxide per unit energy than any other fossil fuel on combustion.

> **In the light of the above statements, choose the correct answer from the options given below:**
> 1. Both (A) and (R) are true and (R) is the correct explanation of (A).
> 2. Both (A) and (R) are true and (R) is not the correct explanation of (A).
> 3. (A) is true, but (R) is false.
> 4. (A) is false, but (R) is true.
>
> **Answer: 1.** Both (A) and (R) are true and (R) is the correct explanation of (A).

Last Minute Revisions

Wind Power

- ✓ Wind Farms are often installed in rows, create noise pollution, can be installed on land or offshore and contribute electricity to power grid. *(Asked in Exam)*
- ✓ Wind farms are large concentrations of wind generators producing electricity. *(Asked in Exam)*
- ✓ Wind energy does not have a high energy density compared to other sources of energy like fossil fuels.
- ✓ Wind energy is an intermittent source of energy. *(Asked in Exam)*
- ✓ Wind Energy is hazardous for birds and bats. *(Asked in Exam)*
- ✓ Thermal Energy is Emission of Green House Gases. *(Asked in Exam)*
- ✓ Hydroelectric is a loss of riparian vegetation. *(Asked in Exam)*
- ✓ Photovoltaic energy is a production of toxic wastes. *(Asked in Exam)*
- ✓ Coastlines are considered as high potential areas for wind energy generation. *(Asked in Exam)*
- ✓ Ocean water can be utilized as coolant during wind energy production. *(Asked in Exam)*
- ✓ As of now, China is the leading country in wind energy-based electricity production. *(Asked in Exam)*

Solar Energy

- ✓ Energy can be harnessed from Sun, and animal excreta. *(Asked in Exam)*
- ✓ Solar Thermal Energy Collectors (STECs) are available in both flat plate and concentrating configurations. These systems are capable of reaching temperatures exceeding one thousand degrees Celsius and are utilised for electricity generation. The parabolic dish collector, a type of STEC, can achieve temperatures up to 2000°C. *(Asked in Exam)*
- ✓ Concept of salt gradient is utilized to store the heat energy in Solar ponds. *(Asked in Exam)*
- ✓ Solar ponds store solar thermal energy by Creating salt gradient. *(Asked in Exam)*
- ✓ Photovoltaic cells are exposed directly to the sun, therefore as temperature rises leakage across the cell increases. *(Asked in Exam)*
- ✓ Photovoltaic (PV) cells produce Direct Current (DC), not Alternating Current (AC). *(Asked in Exam)*

- ✓ Increasingly, photovoltaic panels are being used to supplement electrical energy from the power grid. *(Asked in Exam)*
- ✓ In concentrating type solar collector temperature can be raised upto 500°C. *(Asked in Exam)*
- ✓ A photovoltaic array is a combination of solar panels. *(Asked in Exam)*
- ✓ Photovoltaic cells are often made up of crystal silicon. *(Asked in Exam)*
- ✓ Silicon is widely used in solar cell fabrication. *(Asked in Exam)*
- ✓ Photovoltaic cells are also made up of inexpensive amorphous silicon, which is like ordinary glass and has no crystal properties. *(Asked in Exam)*
- ✓ Photo ElectroChemical (PEC) solar cells are based on Hybrid structure of inorganic semiconductors and an electrolyte. *(Asked in Exam)*
- ✓ Flat plate collectors are examples of simplest and most economic solar collectors. *(Asked in Exam)*
- ✓ Some of the solar concentrating collectors essentially use flat plate collectors. *(Asked in Exam)*
- ✓ 'Solar water still' is a device to Convert saline water to potable water using solar energy. *(Asked in Exam)*
- ✓ Solar flat plate collectors essentially work on the principle of GreenHouse Effect. *(Asked in Exam)*
- ✓ Black absorber plate radiates infrared radiations. *(Asked in Exam)*
- ✓ From the energy security perspective, which of the following energy sources is considered most secure for solar. *(Asked in Exam)*
- ✓ 'Solar Water Still' is a device to produce potable water by using solar energy. *(Asked in Exam)*
- ✓ Solar ponds, store solar energy in the form of heat because solar ponds contain water with a definite gradient of salt concentration. *(Asked in Exam)*

Biomass Energy

- ✓ **Thermal Energy contributes maximum to India's total electricity production.** *(Asked in Exam)*
- ✓ Producer Gas is the result of conversion of solid biomass into gaseous fuels. It can be used as fuel in internal combustion engines. Hydrogen and methane present in Producer Gas determine its heating value. *(Asked in Exam)*
- ✓ Even when a solid waste is buried in landfills, it can still provide energy because buried waste produces natural gas which can be captured and burned. *(Asked in Exam)*
- ✓ Biodiesel can be created from vegetable oils and animal fats. *(Asked in Exam)*
- ✓ Biodiesel has a higher viscosity compared to petroleum diesel. This higher viscosity can affect the flow characteristics of the fuel in engines. *(Asked in Exam)*
- ✓ Pyrolysis produces bio-oil with minimal waste, and the resulting liquid can replace heating oil. *(Asked in Exam)*
- ✓ Biomass has the lowest energy content per unit mass. *(Asked in Exam)*
- ✓ Energy produced from biomass is considered 'carbon neutral'. *(Asked in Exam)*
- ✓ Biomass adds CO_2 to the atmosphere. *(Asked in Exam)*
- ✓ Biomass is considered as carbon neutral because the amount of carbon they emit is equal to the amount of carbon they have consumed during their lifetime. *(Asked in Exam)*

✓ Energy crops are fast-growing plants and can be converted into gaseous and liquid fuel. They generally have high calorific value. *(Asked in Exam)*

✓ An over-fertile lake experiences excessive nutrient enrichment, particularly from nitrates and phosphates, leading to eutrophication. This process results in: Quality of fishes produced is impaired, Increased algal growth (algal blooms, Oxygen depletion and Poor water quality. *(Asked in Exam)*

✓ Energy production from biomass has traditionally been considered carbon neutral because carbon dioxide emissions from combustion of biomass are sequestered by growing biomass. *(Asked in Exam)*

✓ Carbon dioxide emissions from bioenergy. Production has traditionally been excluded from most emission inventories and climate impact studies. *(Asked in Exam)*

✓ Carbon dioxide emissions associated with production of bioenergy are significantly less compared to those from combustion of fossil fuels. *(Asked in Exam)*

✓ Biomass fuels have the potential to form a sustainable carbon-neutral energy source because they produce carbon dioxide on combustion as much as they consume when they grow. *(Asked in Exam)*

✓ A source of renewable power which can be developed with minimum cost Biomass power. *(Asked in Exam)*

✓ The biggest hindrance in using biomass as a major energy source is large amounts of land required to grow energy crops. *(Asked in Exam)*

✓ Natural gas is a very attractive eco-friendly fuel because It Produces fewer pollutants and less carbon dioxide per unit energy than any other fossil fuel on combustion. *(Asked in Exam)*

Chapter 5

Natural Hazards and Natural Disasters: Environmental Protection Act (1986), National Action Plan on Climate Change, and international agreements/efforts

Natural Hazards and Natural Disasters

Here is the refined content for the chapter on Natural Hazards and Natural Disasters. I have integrated the scattered points into their relevant sections, corrected grammatical errors (such as spelling "Draught" to "Drought"), and preserved the exam tags.

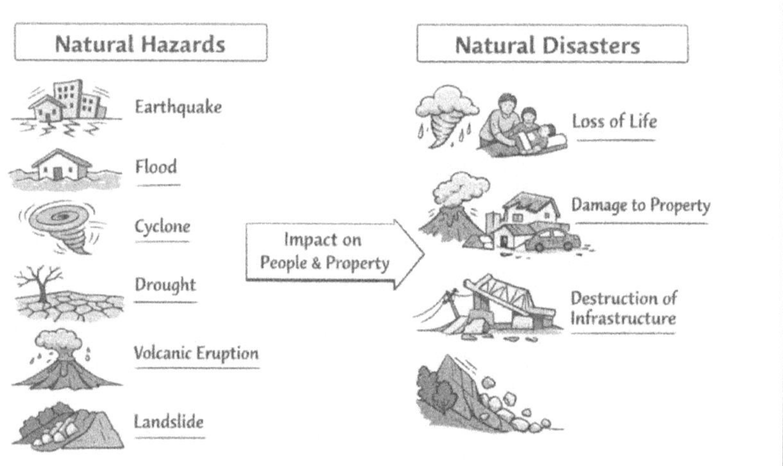

Definitions:

- **Natural Hazard:** A natural event that has the potential to cause damage.
- **Natural Disaster:** Occurs when a natural hazard causes significant damage, and the affected community cannot cope with its resources. **Natural disasters do not discriminate between people of society and other communities.** *(Asked in Exam)*

Types of Natural Hazards:

- **Geophysical Hazards:** Earthquakes, volcanic eruptions, tsunamis, avalanches. **Landslides are of Geo-physical origin.** *(Asked in Exam)* **Avalanches belong to the category of geophysical hazards.** *(Asked in Exam)*
- **Hydrological Hazards:** Floods.

> **Meteorological Hazards:** Cyclones, storms.
> **Climatological Hazards:** Droughts, wildfires. **Droughts are natural hazards and have a relatively slow onset.** *(Asked in Exam)*
> **Biological Hazards:** Pandemics.

Prevention and Mitigation:

> **Prevention:** Ensuring actions or phenomena do not result in disasters. **A measure such as building a plinth wall for floods would be termed as prevention.** *(Asked in Exam)*
> **Mitigation:** Reducing the severity of human and material damage caused by disasters.
> **Challenges: Despite increasing vulnerability to natural disasters, many communities resist adopting mitigation programs and measures.** *(Asked in Exam)*
> **Flood Mitigation: Mitigation measures to cope with floods include elevating or protecting electrical service panels, upsizing culverts to better handle flood surges, protecting facilities with barriers and sandbags, and relocating equipment outside the flood plain.** *(Asked in Exam)*

Structural and Non-Structural Measures:

> **Structural Measures:** Physical constructions or engineering techniques to reduce hazard impacts (e.g., flood barriers, earthquake-resistant buildings).
> **Non-Structural Measures:** Policies, public awareness, training, and education to reduce disaster risks (e.g., disaster preparedness programs, building codes). **Non-structural measures refer to strategies and policies that do not involve physical construction or engineering. They are often related to planning, management, or regulatory measures to reduce disaster risks and impacts.** *(Asked in Exam)*
> **Examples: Land-use zoning and insurance programs can be characterized as non-structural.** *(Asked in Exam)*

National Disaster Management Authority (NDMA):

> **NDMA:** Apex body in India for disaster management policies.
> **Established:** Through the Disaster Management Act on 23 December 2005.
> **Operates Under: National Disaster Management Authority (NDMA) works under the aegis of Ministry of Home Affairs (MHA).** *(Asked in Exam)*

Anthropogenic Hazards:

Hazards caused by human action or inaction. Nuclear Disaster, floods, and forest fires hazards can occur due to anthropogenic causes. *(Asked in Exam)*

- ➢ **Societal Hazards:** Criminality, civil disorder, terrorism, war.
- ➢ **Industrial and Engineering Hazards:** Power outages, fires, industrial accidents.
- ➢ **Transportation Hazards:** Environmental hazards caused by transportation activities.

Natural Hazards by Climate Change / Global Warming:

Global warming can lead to/aggravate drought, flood, and storm natural disasters. *(Asked in Exam)* Additionally, the frequency and intensity of extreme weather events will have serious consequences for food security. *(Asked in Exam)*

Rising Disasters Due to Climate Change:

- ➢ **Floods:** Increased rainfall causes severe urban flooding.
- ➢ **Storms:** Stronger hurricanes and typhoons devastate coasts.
- ➢ **Heat Waves:** Prolonged high temperatures worsen health risks.
- ➢ **Droughts:** Reduced rainfall leads to water shortages.
- ➢ **Wildfires:** Rising temperatures cause frequent forest fires.
- ➢ **Melting Glaciers:** Contributes to rising sea levels globally.
- ➢ **Climate Migration:** Disasters force people to relocate. **Climate change is going to increase social tension in India.** *(Asked in Exam)*

Specific Hazards:

Tsunami:

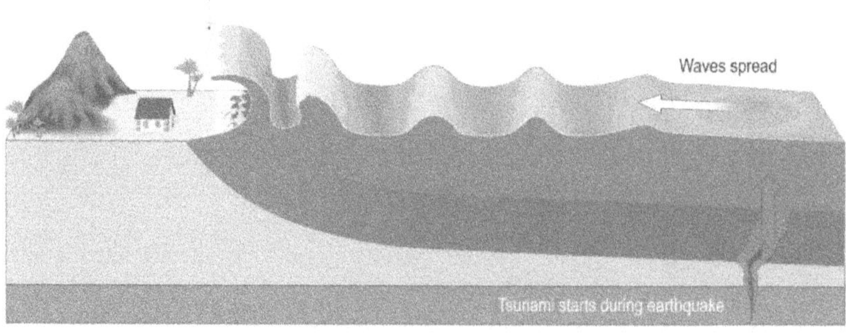

- ➢ **Definition: Meaning of Tsunami is "Harbour Wave".** *(Asked in Exam)*

- ➤ **Caused by Earthquakes:** Seafloor shifts trigger massive waves.
- ➤ **Underwater Volcanic Eruptions:** Lava movement displaces water.
- ➤ **Coastal Devastation:** Floods cities and destroys buildings.
- ➤ **Rapid Speed:** Travels fast in deep oceans.
- ➤ **Warning Signs:** Receding shorelines indicate incoming waves.
- ➤ **High Casualties:** Can kill thousands in minutes.
- ➤ **Global Impact:** Affects multiple countries across oceans.

Cyclones:

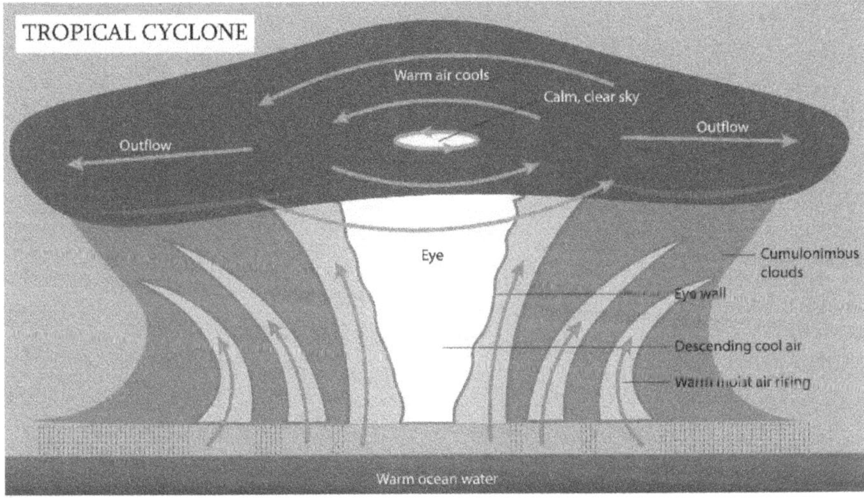

- ➤ **Characteristics: Most cyclones cause widespread damage in coastal areas.** *(Asked in Exam)*
- ➤ **Formation: Warm tropical oceans and moist air mass are prerequisites for the development of tropical cyclones.** *(Asked in Exam)*
- ➤ **Terminology: Hurricanes and typhoons are essentially the same as tropical cyclones.** *(Asked in Exam)*
- ➤ **Rotating Wind System:** Forms around low-pressure areas.
- ➤ **Ocean Heat Transfer:** Fuels storm intensity and duration.
- ➤ **Strong Winds:** Cause infrastructure damage and flooding.
- ➤ **Heavy Rainfall:** Leads to landslides and flash floods.
- ➤ **Storm Surges:** Push seawater inland, flooding cities.
- ➤ **Coastal Destruction:** Homes, crops, and businesses destroyed.
- ➤ **Evacuation Needed:** Early warnings save countless lives.

Human Health Risk Assessment:

The assessment follows a specific sequence: The correct order of risk assessment due to exposure of some chemicals to humans: Hazard Identification → Dose-Response Assessment → Exposure Assessment → Risk Characterization → Estimating the magnitude of the public health. *(Asked in Exam)*

1. Hazard Identification:
- Chemical Risk Analysis: Identifies chemicals causing health effects.
- Health Impact Study: Links substances to specific diseases.
- **Hazard identification is a process of determining whether a particular chemical is linked to a particular health effect.** *(Asked in Exam)*

2. Dose-Response Relationship:
- Higher Dose, Greater Effect: More exposure increases health risks.
- Threshold Level: Some chemicals are harmful above a limit.
- **Dose-response assessment characterizes the relationship between the dose received and the adverse health effect.** *(Asked in Exam)*

3. Exposure Assessment:
- Population at Risk: Identifies exposed groups and locations.
- Toxicant Pathways: Tracks chemicals through air, water, soil.
- **Exposure assessment determines the size and nature of the population that has been exposed to toxicants.** *(Asked in Exam)*

4. Risk Characterization:
- Public Health Impact: Estimates overall risk magnitude.
- Risk Communication: Conveys findings for safety measures.
- **Risk characterization: Assessing the extent of the public health issue.** *(Asked in Exam)*

Environmental Protection Act (EPA) (1986)

The Environment (Protection) Act, 1986 was enacted with the main objective of providing protection and improvement of the environment, and addressing matters connected therewith. Here's an overview of its background, aims, objectives, and main provisions:

Constitutional Amendment: The original Indian Constitution lacked provisions for environmental protection. The 42nd Amendment introduced Fundamental Duties, including environmental protection, and added Directive Principles like Article 48A, directing the State to protect and improve the environment.

Global Influence: These changes were influenced by the **United Nations Conference on Human Environment in Stockholm, 1972.**

Preceding Laws: Before the EPA, India enacted the Wildlife Protection Act (1972), the Water (Prevention and Control of Pollution) Act (1974), and the Air (Prevention and Control of Pollution) Act (1981).

Bhopal Gas Tragedy: The EPA was passed in the wake of the Bhopal Gas Tragedy on December 2, 1984.

Aims and Objectives

- **Implementation of Stockholm Decisions:**
  - Implementing decisions from the 1972 Stockholm Conference.
- **Regulatory Authority:**
  - Creation of a government authority to regulate industry
  - Capable of issuing direct orders including closures.
- **Coordination:**
  - Coordinating activities of various agencies under existing laws.
- **Environmental Laws:**
  - Enacting regular laws for environmental protection.
- **Punishments:**
  - Imposing punishments for endangering the environment, safety, and health.
  - Penalties can include up to five years in prison, fines up to Rs. 1 lakh, or both.
  - In severe cases, imprisonment can extend up to seven years.
- **Sustainable Development:**
  - Engaging in the sustainable development of the environment.
- **Right to Life:**
  - Attaining protection of the right to life under Article 21 of the Constitution.

Main Provisions

- **Central Powers:** The Centre enforces environmental protection measures.
- **Nationwide Programs:** Plans and coordinates environmental initiatives.
- **Quality Standards:** Regulates pollution and emission limits.
- **Industry Restrictions:** Controls industrial locations for environmental safety.
- **Inspection & Analysis:** Government can inspect, test, and analyze pollutants.
- **Pollutant Discharge:** Prohibits emissions beyond set limits.
- **Hazardous Substances:** Regulates handling of hazardous materials.
- **Public Complaints:** Citizens can file legal complaints on violations.

The Environment Protection Act, 1986, is a comprehensive law aimed at safeguarding and improving the environmental quality in India, ensuring sustainable development and public health protection.

International Agreements/Efforts

Before diving into specific protocols, it is important to note the origins of global environmental governance. United Nations Environmental Program (UNEP) was the result of deliberations held during the Human Environmental Conference at Stockholm in 1972. *(Asked in Exam)*

Following this global momentum, nations took individual actions. For instance, **The Environment (Protection) Act, 1986 was the result of India's commitment to take appropriate action for the protection and**

improvement of the environment at the United Nations Conference on the Human Environment, Stockholm, 1972. *(Asked in Exam)*

Montreal Protocol (1987, 1989)

The Montreal Protocol is an international treaty designed to protect the ozone layer by phasing out the production of numerous substances responsible for ozone depletion. The Montreal Protocol was signed specifically to address the issue of the depletion of the ozone layer in the stratosphere. *(Asked in Exam)*

> ➤ **Agreed upon:** 16 September 1987.
> ➤ **Came into force:** 1 January 1989.
> ➤ **Nature of Agreement: The Montreal Protocol is a multilateral environmental agreement that regulates the production and consumption of nearly 100 man-made chemicals.** *(Asked in Exam)* It is also broadly recognized that **the Montreal Protocol is an international treaty designed to protect the environment.** *(Asked in Exam)*

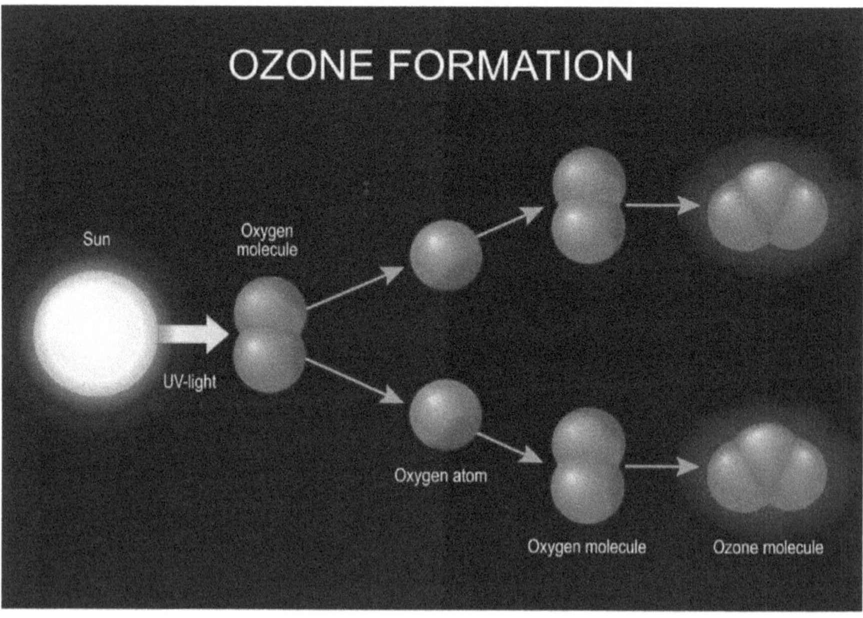

Success and Ratification:

The Montreal Protocol is considered one of the most successful environmental agreements of all time. Former UN General Secretary Kofi Annan once stated that "perhaps the single most successful international environmental agreement to date has been the Montreal Protocol." *(Asked in Exam)*

Its universal acceptance is unique: The only UN treaty related to environmental issues which has been ratified by all 197 UN member states is the Montreal Protocol. *(Asked in Exam)*

Structure and Responsibilities:

The treaty sets specific timetables for phasing down the consumption and production of ozone-depleting substances (ODS).

- **Article 5 Countries: Under the Montreal Protocol, developing countries are referred to as 'Article 5 Countries'.** *(Asked in Exam)*
- **Differentiated Responsibility: Under the Montreal Protocol, developed and developing nations have differentiated responsibilities.** *(Asked in Exam)*

Ozone-Depleting Substances (ODS):

ODS are man-made gases that destroy ozone once they reach the ozone layer. The Montreal Protocol refers to phasing out the consumption and production of ozone-depleting substances. *(Asked in Exam)* These substances include:

- Chlorofluorocarbons (CFCs)
- Hydrochlorofluorocarbons (HCFCs)
- Hydrobromofluorocarbons (HBFCs)
- Halons
- Methyl bromide
- Carbon tetrachloride
- Methyl chloroform

Sources of ODS:

- Refrigerants and vehicle air conditioners and refrigerators
- Foam blowing agents
- Components in electrical equipment
- Industrial solvents
- Solvents for cleaning (including dry cleaning)
- Aerosol spray propellants
- Fumigants

CFCs vs. HFCs and The Evolution of Substitutes

The main aim of the Montreal Protocol is to limit the release of CFCs into the atmosphere by replacing them with safer alternatives.

Hydrochlorofluorocarbons (HCFCs) replaced chlorofluorocarbons (CFCs) after their phase-out due to the Montreal Protocol. *(Asked in Exam)* Eventually, the industry moved toward Hydrofluorocarbons (HFCs).

1. CFCs (Chlorofluorocarbons):

These were commonly used in air conditioning and refrigeration systems. However, they significantly contribute to ozone layer depletion.

2. HFCs (Hydrofluorocarbons):

Used as a replacement for CFCs in air conditioning systems.

> **Ozone Impact: HFCs do not deplete the ozone layer; they were actually introduced as alternatives to ozone-depleting substances like chlorofluorocarbons (CFCs) and hydrochlorofluorocarbons (HCFCs).** *(Asked in Exam)*

> **Chemical Properties: HFCs have a shorter lifetime than CFCs and contain no chlorine and bromine.** *(Asked in Exam)*

> **Climate Impact:** While they save the ozone, **HFCs have a high global warming potential.** *(Asked in Exam)* They are recognized as potent greenhouse gases contributing to global warming.

Co-benefits and Amendments:

> **Climate Co-benefits: The Montreal Protocol, primarily aimed at phasing out ozone-depleting substances, has also had the co-benefit of reducing greenhouse gas emissions.** *(Asked in Exam)*

> **Kigali Amendment:** Because HFCs are potent greenhouse gases, the protocol was updated to address them. **The latest amendment to the Montreal Protocol is the Kigali Amendment.** *(Asked in Exam)*

Stockholm Declaration of 1972

> **Significance:** First UN declaration on environmental protection.
> **Legacy:**
> - Marked a milestone in environmental law.
> - Laid groundwork for future environmental policies.
> - Inspired future global environmental agreements.
> **Key Principles:**
> - Established principles for sustainable development.
> - Emphasized global cooperation for sustainability.
> - Addressed pollution, biodiversity, and resource use.
> - Recognized humans' right to a healthy environment.
> - Encouraged nations to adopt sustainable practices.
> **Institutional Outcome:** Led to the creation of UNEP. **United Nations Environmental Program (UNEP) was the result of deliberations held during the Human Environmental Conference at Stockholm in 1972.** *(Asked in Exam)*

United Nations Environment Programme (UNEP)

> **Establishment:** Established after the Stockholm Conference (1972).
> **Headquarters:** Nairobi, Kenya.
> **Role:**
> - Leads global environmental policy and law.

- o Coordinates UN responses to environmental issues.
- o Oversees major environmental agreements and treaties.
- ➢ **Key Functions:**
  - o Focuses on climate change, biodiversity, and pollution.
  - o Supports sustainable development worldwide.
  - o Promotes resource efficiency and green economy.
  - o Conducts scientific research on environmental trends.
  - o Provides technical and financial support to nations.

Environment Protection Act, 1986 (India)

- ➢ **Context:** Enacted in 1986 after the Bhopal disaster (1984).
- ➢ **International Commitment: The Environment (Protection) Act, 1986 was the result of India's commitment to take appropriate action for the protection and improvement of the environment at the United Nations Conference on the Human Environment, Stockholm, 1972.** *(Asked in Exam)*
- ➢ **Framework:**
  - o Provides a framework for environmental protection.
  - o One of India's most comprehensive environmental laws.
  - o Empowers the central government to act and coordinates state and central authorities.
- ➢ **Scope:**
  - o Covers air, water, and land pollution.
  - o Regulates industrial operations affecting the environment.
  - o Allows penalties for environmental violations.
  - o Encourages sustainable development and conservation.

Rio Summit (Earth Summit 1992)

- ➢ **Event:** Earth Summit 1992 – Held in Rio de Janeiro, Brazil. Also known as the United Nations Conference on Environment and Development (UNCED).
- ➢ **Core Goal: Rio de Janeiro Conference adopted the program of Action for Sustainable Development.** *(Asked in Exam)* Sustainable Development was recognized as a global goal.
- ➢ **Major Agreements & Outcomes:**
  - o **Agenda 21:** A comprehensive sustainability action plan.
  - o **Forest Management:** Principles for sustainable forest use.
  - o **Three Sister Conventions: UN Framework Convention on Climate Change (UNFCCC), UN Convention to Combat Desertification (UNCCD), and Convention on Biological Diversity (CBD) are originated from the Rio Earth Summit.** *(Asked in Exam)*

1. Convention on Biological Diversity (CBD):

- ➢ **The Convention on Biological Diversity (CBD) was opened for signature during the Rio Summit, officially known as the United**

> Nations Conference on Environment and Development (UNCED), held in Rio de Janeiro, Brazil, in 1992. *(Asked in Exam)*
> Convention on Biodiversity was signed during Earth Summit at Rio de Janeiro, 1992. *(Asked in Exam)*
> Purpose: The convention on biological diversity is dedicated to promoting sustainable development conceived as a practical tool for translating the principles of Agenda 21. *(Asked in Exam)*

2. UNFCCC (Climate Change):

> United Nations Framework Convention on Climate Change (UNFCCC) was the outcome of Earth Summit. *(Asked in Exam)*
> Objective: The primary objective of the United Nations Framework Convention on Climate Change (UNFCCC) is to stabilize greenhouse gas concentrations in the atmosphere at a level that would prevent dangerous anthropogenic interference with the climate system. *(Asked in Exam)*

Achievements of the Rio Summit:

> **Equitable Resource Sharing:** Fair use of genetic biodiversity.
> **Climate System Protection:** Prevent human-induced climate change.
> **International Cooperation:** Strengthen global environmental policies.
> **Local Impact Focus:** Governments and stakeholders play key roles.
> **Long-Term Sustainability:** Ensure future generations' environmental rights.

Rio+20 Summit (2012)

> **Event: The Rio + 20 Conference, 2012 is also known as the UN Conference on Sustainable Development (UNCSD).** *(Asked in Exam)*
> **Context:** Held in Rio de Janeiro, Brazil, in June 2012, as a 20-year follow-up to the 1992 Earth Summit.
> **Goal:** Aimed at reconciling the economic and environmental goals of the global community.

Objectives of Rio+20:

> Renew Political Commitment for sustainable development.
> Evaluate Progress and identify remaining gaps.
> Address Emerging Challenges in sustainability.
> Strengthen Global Cooperation for future development.

Key Outcomes of Rio+20:

> **The Future We Want:** Key outcome document of Rio+20.
> **Green Economy Promotion:** Emphasized sustainable economic growth.
> **Institutional Framework:** Strengthened governance for sustainability.
> **Sustainable Development Goals (SDGs):** Initiated their global framework.

> **Progress Beyond MDGs:** Expanded sustainability focus from Millennium Development Goals (MDGs).
> **Corporate Sustainability:** Encouraged businesses to adopt green practices.

The Rio Summits have been pivotal in shaping global policies and strategies towards sustainable development, emphasizing the integration of environmental, economic, and social objectives.

United Nations Framework Convention on Climate Change (UNFCCC)

Overview and Objective:

The UNFCCC was proposed in 1992 during the Earth Summit and entered into force on 21 March 1994.[1] Its ultimate aim is to prevent "dangerous human interference with the climate system."[2]

> **The primary objective of the United Nations Framework Convention on Climate Change (UNFCCC) is to stabilize greenhouse gas concentrations in the atmosphere at a level that would prevent dangerous anthropogenic interference with the climate system.[3]**
> *(Asked in Exam)*
> **Prevent Climate Impact:** Avoid human-caused climate change.

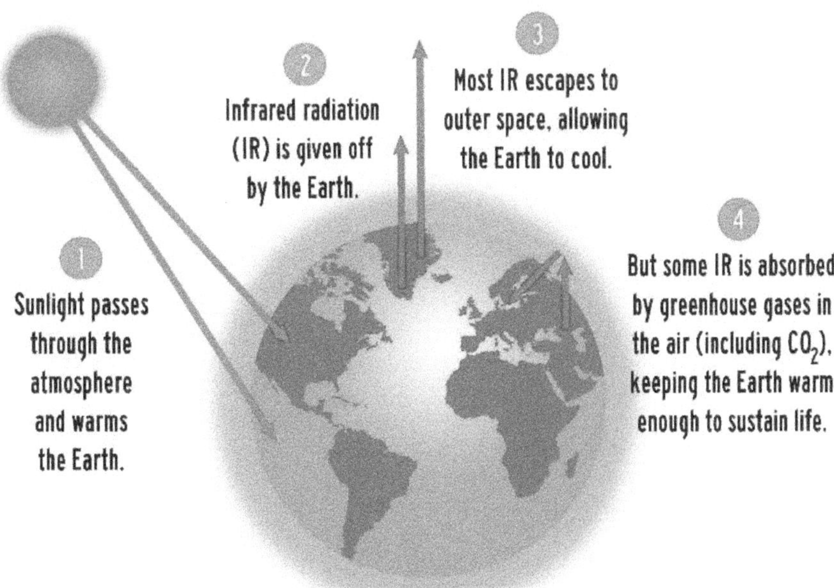

Key Facts:

- **Established:** 1992 (Proposed during the Earth Summit).[4]
- **Came into force:** 21 March 1994.[5]
- **Parties:** 197 Parties (Includes 196 countries and the EU).
- **COP Meetings:** Annual decision-making conferences (Conference of the Parties).[6]

Main Functions:

- Provides a framework for negotiating specific international treaties (protocols) that may set binding limits on greenhouse gases.
- Establishes a process for monitoring and reporting on national efforts to reduce greenhouse gas emissions.[7]
- Promotes financial and technological support to help developing countries mitigate and adapt to climate change.[8]

Commitments by Parties:

- **Developed countries (Annex I parties):** Required to submit regular reports on their climate policies and measures, including annual inventories of greenhouse gas emissions.[9]
- **Developing countries (Non-Annex I parties):** Encouraged to submit national reports on their emissions and climate actions, supported by financial and technical assistance.[10]

Financial Mechanisms:

- **The Global Environment Facility (GEF):** Serves as an operating entity of the financial mechanism of the UNFCCC.[11]
- **The Green Climate Fund (GCF):** Established to assist developing countries in adaptation and mitigation practices to counter climate change.[12]

Global Warming Targets & Scientific Context:

Understanding the urgency behind the UNFCCC requires looking at temperature thresholds:

- **If global average warming is limited to one or two additional degrees, some regions will experience enhanced agricultural productivity.** *(Asked in Exam)*
- **Beyond 2°C to 3°C of global average warming, essentially all impacts become deleterious.** *(Asked in Exam)*
- **To limit the rise in global temperature to 1.5°C over preindustrial levels, IPCC indicates that the world has to reduce the emission of greenhouse gas to the extent of 45% by the year 2030.**[13] *(Asked in Exam)*

Kyoto Protocol

Overview:

The Kyoto Protocol is an international treaty that extended the 1992 UNFCCC and committed state parties to reduce greenhouse gas emissions.14

> - **Adoption: The Kyoto Protocol was adopted during the third Conference of Parties (COP-3) to the United Nations Framework Convention on Climate Change (UNFCCC), which took place in Kyoto, Japan, in December 1997.**[15] *(Asked in Exam)*
> - **Entry into Force: Kyoto Protocol was agreed in 1997 and came into force in 2005.**[16] *(Asked in Exam)* It required 55 countries representing 55% of global emissions to ratify it before activation.[17]

Nature of Commitments:

> - **Legally Binding:** It set binding emission reduction targets for industrialized countries.[18]
> - **Differentiated Responsibility: Kyoto Protocol only binds developed countries and places a heavier burden on them.**[19] *(Asked in Exam)*
> - **Baselines: Kyoto Protocol set up different limits of carbon emissions for individual nations, depending on their output before 1990.**[20] *(Asked in Exam)*

Greenhouse Gases Covered:

The Kyoto Protocol targets six greenhouse gases. Carbon dioxide (CO_2), Methane (CH_4), and Nitrous oxide (N_2O) gases were covered under the Kyoto Protocol.21 *(Asked in Exam)* The full list includes:

1. Carbon dioxide (CO_2)
2. Methane (CH_4)
3. Nitrous oxide (N_2O)
4. Hydrofluorocarbons (HFCs)
5. Perfluorocarbons (PFCs)
6. Sulfur hexafluoride (SF_6)

Commitment Periods:

There are two commitment periods to monitor progress:

First Commitment Period (2008–2012):

> - **The Kyoto Protocol, adopted in 1997, set binding emission reduction targets for developed countries.**[29] **These targets were to be achieved during the first commitment period, which began in 2008 and ended in 2012.**[30] *(Asked in Exam)*
> - **Under Kyoto Protocol, the first commitment period for reduction of greenhouse gas emissions by 37 industrialized and European community countries was 2008–2012.**[31] *(Asked in Exam)*
> - **CO_2 (Carbon Dioxide), N_2O (Nitrous Oxide), and CH_4 (Methane) greenhouse gases were the target gases whose emission was to be**

covered under the first commitment period of the Kyoto Protocol.[32]
(Asked in Exam)

Second Commitment Period (2013–2020): Known as the Doha Amendment period.

Mechanisms under Kyoto Protocol:

To help countries meet targets cost-effectively, the protocol introduced three market-based mechanisms:33

- ➤ **Clean Development Mechanism (CDM):**
    - o Allows industrialized countries to invest in emission reduction projects in developing countries.[34]
    - o Emission Credits Earned are used to meet reduction targets.[35]
    - o Promotes sustainable development in developing nations.[36]
- ➤ **Joint Implementation (JI):**
    - o Allows industrialized countries to implement emission reduction projects in other industrialized countries.[37]
- ➤ **Emissions Trading:**
    - o Allows countries that have emission units to spare to sell them to countries that are over their targets (Carbon Market System).[38]

Challenges Faced:

- ➤ **U.S. Did Not Ratify:** Weakened global participation.
- ➤ **Limited Scope:** Did not include all major emitters in the binding targets initially.[39]
- ➤ **Modest Global Impact:** Insufficient to curb climate change alone.

Paris Agreement

Overview and Objectives:

The Paris Agreement, also known as the Paris Accords or the Paris Climate Accords, is an international treaty on climate change.1 It was adopted on 12 December 2015 and entered into force on 4 November 2016.2

The central aims of the agreement are defined by specific temperature thresholds:

- ➤ **To strengthen the global response to the threat of climate change was the central aim of the Paris Agreement.**[3] *(Asked in Exam)*
- ➤ **The Paris Agreement aims to limit the global temperature rise in this century to well below 2°C above pre-industrial levels.**[4] *(Asked in Exam)*
- ➤ **Paris Agreement was decided to limit the increase in global average temperature to well below 2°C.**[5] *(Asked in Exam)*
- ➤ **The Paris Agreement envisages pursuing efforts to limit global warming this century to 1.5 degrees Celsius above the pre-industrial levels of global average temperature.**[6] *(Asked in Exam)*

> ➤ **Under Paris Agreement, countries by the end of this century will strive to limit the global temperature rise above pre-industrial level to 1.5°C.[7]** *(Asked in Exam)*

To limit global warming to 1.5°C, greenhouse gas emissions must peak before 2025 at the latest and decline by 45% by 2030.

Adoption and Entry into Force:

> ➤ **Adopted on 12 December 2015:** Agreed at COP21 in Paris.[8]
> ➤ **Entered into force on 4 November 2016:** Became legally binding.[9]
> ➤ **Widespread global participation:** Ratified by many countries.[10]

Nationally Determined Contributions (NDCs):

Countries set their own targets, known as NDCs, which outline national climate action.[11] These are updated every five years to reflect progress and higher ambition.[12]

> ➤ **The Nationally Determined Contributions (NDCs) of the European Union (EU) countries aim at a reduction in greenhouse gas emissions by 40% by the year 2030, relative to the levels in 1990.** *(Asked in Exam)*
> ➤ However, it is noted that **Nationally Determined Contributions (NDCs) declared by each country are not sufficient to keep the rise in global temperature up to 2°C above the pre-industrial level.** *(Asked in Exam)*

Long-Term Strategies:

Beyond immediate NDCs, the agreement focuses on the long view.[13]

> ➤ **Long term low emission development strategies by each country are crucial to realizing the goals of the Paris Agreement.[14]** *(Asked in Exam)*
> ➤ **Formulation of long term - low emission development strategies by each country were suggested under Paris Agreement.[15]** *(Asked in Exam)*
> ➤ **Focus on long-term reduction:** Aim for the second half of the century to achieve net-zero emissions.[16]

Global Stocktake:

> ➤ **Conducted every five years:** Measures collective climate progress.[17]
> ➤ **Assesses overall implementation:** Reviews long-term goals.[18]
> ➤ **Guides further climate action:** Helps countries enhance commitments.[19]

Climate Finance:

> ➤ **Developed countries provide financial aid:[20]** Supports developing nations.[21]
> ➤ **$100 billion target per year:** Mobilized from various sources.[22]
> ➤ **Funds mitigation and adaptation:** Addresses climate challenges.[23]

Transparency Framework:

> ➤ **Enhanced reporting requirements:** Countries report emissions and actions.[24]
> ➤ **Flexibility for developing nations:** Supports varying capacities.[25]

> **Ensures accountability in commitments:** Strengthens implementation efforts.

Adaptation, Loss, and Damage:

> **Adaptation:** Builds resilience to climate change and encourages national adaptation plans.[26]

> **Loss and Damage:** Recognizes climate-induced losses and addresses unavoidable climate impacts.

Technology and Capacity-Building:

> **Promotes technology transfer:** Helps reduce emissions and enhance resilience.[27]

> **Supports innovation for climate action:** Develops sustainable solutions.

Key Environmental Agreements Summary

(Quick Revision for Exams)

> **Kyoto Protocol:** Global Warming – Focused on reducing greenhouse gases.[28] *(Asked in Exam)*

> **Montreal Protocol:** Ozone Depletion – Aimed at phasing out CFCs.[29] *(Asked in Exam)*

> **Rio Summit:** Biodiversity Conservation – Promoted sustainable development. *(Asked in Exam)*

> **Paris Agreement:** Solar Alliance – Encouraged renewable energy transition. *(Asked in Exam)*

The Convention on Biological Diversity (CBD)

Overview:

The Convention on Biological Diversity (CBD), also known as the Biodiversity Convention, is a multilateral treaty with three main goals:

1. Conservation of biological diversity (biodiversity)
2. Sustainable use of its components
3. Fair and equitable sharing of benefits arising from genetic resources

The Convention on Biological Diversity (CBD) seeks to promote the conservation of biodiversity; advocate for the sustainable use of its components; and emphasize the fair and equitable sharing of benefits arising from the utilization of genetic resources. *(Asked in Exam)*

The objective of the CBD is to develop national strategies for the conservation and sustainable use of biological diversity. It is considered a key document for sustainable development. **The benefits of biodiversity are contribution to human food supplies, providing important medicines, supporting ecosystem stability, and aesthetic and cultural value.** *(Asked in Exam)*

History:

- ➢ **Opened for Signature:** 5 June 1992, at the Earth Summit in Rio de Janeiro.
- ➢ **Entered into Force:** 29 December 1993.
- ➢ **Notable Exception:** The United States is the only UN member state that has not ratified the Convention.

Supplementary Agreements:

Cartagena Protocol and Nagoya Protocol are supplementary to the Convention on Biodiversity (CBD). *(Asked in Exam)*

- ➢ **Cartagena Protocol on Biosafety:** Governs the movement of living modified organisms (LMOs) resulting from modern biotechnology from one country to another.
  - o Adopted: 29 January 2000
  - o Entered into Force: 11 September 2003
- ➢ **Nagoya Protocol on Access to Genetic Resources and the Fair and Equitable Sharing of Benefits Arising from their Utilization (ABS):** Provides a legal framework for fair and equitable sharing of benefits from genetic resources.
  - o Adopted: 29 October 2010
  - o Entered into Force: 12 October 2014

Conferences of the Parties (COP):

- ➢ **COP 1: In the context of Convention on Biological Diversity (CBD), the first session of Conference of Parties (COPs) was scheduled in the Bahamas.** *(Asked in Exam)* (1994, Nassau)
- ➢ **COP 15:** 2021/2022, Kunming, China, and Montreal, Canada.

Milestones:

- ➢ **2010:** International Year of Biodiversity; The Secretariat of the CBD was the focal point.
- ➢ **2011-2020:** United Nations Decade on Biodiversity (A recommendation from CBD signatories at Nagoya).
- ➢ **Strategic Plan for Biodiversity 2011-2020:** Includes the Aichi Biodiversity Targets.

Marine and Coastal Biodiversity:

- ➢ **Current Focus:** Identifying Ecologically or Biologically Significant Marine Areas (EBSAs) based on scientific criteria.
- ➢ **Goal:** Create an international legally binding instrument (ILBI) under UNCLOS to support the conservation and sustainable use of marine biological diversity beyond areas of national jurisdiction (BBNJ).

International Solar Alliance (ISA)

Overview:

The International Solar Alliance (ISA) is an alliance of more than 120 signatory countries, most of which are located in regions with abundant sunlight. The International Solar Alliance (ISA) is a joint initiative between France and India. It has 121 signatory countries, with most participants being nations that receive abundant sunshine. *(Asked in Exam)*

International Solar Alliance (ISA) is the alliance countries most of which lie partially or completely between the Tropic of Cancer and the Tropic of Capricorn. *(Asked in Exam)*

Key Details:

- ➤ **Proposed by:** Indian Prime Minister Narendra Modi. **The initiative to establish International Solar Alliance was jointly taken by France and India.** *(Asked in Exam)*
- ➤ **First Proposed:** November 2015, Wembley Stadium.
- ➤ **Entry into Force: International Solar Alliance Framework Agreement entered into force in the year 2017.** *(Asked in Exam)* (6 December 2017).
- ➤ **Headquarters:** Haryana, India.
- ➤ **Presidency: International Solar Alliance's present post of President is held by India.** *(Asked in Exam)*
- ➤ **Official Languages: Official languages for International Solar Alliance are Hindi, English, and French.** *(Asked in Exam)*

Vision and Mission:

- ➤ **Vision: International Solar Alliance's vision: "Let us together make the sun brighter."** *(Asked in Exam)*
- ➤ **Mission: International Solar Alliance's mission: "Every home, however far away, will have a light at home."** *(Asked in Exam)*

ISA at COP (Launch):

- ➤ **Launch Event: The International Solar Alliance (ISA) was launched on the sidelines of COP21, not COP24.** *(Asked in Exam)*
- ➤ **Founders: The ISA was indeed launched by Prime Minister Narendra Modi of India and then-President of France, François Hollande, not Emmanuel Macron.** *(Asked in Exam)*
- ➤ **Foundation Stone:** Laid by Narendra Modi and François Hollande in 2016 in Haryana.

Sunshine Countries:

Sunshine countries are those that lie either completely or partly between the Tropic of Cancer and the Tropic of Capricorn. These regions receive high levels of solar radiation, making them ideal for solar energy initiatives. Most of the member countries in the International Solar Alliance are located between the Tropic of Cancer and Tropic of Capricorn. *(Asked in Exam)*Shutterstock

Major Countries in the International Solar Alliance (ISA):

Here are some of the major countries that are part of the ISA, particularly those with significant solar energy initiatives:

- ➢ **India:** Proposed the ISA and hosts its headquarters; significant solar power projects.
- ➢ **France:** Co-launched the ISA with India; active in promoting global solar energy initiatives.
- ➢ **Australia:** High solar potential, extensive installations.
- ➢ **Japan: Japan is a member country of the International Solar Alliance.** *(Asked in Exam)*
- ➢ **Brazil:** Large projects, growing renewable investment.
- ➢ **UAE:** Major investments, large-scale solar parks.
- ➢ **South Africa:** Leading solar projects in Africa.

Note regarding membership:

- ➢ **China has not signed/ratified the International Solar Alliance (ISA) Framework Agreement.** *(Asked in Exam)*
- ➢ **United States:** Joined as the 101st member country (Framework Agreement signed in Nov 2021).

Questions

Natural Hazards and Natural Disasters

Q 1. National Disaster Management Authority (NDMA) works under the aegis of-
1. Ministry of Earth Science (MoES)
2. Ministry of Home Affairs (MHA)
3. Ministry of Environmental Forest and Climatic Change (MoEFCQ)
4. Department of Space- Indian Space Research Organisation (ISRO)

Answer: 2. Ministry of Home Affairs (MHA)

Q 2. Global warming can lead to/aggravate which of the following natural disasters?
(A) Draught
(B) Earthquake
(C) Flood
(D) Storm

Choose the correct answer from the options given below:
1. A, B, C
2. A, C, D
3. B, C, D
4. B, D

Answer: 2. A, C, D

Q 3. Given below are two statements:
Assertion (A): Climate change is going to increase social tension in India.
Reason (R): The frequency and intensity of the extreme weather events will have serious consequences for food security.
1. Both (A) and (R) are true and (R) is the correct explanation of (A).
2. Both (A) and (R) are true and (R) is not the correct explanation of (A).
3. (A) is true, but (R) is false.
4. (A) is false, but (R) is true.

Answer: 1. Both (A) and (R) are true and (R) is the correct explanation of (A).

Q 4. Meaning of Tsunami is ?
1. Oceanic wave
2. Harbour Wave
3. Coastal Wave
4. Oceanic earthquake

Answer: 2. Harbour Wave

Q 5. Given below are two statements:
Assertion A: Most cyclones cause widespread damage in coastal areas.
Reason R: The energy of most cyclones increases after landfall
1. Both A and R are true and R is the correct explanation of A
2. Both A and R are true but R is NOT the correct explanation of A
3. A is true but R is false
4. A is false but R is true

Answer: A is true but R is false

Q 6. Match the column:

A. Hazard identification	I. determining the size and nature of the population that has been exposed to toxicants
B. Dose response assessment	II. estimation of the magnitude of the public health problem
C. Exposure assessment	III. characterizing the relationship between the dose received and the adverse health effect
D. Risk characterization	IV. process of determining whether or not a particular chemical is linked to particular health effect

Choose the correct answer from the options given below:
1. A-IV B-III C-II D-I
2. A-IV B-III C-I D-II
3. A-I B-II C-III D-IV
4. A-I B-II C-IV D-III

Answer: 2. A-IV B-III C-I D-II

Q 7. Which among the following hazards can occur due to anthropogenic causes?
  A. Cyclones
  B. Nuclear Disaster
  C. Floods
  D. Volcanoes
  E. Forest Fires
Choose the correct answer from the options given below:
  1. A B and D only
  2. B, C, and D only
  3. B, D, and E only
  4. B, C, and E only
Answer: 4. B, C, and E only

Q 8. What is the correct order of Risk assessment due to exposure of some chemicals to the humans-
A. Dose-Response Assessment
B. Exposure Assessment
C. Risk Characterization
D. Hazard Identification
Choose the correct answer from the options given below:
1. ABCD
2. DBCA
3. CDAB
4. DABC
Answer: 4. DABC

Q 9. Given below are two statements:
Assertion A: Despite increasing vulnerability to natural disasters many communities resist adopting mitigation programmes and measures.
Reason R: Mitigation is often perceived by communities as being incompatible with their cultural practices.
In the light of the above statements, choose the most appropriate answer from the options given below
  1. Both A and R are correct and R is the correct explanation of A
  2. Both A and R are correct but R is NOT the correct explanation of A
  3. A is correct but R is not correct
  4. A is not correct but R is correct
Answer: 3. A is correct but R is not correct.

Q 10. Mitigation measures to cope with floods include
  A. Elevating or protecting electrical service panels
  B. Upsizing culverts to better handle flood surges
  C. Protecting facilities with barriers and sandbags
  D. Removing trees and debris from the flood plain
  E. Relocating equipment outside the flood plain
Choose the correct answer from the options given below:

1. A, C, D and E only
2. A, B, C and E only
3. A, B, C, D and E
4. B, C, D, and E only

Answer: 2. A, B, C and E only

Q 11. A measure such as building a plinth wall for floods would be termed as
1. Preparedness
2. Prevention
3. Mitigation
4. Adaptation

Answer: 2. Prevention

Q 12. Landslides are of
1. Chemical origin
2. Hydrological origin
3. Hydro-biological origin
4. Geo-physical origin

Answer: 4. Geo-physical origin

Q 13. Given below are two statements:
Statement I: Hurricanes and typhoons are essentially the same as tropical cyclones.
Statement II: Warm tropical oceans and moist air mass are prerequisites for the development of tropical cyclones
In the light of the above statements, choose the most appropriate answer from the options given below:
1. Both Statement I and Statement II are correct
2. Both Statement I and Statement II are incorrect
3. Statement I is correct but Statement II is incorrect
4. Statement I is incorrect but Statement II is correct

Answer: 1. Both Statement I and Statement II are correct

Q 14. From disaster mitigation measures given below, identify the measures which can be characterized as non-structural
A. Flood dykes
B. Land-use zoning
C. Raising of homes in flood-prone areas
D. Insurance programmes
E. Reinforce tornado safe rooms

Choose the correct answer from the options given below:
1. B and D only
2. A, B and D only
3. B, D and E only
4. A, B, D and E only

Answer: 1. B and D only

Q 15. Which among the following natural hazards has a relatively slow onset?
1. Volcanic eruptions
2. Droughts
3. Wild fires
4. Land and slides

Answer: 2. Droughts

Q 16. Given below are two statements - one labelled as Assertion (A) and the other is labelled as Reason (R).

Assertion (A): The impact of natural disasters does not depend on socio economic factors.

Reason (R): Natural disasters do not discriminate between people of a society and other communities.

In the light of the above two statements. choose the correct option :
1. Both (A) and (R) are true and (R) is the correct explanation of (A)
2. Both (A) and (R) are true and (R) is not the correct explanation of (A)
3. (A) is true but (R) is false
4. (A) is false but (R) is true

Answer: 4. (A) is false but (R) is true

Q 17. Which of the following belongs to the category of geophysical hazards?
1. Infestation
2. Invasive species
3. Avalanches
4. Diseases

Answer: 3. Avalanches

Q 18. Which of the following are National Missions of National Action Plan on climate change?
A. National Ozone Mission
B. National Solar Mission
C. National Water Mission
D. National Air Mission
E. National Mission for Green India

Choose the correct answer from the options given below:
1. ABD
2. ADE
3. BCE
4. CDE

Answer: 3. BCE

Q 19. How many 'core national missions' are there in the National Action Plan on Climate Change?
1. 5
2. 6
3. 7

4. 8

Answer: 4. 8

Q 20. Which of the following National missions come under the National Action Plan for climate change?
   A. National Solar mission
   B. National Water mission
   C. National Green Hydrogen mission
   D. National Mission for Sustainable Agriculture
   E. National Mission on Sustainable Habitat
Choose the correct answer from the options given below:
   1. A, B, C and D Only
   2. B, C and E Only
   3. C, D, E and A Only
   4. D, E, A and B Only
Answer: 4. D, E, A and B Only

Q 21. Climate change can have serious consequences for:
   A. Water security
   B. Food security
   C. Erosion of coastal zones
   D. Soil fertility
   E. Respiratory health
Choose the correct answer from the options given below:
   1. Only (a), (b) and (c)
   2. Only (a), (b), (d) and (e)
   3. Only (a), (b), (c) and (e)
   4. (a), (b), (c), (d) and (e)
Answer: 1. Only (a), (b) and (c)

International Agreements/Efforts

Montreal Protocol

Q 22. Given below are two statements - one labelled as Assertion (A) and the other is labelled as Reason (R).
Assertion A: Hydrofluorocarbons (HFCs) need to be phased out to protect the Ozone layer
Reason R: HFCs have a high global warming potential
In light of the above statements, choose the most appropriate answer from the options given below
   1. Both A and R are correct and R is the correct explanation of A
   2. Both A and R are correct but R is NOT the correct explanation of A
   3. A is correct but R is not correct
   4. A is not correct but R is correct
Answer: 4. A is not correct but R is correct

Q 23. Given below are two statements:
Statement I: Montreal protocol is a multilateral environmental agreement that regulates the production and consumption of nearly 100 man-made chemicals.

Statement II: Montreal protocol is an international treaty designed to protect the environment.
1. Both Statement I and Statement II are correct
2. Both Statement I and Statement II are incorrect
3. Statement I is correct but Statement II s incorrect
4. Statement I is incorrect but Statement II is correct

Answer: 1. Both Statement I and Statement II are correct

Q 24. Given below are two statements:
Statement (I): Under Montreal Protocol, developed and developing countries have the same timetable for phasing out of Ozone Depleting Substances (ODS).
Statement (II): Under Montreal Protocol developing countries are referred to as 'Article 5 Countries'
1. Both Statement (I) and Statement (II) are correct.
2. Both Statement (I) and Statement (II) are incorrect.
3. Statement (I) is correct but Statement (II) is incorrect
4. Statement (I) is incorrect but Statement (II) is correct

Answer: 4. Statement (I) is incorrect but Statement (II) is correct

Q 25. Given below are two statements:
Statement (I): Under Montreal protocol developed and developing nations have differentiated responsibilities.
Statement (II): Under Kigali amendment of Montreal protocol, Chloro Fluoro Carbons (CFCs) and Hydro-Chloro Fluoro Carbons (HCFCs) were to be phased out.
1. Both Statement I and Statement II are correct
2. Both Statement I and Statement II are incorrect
3. Statement I is correct but Statement II is incorrect
4. Statement I is incorrect but Statement II is correct

Answer: 3. Statement I is correct but Statement II is incorrect

Q 26. Former UN General Secretary Kofi Annan once stated that "perhaps the single most successful international environmental agreement to date has been the-
1. Rio Summit
2. Montreal protocol
3. Kyoto Protocol
4. Paris agreement

Answer: 2. Montreal protocol

Q 27. Given below are two statements - one labelled as Assertion (A) and the other is labelled as Reason (R).
Assertion A: Hydrofluorocarbons (HFCS) replacements of ozone depleting substances chlorofluorocarbons (CFCs) were also decided to be phased out during copenhagen-1992 conference

Reason R: HFCs have shorter lifetime than CFCs and contain no Chlorine and bromine
1. Both A and R are true and R is the correct explanation of A
2. Both A and R are true but R is NOT the correct explanation of A
3. A is true but R is false
4. A is false but R is true

Answer: 4. A is false but R is true

Q 28. The latest amendment to Montreal protocol is -
1. Kigali Amendment
2. Nairobi Amendment
3. Copenhagen Amendment
4. Bangkok Amendment

Answer: 1. Kigali Amendment

Q 29. Which of the following chemicals replaced chlorofluorocarbons (CFCs) after their phase out due to the Montreal Protocol?
1. Perfluorocarbons (PFCs)
2. Hydrochlorofluorocarbons (HCFCs)
3. Sulphur hexafluoride (SF6)
4. Halons

Answer: 2. Hydrochlorofluorocarbons (HCFCs)

Q 30. The only UN treaty related to environmental issues which has been ratified by all 197 UN member states is
(1) Montreal Protocol
(2) Kyoto Protocol
(3) Paris Agreement
(4) Basel Convention

Answer: 1. Montreal Protocol

Q 31. Identify from the options given below. the co-benefit of Montreal Protocol
1. Impetus to development of energy efficient systems
2. Reduction in carbon dioxide (equivalent) emissions
3. Convergence of efforts of international community in addressing air pollution
4. Control of transboundary movement of hazardous waste

Answer: 2. Reduction in carbon dioxide (equivalent) emissions

Q 32. Montreal protocol was signed in order to address which of the following environmental issues?
1. Tropospheric ozone pollution
2. Depletion of ozone in the stratosphere
3. Global warming
4. Acid rain

Answer: 2. Depletion of ozone in the stratosphere

Q 33. The Montreal Protocol refers to
1. Cooperation among UN member countries to combat climate change
2. Phasing out the consumption and production of ozone depleting substances
3. Ensuring environmental sustainability
4. Safeguarding societal quality of life worldwide

Answer: 2. Phasing out the consumption and production of ozone depleting substances

Q 34. Montreal protocol aims at
1. Reduction in emissions of greenhouse gases
2. Phasing out ozone depleting substances
3. Prohibiting transboundary movement of hazardous waste
4. Enhancing cooperation among UN member states for peaceful uses of nuclear energy

Answer: 2. Phasing out ozone depleting substances

United Nations Environment Programme (UNEP), Environment Protection Act, 1986 and Rio Summit

Q 35. United Nations Environmental Program (UNEP) was the result of deliberations held during
1. Human Environmental Conference at Stockholm in 1972
2. Earth Summit at Rio de Janeiro in 1992
3. Montreal Protocol 1987
4. Kyoto Protocol 1997

Answer: 1. Human Environmental Conference at Stockholm in 1972

Q 36. The Environment (protection) Act. 1986 was the result of India's commitment, to take appropriate action for the protection and improvement of environment, at the:
1. 1985 Vienna convention for protection of ozone layer
2. Convention on long range trans boundary air pollution, 1083
3. Convention on international trade in endangered species, 1975 (CITES)
4. United Nation's Conference on the human environment. Stockholm, 1972

Answer: 4. United Nation's Conference on the human environment. Stockholm, 1972

Q 37. During which one of the following the Convention on Biodiversity was opened for signature?
1. Rio Summit
2. Stockholm conference
3. Ramsar convention
4. Montreal Protocol

Answer: 1. Rio Summit

Q 38. The convention on biological diversity is dedicated to promote sustainable development conceived as a practical tool for translating the principles of :
1. Agenda 20
2. Agenda 21
3. Agenda 22
4. Agenda 23

Answer: 2. Agenda 21

Q 39. United Nations Framework Convention on Climate Change (UNFCCC) was the outcome of:
1. Paris Agreement
2. Montreal Protocol
3. Convention on Biodiversity
4. Earth Summit

Answer: 4. Earth Summit

Q 40. Convention on Biodiversity was signed during
1. Montreal Protocol, 1987
2. Earth Summit at Rio de Janeiro, 1992
3. Kyoto Protocol, 1997
4. Human Environment Conference, Stockholm, 1972

Answer: 2. Earth Summit at Rio de Janeiro, 1992

Q 41. Which of the following conventions and protocols originated from the Rio Earth Summit?
A. UN Framework convention on climate change
B. Ramsar convention on wetlands
C. UN convention to combat desertification
D. Kyoto Protocol
E. Convention on Biological Diversity

Choose the most appropriate answer from the options given below:
1. (A), (B) and (E) only
2. (A), (C) and (E) only
3. (A), (C), (D) and (E) only
4. (B), (C), (D) and (E) only

Answer: 2. (A), (C) and (E) only

Q 42. Which of the following UN Conferences/Summit adopted the programme of Action for Sustainable Development?
1. Stockholm Conference
2. Johannesburg Summit
3. Rio de Janeiro Conference
4. Ahmedabad Conference

Answer: 3. Rio de Janeiro Conference

Q 43. Which one of the following conferences/summits is also known as the UN Conference on Sustainable Development (UNCSD)?

1. The Stockholm Conference, 1972
2. The Rio de Janerio Conference, 1992
3. The Johannesburg Summit, 2002
4. The Rio + 20 Conference, 2012

Answer: 4. The Rio + 20 Conference, 2012

Q 45. Which of the following indicates the objective of the United Nations Framework Convention on Climate Change (UNFCCC)?
1. To stabilize greenhouse gases concentration in the atmosphere
2. To prescribe limits on greenhouse gas emissions for individual countries
3. To lay down enforcement mechanisms
4. To prepare guidelines for formulation of Climate Action Plan by member countries

Answer: 1. To stabilize greenhouse gases concentration in the atmosphere

Kyoto Protocol

Q 46. Which of the following gases were covered under the Kyoto Protocol?
A. Carbon dioxide (CO2)
B. Methane (CH4)
C. Nitrogen dioxide (NO2)
D. Nitrous oxide (N20)
E. Sulfur dioxide (SO2)

Choose the most appropriate answer from the options given below:
1. ABD
2. ABC
3. BCD
4. CDE

Answer: 1. ABD

Q 47. In which one of the following Conference of Parties (COP) Kyoto protocol was adopted?
1. COP-1
2. COP-3
3. COP-7
4. COP-10

Answer: 3. COP-3

Q 48. Given below are two statements:
Statement (I): Kyoto protocol only binds developed countries and places a heavier burden on them.
Statement (II): Kyoto protocol has nothing to do with United Nations Framework Convention on climate change (UNFCCC).
Choose the most appropriate answer from the options given below:
1. Both Statement (I) and Statement (II) are correct.
2. Both Statement (I) and Statement (II) are incorrect.
3. Statement (I) is correct but Statement (II) is incorrect

4.   Statement (I) is incorrect but Statement (II) is correct

Answer: 3. Statement (I) is correct but Statement (II) is incorrect

Q 49. Given below are two statements:
Statement (I): If Global average warming is limited to one or two additional degrees, some regions will experience enhanced agricultural productivity.
Statement (II): Beyond 2 °C to 3°C of global average warming, essentially all impacts become deleterious.
Choose the most appropriate answer from the options given below:
1.   Both Statement (I) and Statement (II) are correct.
2.   Both Statement (I) and Statement (II) are incorrect.
3.   Statement (I) is correct but Statement (II) is incorrect
4.   Statement (I) is incorrect but Statement (II) is correct

Answer: 1. Both Statement (I) and Statement (II) are correct.

Q 50. In which year did the first commitment period of the Kyoto Protocol come to an end?
1. 2011
2. 2012
3. 2014
4. 2008

Answer: 2. 2012

Q 51. Given below are two statements:
Statement I: United Nations Framework Convention on Climate Change (UNFCC) was framed during Kyoto Protocol, 1997.
Statement II: Kyoto Protocol set up different limits of carbon emissions for individual nations, depending on their output before 1990.
Choose the most appropriate answer from the options given below:
1.   Both Statement I and Statement II are true
2.   Both Statement I and Statement II are false
3.   Statement I is true but Statement II is false
4.   Statement I is false but Statement II is true

Answer: 4. Statement I is false but Statement II is true

Q 52. In order to limit the rise in global temperature to 1.5 °C over pre industrial levels, IPCC indicates that the world has to reduce the emission of greenhouse gas to the extent of - % by the year 2030.
1. 65
2. 50
3. 45
4. 40

Answer: 3. 45

Q 53. Given below are two statements:

Statement I: Montreal Protocol was agreed in 1987 and came into force in 1990.

Statement II: Kyoto protocol was agreed in 1997 and came into force in 2005.

Choose the most appropriate answer from the options given below:
1. Both Statement I and Statement II are true.
2. Both Statement I and Statement II are false.
3. Statement I is true but Statement II is false.
4. Statement I is false but Statement II is true.

Answer: 4. Statement I is false but Statement II is true.

Q 54. Under Kyoto Protocol, the first commitment period for reduction of greenhouse gas emissions by 37 industrialized and European community countries was:
1. 1997 - 2005
2. 2008—2012
3. 2000—2012
4. 2005—2025

Answer: 2. 2008—2012

Q 55. Which of the following Greenhouse bases were the target gases whose emission was to be covered under the first commitment period of the Kyoto protocol?
A. SO,
B. CO2
C. N20
D. NH3
E. CH4

Choose the most appropriate answer from the options given below:
1. A, B, C and D only
2. A, B and C only
3. B, C, D and E only
4. B, C and E only

Answer: 4. B, C and E only

Paris Agreement and The Convention on Biological Diversity (CBD)

Q 56. Under which of the following agreements was it decided to limit the increase in global average temperature to well below 2°C?
1. Paris Agreement
2. Kyoto Protocol
3. Montreal Protocol
4. Rio Summit

Answer: 1. Paris Agreement

Q 57. Which of the following was the central aim of the Paris Agreement?
1. To reduce the CFCs emissions
2. To strengthen the global response to the threat of climate change

3. To address biological diversity issues
4. To address the problem of ozone layer depletion

Answer: 2. To strengthen the global response to the threat of climate change

---

Q 58. Formulation of long term - low emission development strategies by each country was suggested under
1. Paris Agreement
2. International solar alliance
3. Montreal Protocol
4. Kyoto Protocol

Answer: 1. Paris Agreement

Q 59. The Paris Agreement aims to limit the temperature rise in this century by how many degrees Celsius above the pre-industrial levels?
1. 1°0
2. 2°C
3. 0.5°0
4. 3°C

Answer: 2. 2°C

Q 60. The Paris Agreement envisages pursuing efforts to limit global warming this century to how many degrees celsius above the pre-industrial levels of global average temperature?
1. 0.5° C
2. 1°C
3. 1.5°C
4. 2.5°C

Answer: 3. 1.5°C

Q 61. Under Paris Agreement, countries by the end of this century will strive to limit the global temperature rise above pre - industrial level to
1. 1.5°
2. 2.5°
3. 3°
4. 4°

Answer: 1. 1.5°

Q 62. Match the column:

List I (International Meetings)	List II (Key objectives)
A. Kyoto protocol	(I) Global warming
B. Montreal protocol	(II) Biodiversity conservation
C. Rio Summit	(III) Ozone depletion
D. Paris Agreement	(IV) Solar Alliance

Choose the most appropriate answer from the options given below:
1. A-I, B-III, C-II, D-IV
2. A-II, B-III, C-I, D-V
3. A-III, B-I, C-IV, D-II
4. A-IV, B-II, C-I, D-III

Answer: 1. A-I, B-III, C-II, D-IV

Q 63. Which of the following are true about Convention on Biological Diversity (CBD)?
- A. It works for the conservation of Biodiversity
- B. It advocates the sustainable use of its components
- C. Its secretariat is in Geneva, Switzerland
- D. It emphasizes on fair and equitable sharing of benefits arising out of the utilization of genetic resources

Choose the most appropriate answer from the options given below:
1. ABC
2. BCD
3. ACD
4. ABD

Answer: 4. ABD

Q 64. Identify the benefits of biodiversity.
- A. Contribution to human food supplies
- B. Providing important medicines
- C. Supporting ecosystem stability
- D. Aesthetic and cultural value

Choose the most appropriate answer from the options given below:
1. ABC
2. BCD
3. ABD
4. ABCD

Answer: 4. ABCD

Q 65. Which of the following protocols/Conventions are supplementary to the Convention on Biodiversity (CBD)?
- A. Basel Convention
- B. Cartagena Protocol
- C. Kigali Agreement
- D. Nagoya Protocol
- E. Bali Summit

Choose the most appropriate answer from the options given below:
1. AE
2. BCE
3. BD
4. ACD

Answer: 3. BD

Q 66. In the context of Convention on Biological Diversity (CBD), the first session of Conference of Parties (COPs) was scheduled in :
1. Montreal
2. Bahamas
3. Geneva
4. Rio de Janeiro

Answer: 2. Bahamas

International Solar Alliance (ISA)

Q 67. International Solar Alliance (ISA) is the alliance countries most of which lie partially or completely -
1. Above tropic of cancer
2. Below tropic of Capricorn
3. Between the tropic of cancer and the tropic of Capricorn
4. Southern hemisphere

Answer: 3. Between the tropic of cancer and the tropic of Capricorn

Q 68. Given below are two statements:
Statement (I): International Solar Alliance's vision: 'Let us together make the sun brighter.
Statement (II): International Solar Alliance's mission: 'Every home how far away, will have a light at home.
Choose the most appropriate answer from the options given below:
1. Both Statement (I) and Statement (Il) are correct.
2. Both Statement (I) and Statement (II) are incorrect.
3. Statement (I) is correct but Statement (Il) is incorrect
4. Statement (I) is incorrect but Statement (Il) is correct

Answer: 1. Both Statement (I) and Statement (Il) are correct.

Q 69. Most of the countries in International Solar Alliance lie
1. Above tropic of cancer
2. Below tropic of cancer
3. Between tropic of cancer and Capricorn
4. In the Southern hemisphere

Answer: 3. Between tropic of cancer and Capricorn

Q 70. Official languages for International Solar Alliance are-
A. Hindi
B. English
C. French
D. Spanish
E. Chinese

Choose the most appropriate answer from the options given below:
1. ABC
2. BDE
3. BCD
4. BCE

Answer: 1. ABC

Q 71. Given below are two statements:
Statement-I: International Solar Alliance's present post of President is held by India.
Statement-II: The United States of America is not a member of International Solar Alliance.
Choose the most appropriate answer from the options given below:
1. Both Statement I and Statement II are true.
2. Both Statement I and Statement II are false.
3. Statement I is true but Statement II is false.
4. Statement I is false but Statement II is true.

Answer: 3. Statement I is true but Statement II is false.

Q 72. Given below are two statements:
Statement I: International Solar Alliance (ISA) was launched on the side-lines of COP24.
Statement II: ISA was launched by Prime Minister Narendra Modi and President of France, Emanuel Macron.
Choose the most appropriate answer from the options given below:
1. Both Statement I and Statement II are True.
2. Both Statement I and Statement II are False.
3. Statement I is true but Statement II is False.
4. Statement I is false but Statement II is True.

Answer: 2. Both Statement I and Statement II are False.

Q 73. Which of the following are true about the International Solar Alliance (ISA)?
A. Its HeadQuarter is in Washington DC
B. It is a join initiative of France and india
C. Most of the participating countries are in southern hemisphere
D. There are 121 signatory countries
E. Mostly sunshine countries are participants in this
Choose the most appropriate answer from the options given below:
1. (A), (B), (D) and (E) only
2. (B), (D) and (E) only
3. (A), (B), (C) only
4. (B), (C), (D) and (E) only

Answer: 2. (B), (D) and (E) only

Q 74. International Solar Alliance Framework Agreement entered into force in the year
1. 2015
2. 2017
3. 2016
4. 2018

Answer: 2. 2017

Q 75. Which of the following countries has not signed/ratified the International Solar Alliance Framework Agreement?
1. Australia
2. Japan
3. United Kingdom
4. China

Answer: 4. China

Q 76. Given below are two statements:

Statement I: Most of the member countries in the International solar Alliance are located between the tropic of cancer and tropic of Capricorn

Statement II: Japan is a member country of the International solar alliance.

Which of the above statements is/are correct?
1. I only
2. Both I and II
3. II only
4. Neither I nor II

Answer: 2. Both I and II

Q 77. The initiative to establish International Solar Alliance was jointly taken by
1. USA and India
2. Sweden and India
3. France and India
4. China and India

Answer: 3. France and India

Last Minute Revisions

Natural Hazards and Natural Disasters

- ✓ National Disaster Management Authority (NDMA) works under the aegis of Ministry of Home Affairs (MHA). *(Asked in Exam)*
- ✓ Global warming can lead to/aggravate Draught, Flood and Storm natural disasters. *(Asked in Exam)*
- ✓ Climate change is going to increase social tension in India. *(Asked in Exam)*
- ✓ The frequency and intensity of extreme weather events will have serious consequences for food security. *(Asked in Exam)*
- ✓ Meaning of Tsunami is harbor Wave. *(Asked in Exam)*
- ✓ Most cyclones cause widespread damage in coastal areas. *(Asked in Exam)*
- ✓ Hazard identification is a Process of determining whether a particular chemical is linked to a particular health effect. *(Asked in Exam)*
- ✓ Dose response assessment Characterize the relationship between the dose received and the adverse health effect. *(Asked in Exam)*
- ✓ Exposure assessment Determine the size and nature of the population that has been exposed to toxicants. *(Asked in Exam)*

✓	Risk characterization: Assessing the extent of the public health issue. *(Asked in Exam)*
✓	Nuclear Disaster, Floods and Forest Fires hazards can occur due to anthropogenic causes. *(Asked in Exam)*
✓	The correct order of Risk assessment due to exposure of some chemicals to the humans: Hazard Identification → Dose-Response Assessment → Exposure Assessment → Risk Characterization → Estimating the magnitude of the public health. *(Asked in Exam)*
✓	Despite increasing vulnerability to natural disasters many communities resist adopting mitigation programs and measures. *(Asked in Exam)*
✓	Mitigation measures to cope with floods include Elevating or protecting electrical service panels, Upsizing culverts to better handle flood surges, protecting facilities with barriers and sandbags and Relocating equipment outside the flood plain. *(Asked in Exam)*
✓	A measure such as building a plinth wall for floods would be termed as prevention. *(Asked in Exam)*
✓	Landslides are of Geo-physical origin. *(Asked in Exam)*
✓	Hurricanes and typhoons are essentially the same as tropical cyclones. *(Asked in Exam)*
✓	Warm tropical oceans and moist air mass are prerequisites for the development of tropical cyclones. *(Asked in Exam)*
✓	Non-structural measures refer to strategies and policies that do not involve physical construction or engineering. They are often related to planning, management, or regulatory measures to reduce disaster risks and impacts. *(Asked in Exam)*
✓	Land-use zoning and Insurance programs can be characterized as non-structural. *(Asked in Exam)*
✓	Droughts are natural hazards and have a relatively slow onset. *(Asked in Exam)*
✓	Natural disasters do not discriminate between people of society and other communities. *(Asked in Exam)*
✓	Avalanches belong to the category of geophysical hazards. *(Asked in Exam)*

National Action Plan on Climate Change (NAPCC)

✓	National Solar Mission, National Water Mission and National Mission for Green India are National Missions of National Action Plan on climate change. *(Asked in Exam)*
✓	There are 8 core national missions in the National Action Plan on Climate Change. *(Asked in Exam)*
✓	National Solar mission, National Water mission, National Mission for Sustainable Agriculture and National Mission on Sustainable Habitat come under the National Action Plan for climate change. *(Asked in Exam)*
✓	Climate change can have serious consequences for Water security, Food security and Erosion of coastal zones. *(Asked in Exam)*

International Agreements/Efforts

Montreal Protocol (1987, 1989)

✓	HFCs do not deplete the ozone layer; they were actually introduced as alternatives to ozone-depleting substances like chlorofluorocarbons (CFCs) and hydrochlorofluorocarbons (HCFCs). *(Asked in Exam)*
✓	HFCs have a high global warming potential. *(Asked in Exam)*

- ✓ HFCs have shorter lifetime than CFCs and contain no Chlorine and bromine. *(Asked in Exam)*
- ✓ Montreal protocol is a multilateral environmental agreement that regulates the production and consumption of nearly 100 man-made chemicals. *(Asked in Exam)*
- ✓ Montreal protocol is an international treaty designed to protect the environment. *(Asked in Exam)*
- ✓ Under Montreal Protocol developing countries are referred to as 'Article 5 Countries' *(Asked in Exam)*
- ✓ Under Montreal protocol developed and developing nations have differentiated responsibilities. *(Asked in Exam)*
- ✓ Former UN General Secretary Kofi Annan once stated that "perhaps the single most successful international environmental agreement to date has been the Montreal protocol. *(Asked in Exam)*
- ✓ The latest amendment to Montreal protocol is Kigali Amendment. *(Asked in Exam)*
- ✓ Hydrochlorofluorocarbons (HCFCs) replaced chlorofluorocarbons (CFCs) after their phase-out due to the Montreal Protocol. *(Asked in Exam)*
- ✓ The only UN treaty related to environmental issues which has been ratified by all 197 UN member states is Montreal Protocol. *(Asked in Exam)*
- ✓ The Montreal Protocol, primarily aimed at phasing out ozone-depleting substances, has also had the co-benefit of reducing greenhouse gas emissions. *(Asked in Exam)*
- ✓ The Montreal Protocol was signed specifically to address the issue of the depletion of the ozone layer in the stratosphere. *(Asked in Exam)*
- ✓ The Montreal Protocol refers to phasing out the consumption and production of ozone depleting substances. *(Asked in Exam)*
- ✓ United Nations Environmental Program (UNEP) was the result of deliberations held during Human Environmental Conference at Stockholm in 1972. *(Asked in Exam)*
- ✓ The Environment (protection) Act. 1986 was the result of India's commitment, to take appropriate action for the protection and improvement of environment, at the United Nation's Conference on the human environment. Stockholm, 1972. *(Asked in Exam)*

Rio Summit
- ✓ The Convention on Biological Diversity (CBD) was opened for signature during the Rio Summit, officially known as the United Nations Conference on Environment and Development (UNCED), held in Rio de Janeiro, Brazil, in 1992. *(Asked in Exam)*
- ✓ The convention on biological diversity is dedicated to promoting sustainable development conceived as a practical tool for translating the principles of Agenda 21. *(Asked in Exam)*
- ✓ United Nations Framework Convention on Climate Change (UNFCCC) was the outcome of Earth Summit. *(Asked in Exam)*
- ✓ Convention on Biodiversity was signed during Earth Summit at Rio de Janeiro, 1992. *(Asked in Exam)*
- ✓ UN Framework convention on climate change, UN convention to combat desertification and Convention on Biological Diversity are originated from the Rio Earth Summit. *(Asked in Exam)*

✓ Rio de Janeiro Conference adopted the program of Action for Sustainable Development. *(Asked in Exam)*

✓ The Rio + 20 Conference, 2012 is also known as the UN Conference on Sustainable Development (UNCSD). *(Asked in Exam)*

✓ The primary objective of the United Nations Framework Convention on Climate Change (UNFCCC) is to stabilize greenhouse gas concentrations in the atmosphere at a level that would prevent dangerous anthropogenic interference with the climate system. *(Asked in Exam)*

Kyoto Protocol

✓ Carbon dioxide (CO2), Methane (CH4) and Nitrous oxide (N20) gases were covered under the Kyoto Protocol. *(Asked in Exam)*

✓ The Kyoto Protocol was adopted during the third Conference of Parties (COP-3) to the United Nations Framework Convention on Climate Change (UNFCCC), which took place in Kyoto, Japan, in December 1997. *(Asked in Exam)*

✓ Kyoto protocol only binds developed countries and places a heavier burden on them. *(Asked in Exam)*

✓ If Global average warming is limited to one or two additional degrees, some regions will experience enhanced agricultural productivity. *(Asked in Exam)*

✓ Beyond 2 °C to 3°C of global average warming, essentially all impacts become deleterious. *(Asked in Exam)*

✓ The Kyoto Protocol, adopted in 1997, set binding emission reduction targets for developed countries. These targets were to be achieved during the first commitment period, which began in 2008 and ended in 2012. *(Asked in Exam)*

✓ Kyoto Protocol set up different limits of carbon emissions for individual nations, depending on their output before 1990. *(Asked in Exam)*

✓ To limit the rise in global temperature to 1.5 °C over preindustrial levels, IPCC indicates that the world has to reduce the emission of greenhouse gas to the extent of 45% by the year 2030. *(Asked in Exam)*

✓ Kyoto protocol was agreed in 1997 and came into force in 2005. *(Asked in Exam)*

✓ Under Kyoto Protocol, the first commitment period for reduction of greenhouse gas emissions by 37 industrialized and European community countries was 2008—2012. *(Asked in Exam)*

✓ CO2 (Carbon Dioxide), N2O (Nitrous Oxide) and CH4 (Methane) greenhouse bases were the target gases whose emission was to be covered under the first commitment period of the Kyoto protocol. *(Asked in Exam)*

Paris Agreement

✓ The Nationally Determined Contributions (NDCs) of the European Union (EU) countries aim at a reduction in greenhouse gas emissions by 40% by the year 2030, relative to the levels in 1990. *(Asked in Exam)*

✓ Long term low emission development strategies by each country are crucial to realizing the goals of the Paris Agreement. *(Asked in Exam)*

✓ Nationally Determined Contributions (NDCs) declared by each country are not sufficient to keep the rise in global temperature upto 2°C above the pre-industrial level. *(Asked in Exam)*

- ✓ Paris Agreement was decided to limit the increase in global average temperature to well below 2°C. *(Asked in Exam)*
- ✓ To strengthen the global response to the threat of climate change was the central aim of the Paris Agreement. *(Asked in Exam)*
- ✓ Formulation of long term - low emission development strategies by each country were suggested under Paris Agreement. *(Asked in Exam)*
- ✓ The Paris Agreement aims to limit the global temperature rise in this century to well below 2°C above pre-industrial levels. *(Asked in Exam)*
- ✓ The Paris Agreement envisages pursuing efforts to limit global warming this century to 1.5 degrees celsius above the pre-industrial levels of global average temperature. *(Asked in Exam)*
- ✓ Under Paris Agreement, countries by the end of this century will strive to limit the global temperature rise above pre-industrial level to 1.5° *(Asked in Exam)*
- ✓ Kyoto Protocol – Global Warming – Focused on reducing greenhouse gases. *(Asked in Exam)*
- ✓ Montreal Protocol – Ozone Depletion – Aimed at phasing out CFCs. *(Asked in Exam)*
- ✓ Rio Summit – Biodiversity Conservation – Promoted sustainable development. *(Asked in Exam)*
- ✓ Paris Agreement – Solar Alliance – Encouraged renewable energy transition. *(Asked in Exam)*

The Convention on Biological Diversity (CBD)

- ✓ The Convention on Biological Diversity (CBD) seeks to Promote the conservation of biodiversity; Advocate for the sustainable use of its components; and emphasize the fair and equitable sharing of benefits arising from the utilization of genetic resources. *(Asked in Exam)*
- ✓ The benefits of biodiversity are Contribution to human food supplies, providing important medicines, Supporting ecosystem stability and Aesthetic and cultural value. *(Asked in Exam)*
- ✓ Cartagena Protocol and Nagoya Protocol are supplementary to the Convention on Biodiversity (CBD). *(Asked in Exam)*
- ✓ In the context of Convention on Biological Diversity (CBD), the first session of Conference of Parties (COPs) was scheduled in Bahamas. *(Asked in Exam)*

International Solar Alliance (ISA)

- ✓ International Solar Alliance (ISA) is the alliance countries most of which lie partially or completely Between the tropic of cancer and the tropic of Capricorn. *(Asked in Exam)*
- ✓ International Solar Alliance's vision: 'Let us together make the sun brighter. *(Asked in Exam)*
- ✓ International Solar Alliance's mission: 'Every home, how far away, will have a light at home. *(Asked in Exam)*
- ✓ Most of the countries in International Solar Alliance lie between tropic of cancer and Capricorn. *(Asked in Exam)*
- ✓ Official languages for International Solar Alliance are Hindi, English and French. *(Asked in Exam)*
- ✓ International Solar Alliance's present post of President is held by India. *(Asked in Exam)*

- ✓ The International Solar Alliance (ISA) was launched on the sidelines of COP21, not COP24. *(Asked in Exam)*
- ✓ The ISA was indeed launched by Prime Minister Narendra Modi of India and then-President of France, François Hollande, not Emmanuel Macron. *(Asked in Exam)*
- ✓ The International Solar Alliance (ISA) is a joint initiative between France and India. It has 121 signatory countries, with most participants being nations that receive abundant sunshine. *(Asked in Exam)*
- ✓ International Solar Alliance Framework Agreement entered into force in the year 2017. *(Asked in Exam)*
- ✓ China has not signed/ratified the International Solar Alliance (ISA) Framework Agreement. *(Asked in Exam)*
- ✓ Most of the member countries in the International solar Alliance are located between the tropic of cancer and tropic of Capricorn *(Asked in Exam)*
- ✓ Japan is a member country of the International solar alliance. *(Asked in Exam)*
- ✓ The initiative to establish International Solar Alliance was jointly taken by France and India. *(Asked in Exam)*

End

www.ingramcontent.com/pod-product-compliance
Lightning Source LLC
Chambersburg PA
CBHW041310120726
48005CB00014B/1946